Martial Arts
FOR
DUMMIES®

by Jennifer Lawler

Wiley Publishing, Inc.

Martial Arts For Dummies®

Published by
Wiley Publishing, Inc.
909 Third Avenue
New York, NY 10022
www.wiley.com

Copyright © 2003 by Wiley Publishing, Inc., Indianapolis, Indiana

Published by Wiley Publishing, Inc., Indianapolis, Indiana

Published simultaneously in Canada

No part of this publication may be reproduced, stored in a retrieval system, or transmitted in any form or by any means, electronic, mechanical, photocopying, recording, scanning, or otherwise, except as permitted under Sections 107 or 108 of the 1976 United States Copyright Act, without either the prior written permission of the Publisher, or authorization through payment of the appropriate per-copy fee to the Copyright Clearance Center, 222 Rosewood Drive, Danvers, MA 01923, 978-750-8400, fax 978-750-4744. Requests to the Publisher for permission should be addressed to the Legal Department, Wiley Publishing, Inc., 10475 Crosspoint Blvd., Indianapolis, IN 46256, 317-572-3447, fax 317-572-4447, or e-mail permcoordinator@wiley.com

Trademarks: Wiley, the Wiley Publishing logo, For Dummies, the Dummies Man logo, A Reference for the Rest of Us!, The Dummies Way, Dummies Daily, The Fun and Easy Way, Dummies.com and related trade dress are trademarks or registered trademarks of Wiley Publishing, Inc., in the United States and other countries, and may not be used without written permission. All other trademarks are the property of their respective owners. Wiley Publishing, Inc., is not associated with any product or vendor mentioned in this book.

For general information on our other products and services or to obtain technical support, please contact our Customer Care Department within the U.S. at 800-762-2974, outside the U.S. at 317-572-3993, or fax 317-572-4002.

Wiley also publishes its books in a variety of electronic formats. Some content that appears in print may not be available in electronic books.

Library of Congress Cataloging-in-Publication Data:

Library of Congress Control Number: 2002110320

ISBN: 0-7645-5358-5

Manufactured in the United States of America

10 9 8 7 6 5 4 3 2 1

Ⓦ**Wiley Publishing, Inc.** is a trademark of Wiley Publishing, Inc.

About the Author

Jennifer Lawler earned her black belt in Tae Kwon Do in 1994, much to the astonishment of friends and family who thought she would be a couch potato for the rest of her life. She has been kicking, punching, throwing and grappling ever since, gaining experience in arts such as Escrima, Hapkido, and Aikijutsu. She has taught Tae Kwon Do and self-defense for many years.

Lawler earned a Ph.D. in English (medieval literature) from the University of Kansas and taught college literature and writing classes for six years before becoming a full-time writer.

She has written more than 15 books, many of them about the martial arts, including *The Martial Arts Encyclopedia, Secrets of Tae Kwon Do,* and *Martial Arts for Women.*

She lives outside of Kansas City with her daughter, who kicks and punches on her own heavy bag right beside her mother's.

Dedication

As always, this is for my daughter Jessica, the lion-hearted.

Author's Acknowledgments

Many thanks to Debz Buller, for organizing the photo shoot and for supplying much-needed equipment, supplies and models, and for making sure the shoot ran smoothly.

Thanks also to Gold's Gym in Merriam, Kansas; and to Four Eras Jun Fan Jeet Kune Do, Independence, Missouri, for letting me shoot photos on site.

Much appreciation to the models, all of them terrific martial artists: Robin W. Bailey, Ronnie Williams, Jr., Isabel Hernandez, Mark Samuel, Gerald M. Allen, Shari Elliott, Juan Fernandez, Nabil Cherif, Jonathan P. Merz, Kelly Miller, Bryan Stevenson, Jeffrey Holmes, Christopher Kuhl, Debz Buller, Krista McGowan, Chantal Anderson, Stephen Diamond, Sr., Dave Buller, Cody Szuwalski, and John Hileman.

Special thanks to Nabil Cherif, John Hileman, and Bryan Stevenson for sharing their extensive knowledge of and expertise in the martial arts with me.

In addition, I have to express my gratitude to my agent, Carol Susan Roth, whose perfectly timed arrival in my life epitomizes the old martial arts saying, "When the student is ready, the master appears." She has done more for my writing career in six months as my agent than I managed in the previous six years.

To the staff at Wiley, including Tracy Boggier and Sherri Fugit, for making this a much better book than I could have done on my own.

Finally, no martial arts book of mine would be complete without honoring Masters Donald and Susan Booth, who taught me my very first sidekick all those years ago, and Grandmaster Woo Jin Jung, who has inspired countless martial artists in the last three decades.

Pilsung!

Jennifer Lawler

Publisher's Acknowledgments

We're proud of this book; please send us your comments through our Dummies online registration form located at www.dummies.com/register/.

Some of the people who helped bring this book to market include the following:

Acquisitions, Editorial, and Media Development

Project Editors: Sherri Fugit, Tim Gallan

Acquisitions Editor: Tracy Boggier

Copy Editors: Esmeralda St. Clair, Greg Pearson, Chad Sievers

Technical Editor: Loren Franck

Editorial Manager: Christine Meloy Beck

Editorial Assistants: Melissa Bennett, Carol Strickland

Cover Photos: Allsport Concepts / Markus Boesch

Cartoons: Rich Tennant, www.the5thwave.com

Production

Project Coordinator: Maridee Ennis

Layout and Graphics: David Bartholomew, Sean Decker, Carrie Foster, Joyce Haughey, LeAndra Johnson, Tiffany Muth, Jackie Nicholas, Barry Offringa, Jacque Schneider, Scott Tullis, Jeremey Unger

Proofreaders: Laura Albert, John Greenough, Andy Hollandbeck, TECHBOOKS Production Services

Indexer: TECHBOOKS Production Services

Publishing and Editorial for Consumer Dummies

Diane Graves Steele, Vice President and Publisher, Consumer Dummies

Joyce Pepple, Acquisitions Director, Consumer Dummies

Kristin A. Cocks, Product Development Director, Consumer Dummies

Michael Spring, Vice President and Publisher, Travel

Brice Gosnell, Publishing Director, Travel

Suzanne Jannetta, Editorial Director, Travel

Publishing for Technology Dummies

Andy Cummings, Vice President and Publisher, Dummies Technology/General User

Composition Services

Gerry Fahey, Vice President of Production Services

Debbie Stailey, Director of Composition Services

Contents at a Glance

Introduction 1

Part 1: Martial Arts Essentials 7
Chapter 1: Better than a Barroom Brawl 9
Chapter 2: Martial Arts Culture 27
Chapter 3: Choosing a Style 39
Chapter 4: Choosing a School or Instructor 47
Chapter 5: Go Get 'Em: Goals and Ranking Systems 61
Chapter 6: Clothes, Shoes, and Equipment 73
Chapter 7: Playing It Safe and Avoiding Injury 81

Part 11: Walking the Walk and Talking the Talk 89
Chapter 8: Getting the Most from Your Training 91
Chapter 9: Protecting Yourself: Self-Defense Details 111
Chapter 10: Preparing for Competition without Losing Your Head (Literally) 131
Chapter 11: Working the Mind-Body-Spirit Connection 147
Chapter 12: Just Like in the Movies: The Lowdown on Weapons 159
Chapter 13: Using Martial Arts Outside of Class 169

Part 111: Styles, Techniques, and Tactics: An Up-Close Look 181
Chapter 14: Karate 183
Chapter 15: Kung Fu 197
Chapter 16: Tae Kwon Do 209
Chapter 17: Judo 223
Chapter 18: Aikido 235
Chapter 19: Escrima 249
Chapter 20: Hapkido 263
Chapter 21: Muay Thai 275
Chapter 22: Jeet Kune Do and Eclectic Martial Arts 289
Chapter 23: T'ai Chi Chuan 301

Part 1V: The Part of Tens 313
Chapter 24: Ten Rules for the Martial Arts Classroom 315
Chapter 25: Ten Qualities a Good Instructor Must Have 319

Chapter 26: Ten Tips from the Master 323
Chapter 27: Ten Cool Martial Arts Movies 327

Part V: Appendixes 329

Appendix A: Glossary 331
Appendix B: Sources and Resources 337

Index 343

Table of Contents

Introduction 1

  About This Book 2
  Conventions Used in This Book 2
  Foolish Assumptions 3
  How This Book Is Organized 3
    Part I: Martial Arts Essentials 4
    Part II: Walking the Walk and Talking the Talk 4
    Part III: Styles, Techniques, and Tactics: An Up-Close Look 4
    Part IV: The Part of Tens 4
    Part V: Appendixes 4
  Icons Used in This Book 5
  Where to Go from Here 5

Part 1: Martial Arts Essentials 7

Chapter 1: Better than a Barroom Brawl 9

  Kicks, Flips, and Other Stuff: What Are the Martial Arts? 10
    Starting on the path 10
    Achieving harmony and balance: It's more than self-defense 11
  What It Ain't: Martial Arts Misconceptions 11
    Clarifying the spiritual aspect 12
    Demystifying the black belt mystique 12
    Violence: Turning the other cheek 12
    Why all the board-breaking stuff? 13
  Pick a Flavor, Any Flavor: The Different Types 14
    Chinese martial arts 14
    Japanese martial arts 16
    Okinawan martial arts 18
    Korean martial arts 19
    Indonesian, Filipino, and other martial arts 20
  Who, Me? Anybody Can Succeed! 21
    It takes all kinds: Diversity "R" Us 21
    See your physician first 22
  It's All About You: The Benefits 22
    Sitting couch potato, hidden tiger: Physical benefits 23
    Peaceful warrior: Mental and emotional benefits 23
  Preconditioning Your Mind and Body 25
    Work out (or at least get off the couch) 25
    Condition your mind 26

Chapter 2: Martial Arts Culture 27

Martial Arts Wildlife 27
  Lions and tigers and bears, oh my! 28
  And that's not all 28
Coffee, Chi, or Me? 28
Yin-Yang and You 29
  The eternal conflict: Not "Tastes great" versus "Less filling" 29
  Walking the balance beam 30
Character Building Beliefs: Resolute in Five Respects 30
  Resolution #1: You must believe in the philosophy
    of your school 30
  Resolution #2: You must stay fit, regardless of circumstances 31
  Resolution #3: You must commit to mastering the martial art 31
  Resolution #4: You must be willing to endure hard training 31
  Resolution #5: You must do your best in competition 32
The Five Tenets of Tae Kwon Do 32
  Tenet #1: Courtesy 32
  Tenet #2: Integrity 32
  Tenet #3: Perseverance 33
  Tenet #4: Self-Control 33
  Tenet #5: Indomitable Spirit 33
Chinese Martial Arts and Tao 33
  Tao who? 33
  The Tao of washing dishes 34
  The Tao ethical tradition 34
  The Tao and the warrior arts 35
Martial Arts Mindsets 35
  Fudoshin 35
  Heijo-Shin 36
  Kokoro 37

Chapter 3: Choosing a Style 39

How Do You Pronounce That Again? Discovering
  Martial Arts Styles 40
  The public library is the place to be 40
  Let's go surfing now 41
  Make it a blockbuster night 41
All Around the Town 41
Kick, Punch, or Grapple? 42
Watching and Analyzing Classes 43
  Hey, I can do that! 43
  White belts as role models 43
Interviewing Students and Instructors 44
  Grill the instructor (gently) 44
  Talk to students 44
Don't Stop Now! 45
The Chosen Style 45

Chapter 4: Choosing a School or Instructor 47

Locating a Good School 48
   Fundamentals that all good schools share 48
   Differences in types of schools 49
   Going for your goals 50
Finding a Good Instructor 51
   Who teaches what and when 51
   The head instructor's role 51
   The nitty-gritty details 51
The Gender-Neutral Zone: Finding a Female-Friendly School 52
   Female students 52
   Female instructors 53
   Partnering with prejudices 53
   Condescending to the "weaker" sex 53
Visiting Schools 53
   Checking out the scenery 54
   Choosing the right size 54
   Do you prefer formal or laid-back? 55
   Comparing yourself to others 56
Interviewing Instructors 56
   Instructor qualifications 56
   Competition: Thumbs up or thumbs down? 57
   Achieving rank 58
Paying a Pretty Penny 58
Equipping Yourself 59

Chapter 5: Go Get 'Em: Goals and Ranking Systems 61

Setting Martial Arts Goals 62
   Long-term and short-term goals 62
   Sharing your goals with others 63
Planning the Steps to Reach Your Goals 63
   Considering how goals are reached 64
   Breaking down every goal: Forms 64
   Planning for the long term 65
   Trying the quarterly approach 66
I Have a Black Belt . . . and Green Suspenders:
  The Ranking System 67
   White-belt wannabe 67
   The blue-belt blues 67
   Black-belt beginners 68
   Ranking systems 68
   The kyu/dan system 69
Testing 1, 2, 3 . . . Testing 1, 2, 3 70
   What the judges are looking for 70
   Preparing for your ordeal by fire 71
   Coming out with flying colors 71

Chapter 6: Clothes, Shoes, and Equipment **73**

Pajama Paradise 73
    Using regular workout clothes 74
    Finding a uniform: Plain or with sprinkles? 74
Something's Afoot: Martial Arts Shoes 75
The Right Rigging 75
    Sparring equipment 76
    Weapons 77
Grasshopper's Home Gym 78

Chapter 7: Playing It Safe and Avoiding Injury **81**

Attitude? I'll Give You Attitude! 81
Unnecessary Roughness 82
    I'll have light contact, please 82
    It's not sparring if you don't bruise 83
    Safe sparring 83
Injury Prevention 84
    Watching like a hawk 84
    Treating your body right 86
    Understanding common injuries 86
    Taking simple precautions 87

Part II: Walking the Walk and Talking the Talk 89

Chapter 8: Getting the Most from Your Training **91**

A Martial Artist in Training 91
    Training consistently 91
    Developing the right attitude 92
    Perfect practice makes perfect 94
    Treating yourself right 94
Supplemental Training 97
    Cardiovascular training 97
    Conditioning for flexibility 98
    Speed training 100
    Strength-training techniques 102
    What's a weekend warrior to do? 109

Chapter 9: Protecting Yourself: Self-Defense Details **111**

The Philosophy of Self-Defense 111
    Just walking away 112
    Using only the necessary amount of force 112
    Fighting only for what's worth fighting for 113
    De-escalating a potential conflict 113

Kiai! 113
Stand and deliver 115
Preparation and Planning 115
Simple Precautions 116
Choosing your friends wisely 117
Being aware 117
Listening to intuition 117
Anticipating danger 118
Responding quickly 118
The Three Levels of Self-Defense 119
Basic Self-Defense Techniques 120
The wrist-grab defense 120
The double-wrist grab defense 121
The shoulder- or sleeve-grab defense 123
The shirt- or lapel-grab defense 124
Defending yourself in a chokehold from the front 125
Defending yourself in a chokehold from behind 126
Defending yourself while seated 128
Defending yourself while prone 129

**Chapter 10: Preparing for Competition without
Losing Your Head (Literally)** **131**
Making an Idiot of Yourself and Why You Should Risk It 131
Getting the hang of it 132
Finding out who's doing what 132
Beating the jitters 133
Tournament Events 133
Forms competition 134
Sparring competitions: Mock combat 134
Breaking contests 139
What to Expect When You're Expecting to Compete 139
On the day of the contest 140
Long division 140
Finding Tournaments 142
Choosing the right tournament 143
Doing a dry run 144
Preparing to Strike Oil 144
Being aware of the peak season 144
Knowing the rules 145
Keeping your head in the game 146

Chapter 11: Working the Mind-Body-Spirit Connection **147**
The Way of Martial Arts 147
The mental aspects of the Way 148
The physical aspects of the Way 148

Meditation and Breathing Exercises 150
    Meditation basics 150
    Visualization 151
    Controlled breathing 152
    Rooted-tree breathing 153
Developing Focus and Discipline 153
    Getting organized 155
    Setting priorities 155
Martial Arts as Therapy 156
    Confronting your fears 156
    Building blocks: Confidence and self-esteem 157
    Developing emotional muscle memory 157

**Chapter 12: Just Like in the Movies: The Lowdown
on Weapons 159**
Weapons Disclaimer 159
What's a Weapon? 160
    Weapon categories: Would you like a blade with that? 160
    Weapon ranges: Going my way? 160
Traditional Weapons 161
    Using traditional weapons 162
    Defense against traditional weapons 165
Modern Weapons 165
    Using modern weapons 165
    Defending against modern weapons 166
Environmental Weapons 166
    Look around 167
    What you know, the attacker can know 167

Chapter 13: Using Martial Arts Outside of Class 169
Representing Your Art in the World 169
    Keeping your cool 170
    Wearing your uniform with caution 170
    No kicking your boss 171
    Entering the no-boasting zone 171
    Keeping the trade secrets secret 172
    Giving back to your school and your art 173
Incorporating Martial Arts Beliefs into Your Daily Life 173
    Finding balance 173
    Using the tenets 174
Using Martial Arts Training Every Day 178
    Let's get physical 178
    Looking outside yourself 179
    Achieving your goals 180

Part III: Styles, Techniques, and Tactics: An Up-Close Look 181

Chapter 14: Karate 183
Physical Considerations 183
Okinawan versus Japanese Karate 184
    Okinawan characteristics 184
    Japanese characteristics 185
Traditional Training Methods 185
Basic Training 186
Techniques of Karate 187
    Stances 187
    Guards, guards! 188
    Blocks 189
    Punches 189
    Other hand techniques 190
    Just for kicks 190
    Smash-mouth Karate 193
    Sweeps, throws, and takedowns 193
    Weapons, we've got weapons 194

Chapter 15: Kung Fu 197
Categories of Kung Fu Styles 198
    Northern versus Southern styles 198
    Internal versus External styles 198
Don't Get Bent Out of Shape 199
Popular Kung Fu Styles 199
    Northern Praying Mantis 199
    Monkey style 200
    Choy-Li-Fut 200
    Wing Chun 202
    White Crane 203
Chi Kung Exercises 204
Traditional Training 204
Kung Fu Weapons 206
Kung Fu Techniques 208

Chapter 16: Tae Kwon Do 209
Hard Bodies, Hard Heads 209
The Five Tenets 210
Tae Kwon Do versus Tae Kwon Do 210
    Traditional Tae Kwon Do 211
    Sport or Olympic style Tae Kwon Do 212
    Other Tae Kwon Do approaches 212

Training Methods 213
Strength and endurance training 213
Stretching techniques 213
Basic Techniques 214
Stances 215
Blocks 216
Kicks 217
Hand strikes 220

Chapter 17: Judo 223

Complex Simplicity 223
Physical Fitness Requirements 224
Categories of Techniques 225
Class Is Now in Session 225
Doing the basics 225
Typical training 226
Mobility and Stretching Exercises 226
Breakfalls (Ukemi) 227
Avoiding injury 227
Frustrating your opponent 228
Throwing Techniques 228
Gripping the Gi 229
In the throes of throwing 229
Defending against throws 232
Groundwork (Grappling) Techniques 232
Combining Techniques 233

Chapter 18: Aikido 235

Your Physical Resources 236
Hard and Soft Aikido 236
Showing Rank 236
Ready, Set, Relax! 237
Aikido Curriculum 238
The Best Defense Is a Good Defense 238
Flexibility Training 239
Seated toe touches 239
Kneeling stretches 239
Side bends 240
Upper-body twist 240
Eight-direction exercise 240
Rolls (But No Donuts) 241
Backward rolls 241
Forward rolls 242
Basic Techniques 243
Stances 243
Footwork 244
Basic immobilizations 245
Throwing techniques 246

Chapter 19: Escrima 249

Different Strokes for Different Folks 250
Getting Started 250
Escrima Fitness 251
Mental Attributes 251
Traditional Training 252
    Pandalag 252
    Sombra Tabak 252
Twelve: Your Lucky Number 252
Basic Techniques 253
    Empty-hand techniques 254
    Using the Escrima stick 254
    Stances 254
    Footwork and body-shifting 256
    Stick strikes 257
    Blocking with the stick 257
    Without a stick: Unarmed techniques 259

Chapter 20: Hapkido 263

Well-Rounded Fitness 264
Chi for Me 264
    Vital points (Kup so) 264
    Danjon rules 265
    Chi breathing 265
    You make me wanna shout (Kihop) 265
Defensive Strategy 266
Basic Techniques 266
    Breakfalls (Nakbeop) 267
    The natural stance 268
    Hand techniques 268
    Disengaging techniques 269
    Joint-locking techniques 269
    Throwing techniques 270
    Defense against strikes 271

Chapter 21: Muay Thai 275

Fighting Fit 275
Conditioning Versus Competition: Kickboxing Styles 276
Training Methods 276
    Weight training 277
    Body conditioning 277
    Cardio training 277
    Flexibility training 278
    Balance 278
    Fitting it all in 279
A Kickboxing Workout Routine 279

Sparring for Fun and Profit 280
    Safety considerations 280
    Competitive sparring 281
Basic Techniques 281
    Fighting stance 282
    Punches 282
    Elbows and knees 284
    Kicks 284
    Leg sweeps and throws 287

Chapter 22: Jeet Kune Do and Eclectic Martial Arts **289**

Defense by Interception 289
Let Me Count the Eclectic Ways 290
    Drawbacks to the traditional approach 290
    Eclectic styles 291
Physical Facts 292
Jeet Kune Do Concepts 292
Jeet Kune Do Curriculum 293
Typical Training 293
Creating Your Own Martial Art 294
    Developing a solid background 294
    Finding other techniques 294
Basic Techniques of Jeet Kune Do 295
    The way of no stances 295
    Evasion 295
    Trapping 296
    Attacking by combination 296
    Attacking by drawing 297
    Kicks 297
    Punches 299

Chapter 23: T'ai Chi Chuan **301**

Martial Art or Not? 302
Weapons Use 302
Benefits of T'ai Chi 302
Physical Factors 303
Schools of Thought 303
T'ai Chi Concepts 304
    Dan tien 305
    Extend chi 305
    Meditation 305
The Typical T'ai Chi Class 306
    What to expect 306
    Training tips 307
Techniques of T'ai Chi 307
    Sinking a horse stance instead of a basket 307
    Free flows, not free throws 307
    The first movements 308
    Push hands 310

Part IV: The Part of Tens 313

Chapter 24: Ten Rules for the Martial Arts Classroom 315

Listen More than You Talk 315
Watch and Learn 315
Visualize 316
Accept Criticism 316
Practice, Practice, Practice 317
Respect Yourself (And Others) 317
Remember That Persistence Beats Talent 317
Eat Humble Pie 318
Cultivate Patience 318
Have Fun 318

Chapter 25: Ten Qualities a Good Instructor Must Have 319

Commitment 319
Patience 320
Enthusiasm 320
Humor 320
Acceptance 320
Creativity 321
Selflessness 321
Respect 321
Knowledge 321
Focus 322

Chapter 26: Ten Tips from the Master 323

Setting Goals 323
Committing to Training 323
Learning to Breathe 324
Finding and Using Your Chi 324
Developing a Good Kiai (Shout) 324
Being a Good Role Model 325
Contributing to the Art 325
Honoring Your School 325
Discovering All Aspects of Martial Arts 326
Accepting Hard Training 326

Chapter 27: Ten Cool Martial Arts Movies 327

Why Watch Them? 327
Who Can You Watch? 328
What to Watch 328

Part V: Appendixes *329*

    Appendix A: Glossary 331

    Appendix B: Sources and Resources 337

Index *343*

Introduction

*T*he practice of martial arts is thousands of years old, yet it is just now becoming mainstream in the West. When I was a child (not *that* long ago), all martial arts were called *Kung Fu* or *Karate*. If you were a girl, you'd never ever be able to talk your parents into letting you take lessons. If you were a boy, you had a slight chance. Martial artists and martial arts schools just weren't around much. An occasional serviceman would return from an Asian tour of duty and set up shop somewhere, but these were few and far between.

All that has changed now. You can hardly drive down a block without seeing a martial arts school on the corner, and you can hardly watch an action movie without seeing the hero use martial arts moves against the bad guys. Half the kids in the country are going to the *dojo* (training hall) instead of the baseball diamond.

How did this happen? Thanks to the efforts of martial artists, such as Bruce Lee, Jhoon Rhee, Bill Wallace, Remy Presas, and others, it isn't considered odd anymore to want to kick and punch and grapple for fun (and sometimes profit). These people helped bring what was an Eastern way of life to the West — where now we, too, can benefit from learning combat techniques and the martial arts way of life.

Practicing martial arts helps you achieve a healthy life and a rewarding balance between mind, body, and spirit. Mastering a martial art requires discipline, perseverance, and hard work. A slight loss of sanity never hurts either. (Why else would you think breaking three concrete blocks with a single punch is a good thing to do on a Saturday afternoon? You could be washing the car.)

When you choose to begin training in a martial art, you choose a life of adventure in a real sense. You take more risks, become more open to new ideas, and stop being fearful in your life. You learn to become the person you always wanted to be, and you acquire the courage to pursue the goals and dreams that always seemed just out of your reach before.

Welcome to the most incredible journey of your life, and good luck on the way.

About This Book

The martial arts are systems of combat techniques designed for self-defense. Each martial art has a philosophical foundation. Although the precise nature of this foundation varies from martial art to martial art, and even to some degree from teacher to teacher, all martial arts have a philosophical foundation. Understanding this aspect of martial arts training is important, and that's one of the goals of this book.

Students of the martial arts consider the practice of martial arts to be a way of life. This book is designed to help you understand the purpose of martial arts training and to help you get the most out of it.

Although you may want to curl up with *Martial Arts For Dummies* and read it from cover to cover, that's not essential. If you're already involved in the martial arts, you may want to start with Chapter 5 to focus on what you want to get out of training. If you're new to the martial arts, you may want to turn to Chapter 3 and check up on choosing the right style for you.

Don't worry; skipping around in the book won't leave you totally confused. Each part can stand alone, and so can each of the chapters. Thus, you don't have to worry about missing something that I said in Chapter 1 if you decide to start with Chapter 6. However, I do cover many interesting topics in Chapter 1, and you may not want to miss them.

When a foreign word or concept is introduced for the first time, a definition is given. You can always flip to the Glossary in the back to look up a term in case you haven't seen the definition yet or you forgot what it means. Oh, yeah, and on Friday, you'll be taking a test . . . just kidding.

Conventions Used in This Book

Suppose you're interested in a particular martial art called *Escrima*. You go to your neighborhood *Escrimador* (that would be a person who practices Escrima), ask about training, learn what equipment you need, pay a fee, and sign up for lessons. All this time you've been talking to the Escrimador in English . . . so why is she shouting commands at you in *Spanish* during class? Because that's how Escrima is taught.

While you don't need to know Spanish, Japanese, or Korean (or Chinese or Hindi . . .) to practice a martial art, many classes are conducted in the language of the country that gave birth to the martial art being taught. This means that sooner or later, you're going to have to say the word "dojo" out loud. (That would be a training hall, called a *dojang* in the Korean martial arts.)

In the book, foreign terms such as these are italicized to make them stand out. I define each such term in the text. Appendix A at the back of the book is a glossary that defines each of these terms just in case your memory is as bad as mine, and you can't remember anything without writing it down.

When a specific technique is described, photos are provided to illustrate it. Each photo is called a *figure* and is numbered according to chapter and verse, so to speak. So if I say, "See Figure 14-3," that means you want turn to Chapter 14 and look at the third photo. The caption next to each photo tells you what the figure number is and offers a brief description of what you're seeing.

Foolish Assumptions

Some people have always dreamed of earning a black belt in Karate but never tried because they thought you had to be a 20-year-old man in fantastic shape in order to participate. Not so. Anyone can become a martial artist . . . you just have to try. If you knew what I looked like and what a total klutz I was before I started martial arts training, you would believe in miracles.

Most martial arts instructors offer beginner classes or allow you to modify the workout to suit your needs. So if you're older, have a medical problem, or are simply a bit overweight and out of shape, you'll still be able to learn how to be a martial artist, and impress all your friends and co-workers (and maybe even your Saturday-night date).

However, some 20-year-old men claim to be ninth-degree black belts in Karate, and believing them would be a foolish assumption. Gaining rank in martial arts takes time as well as effort, so don't be impressed when someone claims high ranking and impressive credentials and doesn't shave yet. Instead, be suspicious. In martial arts, older is better or at least better qualified.

How This Book Is Organized

Martial Arts For Dummies has five parts, each covering a different aspect of martial arts. You don't need to read the book in order. I certainly didn't write it in order, why should you have to read it in order? Just pick a part and jump in. Figuratively speaking, of course.

Part 1: Martial Arts Essentials

In addition to an overview of martial arts history and culture, the chapters in this part also show the martial arts rookie what to look out for. You get the lowdown on martial arts schools, styles, and instructors, as well as pointers on how to equip yourself and the payoffs of training. Chapter 5 also describes ranking systems and goal-setting.

Part II: Walking the Walk and Talking the Talk

In this part, Chapter 8 shows you how to get the most from your training. Chapter 9 describes basic and advanced self-defense techniques, including self-defense with and against weapons. Then Chapter 12 tells you even more about weapons. You can find out whether you want to be part of a tournament in Chapter 10. Then Chapter 11 examines the connection between mind, body, and spirit, and Chapter 13 shows you how to use your judgment instead of your side kick when provoked.

Part III: Styles, Techniques, and Tactics: An Up-Close Look

Each chapter in this section offers an in-depth look at one of the ten most-popular martial arts, including the history of the art, basic moves, and training methods.

Part IV: The Part of Tens

In this part, I provide ten rules for learning, ten qualities a good instructor has, and ten tips from the master, and ten fun martial arts movies to watch when you feel like kicking back.

Part V: Appendixes

Appendix A is a glossary of martial arts terms, so when the instructors barks, "Charyehet!" you'll know exactly what to do (come to attention). Finally, Appendix B tells you where to get the goodies, find more information, and meet other martial artists.

Icons Used in This Book

Martial artists bandy foreign words and concepts about on a regular basis. This icon alerts you to the meaning of these terms.

Practicing martial arts means that you have plenty to learn about, so this icon alerts you to the most important information that you should keep in mind.

This icon lets you know when I'm giving you special information about martial arts culture, philosophy, teaching, and learning. By the way, *sensei* means *teacher*.

Let's just say that when I started training in martial arts, I didn't have any gray hair. In all the years since, I have accumulated some wisdom along with some bruises. This icon signals helpful hints to help you improve your training and avoid some of the bruises.

You can hurt yourself breaking bricks with your forehead, so this icon signals information that you should pay attention to in order to stay safe mentally, emotionally, physically, and financially.

Where to Go from Here

If you want to know where martial arts came from, start with Part I for an introduction to the martial arts, as well as the essentials on choosing a style and school if you're ready to get started. If you have some experience, dig into Part II and learn how to get more from your training. If you want to know what to expect from the different martial arts, check out Part III. Then Part IV offers ten learning basics and the ten traits that quality instructors have in common. The resources listed in Part V, Appendix B, can also help as a guide to information that may help you make informed decisions, such as choosing the right martial arts style for you.

Even though popular culture tends toward immediate gratification, some people are dissatisfied with that approach to life and find that they want to achieve something meaningful — of lasting value. Martial artists recognize that mastery of any kind takes time, effort, hard work, and perseverance. But all that's required to start is an interest in martial arts and the willingness to step into the training hall.

Part I
Martial Arts
Essentials

The 5th Wave   By Rich Tennant

As a practitioner of Tae Quik Cash, Jerry performs several well executed finger strikes to enter his PIN.

ATM

In this part . . .

These chapters give you basic information about martial arts, including a brief history, the benefits of training, misconceptions about martial arts, and concepts that are important to martial arts culture. These chapters also help you choose a martial arts style, select the right school and instructor for you, guide you to the right equipment, and describe ranking systems and how to set martial arts goals.

Chapter 1

Better Than a Barroom Brawl

In This Chapter

▶ Understanding what the martial arts are

▶ Finding out about martial arts history

▶ Recognizing that anyone can succeed

▶ Dispelling misconceptions

▶ Preconditioning to get ready for training

The martial arts, as systems of combat techniques, have been around for at least 4,000 years. (The ability to punch someone has been around much longer than that, but I'm talking about complete systems of martial arts techniques.)

How do I know that the martial arts are at least 4,000 years old? I know it, not because *I'm* 4,000 years old, but because ancient stories describe martial arts competitions, and old, old poems recount the deeds of brave martial artists. Sculptures, drawings, and paintings from eons ago show people punching and kicking each other in a stylized way that suggests competition, not combat.

Chinese swordsman Sun T'zu's book of strategy, *The Art of War,* is more than 2,000 years old. Other combat manuals were written hundreds of years ago in China and Korea. All these things tell us that for thousands of years, people have been interested in learning ways to protect themselves and the ones they love. *The Book of Five Rings,* written 400 years ago by the warrior Miyamoto Musashi, is a classic treatise on combat strategy. The *Muye Dobo Tongji,* which was recently translated into English, is a Korean combat manual from 200 years ago.

Anything that has been around for such a long period of time has to have something going for it. Over thousands of years, the martial arts have become refined and organized. Now they're highly efficient methods for defending yourself, becoming physically fit, and impressing your friends with your jump-spinning kick.

Kicks, Flips, and Other Stuff: What Are the Martial Arts?

The martial arts aren't just collections of combat techniques that are taught along with some combat strategy — although you can learn combat techniques and combat strategy. The martial arts aren't just for self-defense — although self-defense can seem pretty pertinent when a mugger is standing between you and your car. But martial arts themselves are more than just methods of combat. They're systems that promote physical, spiritual, and psychological values.

In fact, early martial arts may have begun life as a ritual aspect of religion, according to many historians. Until recently, Sumo wrestling in Japan was performed as a Shinto divination ceremony. Who won and who lost, and how they did so, told the Shinto diviners a great deal about the world and what to expect in the near future. This is just one example of how what appear to be methods of kicking and throwing other people took on moral and philosophical elements.

This is not to say that martial arts as they're practiced today are some form of religion. They're not. They do have spiritual elements, and they do invite practitioners to become better people. Respecting your teacher, learning to work hard, accept criticism, and finding out that you can do more than you ever thought possible helps you to grow as a person. How deeply you delve into the philosophical and character-building aspects is up to you — dig in!

Starting on the path

The names of most martial arts end with the word *do* — Tae Kwon Do, Judo, and so on. Even Karate used to be called *Karate-do,* but the *do* has been dropped in recent times. The word *do* means *way of.* Thus, Tae Kwon Do can be translated to mean, "the way of the hand and foot."

The way simply means *the path.* A martial art is a path that you take, a journey that you embark on . . . and you don't even know where the heck you're going. You just have to take it on faith that it's somewhere that you want to be.

If you think about it, the use of *the way* makes sense. If martial arts were just sports or a means of keeping fit, we wouldn't call them *the way of.* . . . After all, no one calls soccer "the way of the head and feet."

Martial arts mythology

Once upon a time, as folklore from Asia tells us, supernatural creatures called the *Tengu* practiced the warrior arts. The Tengu deigned to instruct worthy humans in these secret arts (no word on who instructed the Tengu). To gain credentials for their martial arts (this was long before the International Sport Karate Association was founded), teachers often claimed that the Tengu had taught them their arts.

I don't mean to suggest that these early teachers were liars, but you can draw your own conclusions.

Achieving harmony and balance: It's more than self-defense

Martial arts incorporate a complete way of living in harmony and balance, within you and in relation to the outside world. This harmony and balance is achieved through physical effort, meditation, and character-building exercises and requirements.

All martial arts teachers expect practitioners to become "better" people. Each style has a method for teaching students to better themselves. For instance, in Tae Kwon Do, the *five tenets* are taught. All Tae Kwon Do practitioners are expected to follow the five tenets and display the qualities of courtesy, integrity, perseverance, self-control, and indomitable spirit. The five tenets are more important — much more important — than the ability to do a flying side kick.

People sometimes confuse aerobic-class martial arts, such as cardio-kickboxing, with the real thing. Just because you work out with your Tae Bo tape each day, does not mean that you're prepared to defend yourself against a mugger. Only specific self-defense or martial arts training can give you the knowledge and experience that you need to defend yourself.

What It Ain't: Martial Arts Misconceptions

Frankly, its slightly sinister reputation was one of the reasons that I began training in the martial arts. I knew martial arts were *not* aerobics, and that appealed to me.

Martial arts are definitely not for people who are unwilling to work hard, sustain a bruise or two, and cultivate a certain toughness of mind and body. On the other hand, misconceptions abound about the martial arts that might stop a person from trying them. I try to dispel some of these misconceptions in the following sections.

Clarifying the spiritual aspect

Martial artists are not all Buddhists or followers of some obscure religious sect (although some of them are and do). Many martial artists are Presbyterians. I know one who is a Methodist minister. Others are Muslims, Catholics, Zoroastrians, agnostics, and atheists. It doesn't matter what religion you practice: Anyone can be a martial artist. When martial artists talk about spiritual matters, they mean a higher being or a higher level of existence — not a specific religious creed.

Demystifying the black belt mystique

The idea of the black belt "lethal weapon" is sorely misunderstood. To become a black belt, you don't have to be initiated by doing any of the following:

- Defeating a black belt in a no-holds-barred fight to the finish
- Injuring or maiming innocent (or even guilty) people
- Firewalking across burning coals

You don't have to do anything remotely like the misconceptions that are listed. I know it may sound boring, but you become a black belt through dedicated practice and perseverance. And no, you don't have to register with the local police department when you earn your black belt. Although you can if you want.

Violence: Turning the other cheek

It seems hard to believe, but martial artists may be, as a group, the most peace-loving, laid-back bunch of pacifists you ever met. All martial arts emphasize nonviolence. Using martial arts techniques to attack another person is never acceptable. The martial arts are to be used only to defend or counterattack.

Martial artists are taught to use their skills only in self-defense (or in defense of someone else). They should never attack another person. If an option to fighting is available, such as running away, they're trained to take it.

However, martial artists who must fight use only the amount of force necessary to end the fight. Along with fighting skills come certain responsibilities. People are justly outraged when trained boxers or other fighters use their skills outside the ring in an unprovoked attack or excessively in self-defense.

Trained fighters who go beyond what's called for are more severely punished than untrained people who panic and lose control. The punishment is more extreme because trained people know what they're doing and are intentionally inflicting more physical damage than is absolutely necessary.

Why all the board-breaking stuff?

Some martial arts styles, such as Tae Kwon Do and some forms of Karate, require board and brick breaking. Martial artists joke about breaking boards with their foreheads, but it's never attempted — at least not by legitimate martial artists. What they do at the circus is their own business.

Boards, bricks, or concrete blocks are broken using combat techniques, such as punches and kicks. You may be wondering, "Why break boards? How many times has a board attacked you?" The answer is that a board-wielding maniac has never attacked me, but I will be perfectly prepared should I ever encounter one. In fact, martial artists break boards for several reasons.

Full contact application

First, martial artists usually don't spar full contact with sparring partners, at least not on a daily basis. You can run through sparring partners pretty quickly if you knock one out every afternoon. Breaking a pine board that's one-inch thick, which is the equivalent of breaking a person's ribs, gives you a sense of the power that you need to actually stop an attacker. Being able to break boards consistently, under different circumstances, gives the martial artist confidence that she can produce the same amount of power against an attacker.

Developing correct technique

In addition, you must execute techniques correctly to break a board. If you don't execute the technique properly, your hand or foot will bounce off the board — and that stings . . . plenty. Board-breaking, therefore, helps martial artists correct and perfect their technique. Further, to break a board, you must strike through the target, thus doing the greatest amount of damage. It can be difficult to learn this skill using any other method.

Peer pressure: Mental discipline

Finally, board-breaking improves mental discipline. If you tell yourself that this board is never going to break, then you're right. You have to decide that you want to hit the block of wood hard enough to break it and that you *can* hit it hard enough to break it. And if you give up at the last minute, everyone watching will know.

More than one person has watched a martial artist break a board or a brick and then tried to do the same thing with the scrap lumber in the garage. Don't try this at home. Board-breaking should only be done by trained martial artists under the supervision of a trained instructor.

Although many misconceptions about martial arts circulate, a student at a well-run school will always feel safe and confident during practice (see Chapter 4).

Pick a Flavor, Any Flavor: The Different Types

This section supplies you with a brief rundown of many of the different types of martial arts that exist today. This section gives you the basic defining characteristics of each type. For more information about the different types of martial arts, get something to drink, get comfy, and flip on over to the appropriate chapter in Part III.

Chinese martial arts

Over the thousands of years that martial arts have been practiced, hundreds of Chinese martial arts have developed. Unfortunately for people who like clearly defined categories, most Chinese martial arts fall under the name *Kung Fu* or *Wushu,* broad terms meaning something like *human effort.* Practically anything can, and does, fall into this category, including cleaning the kitchen and doing the laundry. But we still use the term *Kung Fu* for lack of a better one.

Jeet Kune Do

Bruce Lee, the founder of Jeet Kune Do, was a Wing Chun Kung Fu practitioner for many years before he became dissatisfied with the style — he felt that it was somehow incomplete as a fighting system. He was interested in the purely defensive aspect of martial arts, so he developed a system of fighting that was, in essence, tailored by each individual to suit his needs. He advocated learning from many different martial arts and keeping only those techniques and tactics that work well for you.

Everybody was Kung Fu fighting

The Kung Fu types are all different from each other. The different types tended to be passed on in family groups. Sometimes, the teacher would refrain from teaching his students all the techniques in a system. I suspect that this was so the teacher could always defeat any student who challenged him.

Monastery-based martial arts were usually taught to others in secrecy. In Zen Buddhism, physical effort and movement, when done correctly, is thought to aid enlightenment, which explains why all the monks and nuns spent so much time learning some pretty hairy techniques and tactics. See, David Carradine and *Kung Fu* weren't that far off the mark

Along the same lines, many martial artists begin training in a traditional martial art and then alter or modify it to better suit their needs. Then they begin teaching this "eclectic" art to others. (For more on Jeet Kune Do, see Chapter 22.)

Kung Fu

A complete understanding of Kung Fu (Chapter 15) takes a lifetime to develop. Over 400 different kinds of Kung Fu exist, with some resembling Karate or Aikido (see the following). Generally, grappling techniques aren't taught. Weapons are used in some kinds of Kung Fu but not all. Chinese weapons vary widely from chain whips to paired swords to segmented staffs.

All Kung Fu schools teach postures, guards, and fist and foot attacks, as well as *forms* (predetermined patterns of movement). Sometimes, Kung Fu styles are classified as Northern or Southern style, with *Northern styles* emphasizing foot techniques and *Southern styles* emphasizing hand techniques. A distinction is also made between inner and outer Kung Fu styles. *Inner-style* Kung Fu focuses on chi and philosophical elements of training, and *outer-style* Kung Fu focuses on force and rapid movement.

T'ai Chi

T'ai Chi (Supreme Ultimate Fist) is one of the oldest martial arts in the world. It's so ancient that its origins have been lost. Nothing is known about its early history, although its legendary founder is the Taoist Chang Zhangfeng. T'ai Chi consists of slow, connected movements used mainly as a means for keeping the body in shape and relieving stress. Truly accomplished practitioners can also use its techniques in self-defense.

The three segments of T'ai Chi practice are weapons training, push hands training, and *forms* (often called *kata* or *hyung*, these are precise patterns of specific martial arts movements). The art emphasizes practicing moderation in all things, following the Middle Way — the Way of Balance and Harmony —

instead of going from one extreme to another, such as extreme austerity or complete indulgence, and understanding the importance of yielding, thus allowing the attacker to defeat himself. (For more on T'ai Chi, see Chapter 23.)

Japanese martial arts

Formal martial arts systems sprang into being in Japan in a more militarized way than they did in China. These systems were formed around combat methods to be used in battle. The Samurai, for example, were mounted warriors trained in attacking techniques, self-defense techniques, and all aspects of sword fighting.

The Japanese Samurai were high-ranking noble warriors who practiced the combat arts and controlled the government of Japan for many centuries. Like medieval chivalric knights in Europe, the Samurai were expected to follow a strict code of conduct. The Samurai ideal was difficult to actually practice — many warriors failed to attain it.

Peasantly surprised

Peasants, on the other hand, learned martial arts techniques mostly to defend themselves (often against the Samurai). The Samurai were clever: They forbade peasants from owning weapons, such as swords. The peasants were even cleverer: They used anything that they could get their hands on as weapons.

Japanese weapons

Japanese martial arts weapons are unusual, to say the least. *Nunchuku,* the Karate weapon consisting of two short sticks linked by a chain, was actually a flail used for threshing rice. It became a martial arts weapon when some enterprising peasant used it to thresh a Samurai (or maybe just an irritating neighbor).

Out of the closet

The *Boxer Rebellion of 1900* was a rebellion by Chinese nationalists against foreign rule. These "boxers" were martial artists who had been trained in secret societies, some of which still exist today. When an international army crushed the rebellion, many of the boxers fled to California, where they joined the Chinese-American community. In California, they continued to teach their martial arts in secret.

Bruce Lee was one of the first individuals to teach Chinese martial arts to people who weren't Chinese. He felt that the knowledge should be shared with anyone willing to put forth the effort. As a result, Lee was threatened and even severely beaten at one time. But in true Bruce Lee fashion, he didn't let it stop him.

The *tonfa,* a stick with a handle attached at a right angle, started out as a crank on a handmill that was used to grind rice. Fighting staffs, in all their variations, were originally walking sticks. In the hands of peasants, chains became whips, scythes served as swords, and scraps of metal became throwing stars.

Women of high rank also had to contend with the Samurai and other hoodlums. Because the noble women could possess weapons, they often chose the *naginata,* a bladed weapon similar to a halberd. The naginata could effectively counter a sword. Women routinely trained in naginata-do, so they could defend their homes. Women also concealed short daggers, called *kaiken,* in their clothes. Now you know why the Samurai treated high-ranking women with respect. (For more on weapons, see Chapter 12.)

Aikido

When translated, Aikido means "the Way of Harmony with Universal Energy." Aikido stresses the harmony of mind, body, and moral outlook. This martial art, founded in 1931 by Ueshiba Morihei, is based on elements of Jujutsu, a grappling art. Aikido, however, is a purely defensive art. Its quick, decisive movements are designed to use the attacker's momentum against himself. Aikido doesn't teach punches or kicks, although sometimes weapons — especially the fighting staff — are taught.

Aikido techniques fall into two categories: *controlling techniques* and *throwing techniques.* The techniques are taught in a way that's intended to help students surmount any physical or emotional barriers. Aikido practitioners are trained to become more relaxed and harmonious within themselves and within the outside world. (Turn to Chapter 18 for more on Aikido.)

Judo

Judo (the Way of Gentleness) is a defensive martial art that was created in 1882 by Jigoro Kano. It is based on Jujutsu, an ancient martial art that relies on grappling, throwing, and joint-locking. Judo emphasizes throwing an attacker off balance and using the attacker's momentum against himself. Judo practitioners work on flexibility, balance, speed, and finesse. Alertness, serenity, calmness, and self-discipline are essential elements of Judo practice. No weapons are used in Judo.

Although the founder of Judo discouraged competition — he felt that Judo was a personal means of training oneself — Judo competition has become increasingly popular. It first appeared as an Olympic sport in 1964. Judo, which is an obligatory sport in Japanese schools, is one of the most popular martial arts in the world. (See Chapter 17 for more on Judo.)

Okinawan martial arts

Settlers and monks brought Chinese martial arts with them when they traveled to Okinawa, an island off the coast of Japan. A style of unarmed combat called *Te* had been practiced in Okinawa for many years. The Chinese techniques were combined with Te to create *Kara-te* or *Chinese hand.* Although Karate is famous as a martial art from mainland Japan, it actually originated in Okinawa.

From China hand to empty hand

In the twentieth century, the meaning of the word *Kara-te* was changed from *China hand* to *empty hand* by using a different set of characters that were pronounced the same way. In other words, the founder of modern Karate, a patriotic Japanese martial artist, didn't want his students to think that they were learning a Chinese martial art.

Karate

Karate is a centuries-old style of martial art that incorporates techniques from Chinese and Japanese martial arts. Karate (see Chapter 14) sometimes uses Japanese weapons, such as nunchuku, but bare hands and feet are the primary fighting implements.

Although many different styles of Karate exist, they all have some things in common. Karate uses striking techniques such as kicks, punches, and sweeps. *Grappling* — throws, pins, and holds similar to wrestling — isn't used; the Karate practitioner intends to stay on his own two feet. Speed of movement, power of techniques, and timing of attack are all taught. Mastery can take years, and many advanced *Karate-ka* (Karate practitioners) say you can never master the art.

Make love, not war

In Silla Kingdom Korea (A.D. 668–935), young nobles who were preparing for military leadership were called the *Hwarang* (flowering youth.) Like the Japanese Samurai, they were instructed in martial strategy and were expected to live up to an ideal of loyalty, courage, and justice. This code of conduct was called *Hwarang-do.*

In 1231, the Mongols invaded and occupied Korea. Later, they were expelled. Korea then closed itself off to the outside world. Only China was allowed access to Korea. Because of its isolation, Korea was nicknamed the *Hermit Kingdom.*

Military leaders and all high-ranking individuals were expected to train in martial arts until late in the fourteenth century. What happened then? Confucianism replaced Buddhism as the dominant philosophical belief among Koreans. Confucianism, as a philosophy, disapproves of war and martial deeds and would happily do away with warriors. Cultural and intellectual achievements are considered more important than any battle.

Korean culture rises again

Japan occupied Korea at the beginning of the twentieth century and could not be persuaded to let go of the country until after World War II. During this time, the practice of martial arts was forbidden, as were most Korean cultural practices. Apparently the Japanese wanted the Koreans to forget that they were Korean.

No such luck. After the Japanese left Korea, the previously banned martial arts flourished. General Hong Hi Choi, the founder of modern Tae Kwon Do, consolidated many of the different Korean styles into one. In the 1950s, the name *Tae Kwon Do* was given to this new martial art. Now, it's as popular as Karate.

Korean martial arts

In Korea, Chinese martial arts affected the development of Subak and Tae Kyun, the early Korean martial arts. Korea had isolated itself from everyone except China, so China's martial arts influence was the only one that it absorbed.

Hapkido

Hapkido (the Way of Coordinated Power) is a modern martial art based on the traditional Korean art of Yu-Sol. All techniques are chosen and used solely for their practical application in self-defense. The unnecessary, difficult, and flashy techniques have been eliminated, leaving a set of highly effective techniques that can be used in any fighting situation.

Hapkido was organized and systematized in the 1930s by Choi Yong Shul. He polished the techniques of Yu-Sol and added techniques from Aikido to develop an art that uses both direct linear attacks and circular movements to redirect an attacker's energy. (For more on Hapkido, see Chapter 20.)

Tae Kwon Do

When Tae Kwon Do was first introduced to the United States, it was called *Korean Karate* to show its relationship to the well-known martial art. Now Tae Kwon Do is recognized in its own right as a complete fighting system. Like Karate, Tae Kwon Do teaches punches and kicks. Tae Kwon Do is sometimes thought to be a kicking art, but numerous hand techniques are taught as well. They just don't look as cool as the spectacular jumping kicks.

Tae Kwon Do teaches techniques similar to Aikido, such as *joint-locking* (manipulating the joints to control and attacker) and *vital point-striking* (attacking vulnerable parts of the body, such as the throat and groin). Tae Kwon Do stresses the importance of the correct balance of mind, body, and spirit. (See Chapter 16 for more on Tae Kwon Do.)

From India with love: Flying monks and nuns

Martial arts first developed in India. Historians know that martial arts first developed in India because . . . well, trust me, they know it. From India, martial arts spread throughout China, Japan, and Korea over a period of centuries. Bodhidharma (A.D. 460–534), an Indian monk, founded Zen Buddhism and left India to spread his message. According to legend, he taught martial arts, as well as Zen Buddhism, to the monks he encountered. During his travels, Bodhidharma arrived at the famous Shaolin temple, a monastery in the Hunan province of China. The Shaolin monastery was founded in the late fifth century to honor Bodhiruchi, a devout Buddhist monk. According to legend, Bodhidharma taught his martial arts techniques to the monastics at the temple. This aspect of the legend is in dispute, although it's possible, even probable, that he brought some method of physical exercise — perhaps a form of yoga — with him.

What is not in dispute is that the Shaolin monastery and its inhabitants managed to irritate the unstable government of the region an average of about once a week. Because the monastery sheltered rebels and dissidents, as well as monks and nuns (some of the monks and nuns were also rebels and dissidents), government forces destroyed it repeatedly. Eventually, it was moved to the Fukien province in the south. The second Shaolin temple was also destroyed. This time, the monks and nuns scattered permanently, becoming itinerant martial arts teachers who earned a precarious living. (Most martial arts instructors will tell you that little has changed today.)

Many modern martial arts claim to have originated at the Shaolin temple — much like in earlier times, when teachers claimed that the Tengu had taught them. Although martial arts historians (yes, there is such a thing as a martial art historian) dispute which aspects of the Bodhidharma/Shaolin temple legend are true, doubt doesn't cloud the belief that the practice of martial arts steadily grew and spread throughout China and all of Asia.

Indonesian, Filipino, and other martial arts

As the practice of martial arts spread throughout the world, many cultures became influenced by it, including Indonesian, Thai, and Filipino cultures, which developed their own indigenous styles of martial arts. These styles are less well-known than Japanese, Chinese, and Korean martial arts, but they're becoming more popular and more widely recognized in the West.

Escrima

Escrima, meaning *skirmish,* is a Filipino martial art that teaches stick fighting. Two other arts, *Arnis* and *Kali,* are also common in the Philippines. All three arts teach many of the same techniques, strategies, and tactics. They just go by different names in different parts of the country. In the West, the name that is most well-known is Escrima. This martial art came into existence in the ninth century and was influenced by Indonesian and Chinese warriors.

In the sixteenth century, Spain invaded the Philippines. The Philippine natives had mostly wooden weapons to defend themselves against the swords, so they learned how to strike to the attacker's body (rather than the attacker's sword) with their sticks. Techniques of fencing and swordsmanship influenced the development of Escrima. Escrimadors (Escrima practitioners) use sticks and their hands and feet to fight. One form of Escrima also uses a sword and dagger. (For more on Escrima, see Chapter 19.)

Muay Thai

A martial art called Muay Thai (see Chapter 21) developed in Thailand hundreds of years ago. It may have developed from Chinese martial arts, and soldiers may have used it as a part of military training. Excellent Muay Thai boxers could draw huge crowds of people. The boxers often performed to honor the king. Even now, modern Thai boxers are able to draw huge crowds.

Muay Thai is the forerunner of modern kickboxing. But unlike kickboxing, Muay Thai has a ritual and philosophical background. It's also an extremely brutal martial art. Muay Thai boxers use elbows, knees, and shins, as well as hands and feet to strike. Muay Thai boxers generally have short careers.

Who, Me? Anybody Can Succeed!

People often believe that they have to be a buff 20-year-old man to succeed at Karate (or Escrima or Muay Thai . . .). Or they think that a medical condition or disability means that they have to sit on the sidelines and watch their kids have all the fun. Not so.

It takes all kinds: Diversity "R" Us

Anyone can participate in martial arts, and anyone can succeed. The buff 20-year-old men are often the ones who *don't* succeed because they're not willing to learn the lessons. They think they already know it all.

If you can commit to training, persevere, and simply try to become better than you were yesterday, you can be a success no matter where you're starting.

A typical martial arts school has students of both sexes, as well as students of all ages, abilities, physical conditions, and ethnic groups. I've taught children as young as 4 years old — and they also taught me . . . patience, that is. I've also taught 70-year-old white belt beginners. (On some days, I felt like a 70-year-old white belt beginner.)

Medical problems and disabilities

People with medical problems ranging from asthma to heart disease have participated in martial arts training. When I started, I had been suffering from rheumatoid arthritis for eight years. My condition actually improved the harder that I trained my body.

Those who are physically different can also succeed. One White Crane Kung Fu practitioner has been training from his wheelchair and recently received his teaching certificate. A high-ranking martial artist who taught me a great deal about sparring is deaf. I know of one martial arts instructor who is blind. People with muscular dystrophy, limited mobility, and other problems have succeeded in their martial arts training.

Focusing on the positive: Modification and adaptation

How can it be that so many people with differing abilities have succeeded in martial arts? Simple. Martial arts are about becoming a better person. The martial arts are also about becoming more skilled and more capable of defending yourself. You can accomplish these goals in an infinite number of ways. I know of one black belt in Tae Kwon Do who has a permanent hand injury that prevents him from closing his hand to make a fist. He simply uses open hand techniques instead of punches.

Don't assume that just because you have a medical problem or disability you can't do certain techniques. It never hurts to try. But if you really *can't* do certain techniques, make sure that you speak with your instructor about good ways to modify and adapt the techniques that you're learning.

All techniques can be modified and adapted for people of differing abilities. Your progress and success is based on finding what you can do rather than focusing on what you can't do.

See your physician first

Of course, before you embark on any physical exercise program, you should clear it with your physician first. Yes, you may have to admit that you want to take Kung Fu lessons, but that's better than fainting in the middle of your first class and then finding out that you're hypoglycemic.

It's All About You: The Benefits

So why should you train in the martial arts? (Besides wanting to pull a Steven Seagal armlock on your boss the next time that he opens his big mouth.)

Practicing the martial arts has many benefits. Some of these benefits are obvious. Knowing how to kick an attacker in the groin can come in handy in a deserted parking lot on an early Monday morning. Exercising regularly improves your fitness level and can help you lose those extra pounds that you've put on since college.

But wait! There's more. Martial arts are intended to teach three things:

- ✔ Character
- ✔ Combat techniques
- ✔ Self-confidence

The benefits go beyond losing a dress size and improving your cardiovascular fitness. When you train in martial arts, you're expected to adhere to a certain code of conduct. You're expected to follow this code of conduct every day in all aspects of your life. You learn to be proud of yourself and the things that you can do.

Sitting couch potato, hidden tiger: Physical benefits

Even if you're already in pretty good shape — heck, even if you're one of those buff 20-year-old men that I keep picking on — martial arts practice demands much more from your body than weight lifting regimens or standard aerobics classes.

When you practice martial arts, you develop strength, agility, flexibility, and endurance. These physical benefits can help make ordinary tasks, such as running after a mischievous 3-year-old, much easier. They can also improve your competence at other sports. You may even be able to beat your teenager at basketball now and then. (But I make no promises.)

Peaceful warrior: Mental and emotional benefits

Mental and emotional benefits are also associated with training in the martial arts. You increase your self-confidence as you learn to control your body. Your self-esteem grows as you master new skills. Being able to see your ribs again, after they've been buried under fat for years, can lift even the most downtrodden of spirits.

Self-defense skills may make you braver and more courageous, not just in the training hall but in the outside world, as well — and not just when confronting knife-wielding attackers, but when handling nasty bosses and edgy spouses.

I often tell people that the most dangerous martial artists are green belts, not black belts. In Tae Kwon Do, my main martial art, a green belt is an intermediate rank. At this stage, students have learned the basic techniques and are starting to feel tremendously confident of their physical skills — but they haven't developed much humility yet, so their judgment is poor. Watch out for this stage — don't let confidence become overconfidence and get you into situations you'd do better to avoid.

Becoming empowered

Martial arts training can be empowering and liberating. When you train in the martial arts, you may be more willing to take risks and open up to new experiences. You may also become more assertive.

As Confucius once said, practice moderation in all things, including assertiveness. After a few months of training, I went from Walking Doormat to Crouching Tiger. The change seriously annoyed my friends and startled innocent co-workers. It was some time before I found the right balance and became assertive with important things and easygoing with unimportant things. (Although some would dispute that I'm ever easygoing with anything.)

New strength and beauty ideals: Who needs supermodels, anyway?

Martial arts training teaches you that we're all beautiful when we do our forms right and that we're all strong when we execute our techniques correctly. We don't all have to be strong and beautiful in the same way — such as whatever version this month's *Glamour* or *Esquire* is pushing.

Discovering your inner stupidity

When training in the martial arts, you may tap into sides of your personality that you never knew you had. For instance, I never knew that I had a stupid side until I began training. I injured my knee once, and my doctor told me to rest it for two weeks.

"But I have a competition this weekend!" I wailed. I went to the competition anyway, made the injury worse and ended up having to stay off my knee for *three* weeks.

Prior to this time, I had never been interested in physical competition. Any excuse to avoid physical exertion was a good excuse. For me, to choose to compete when I had been advised not to was a change of mind-altering proportions, at least according to certain family members who knew me when.

I hope you react in a slightly healthier way and listen to what your doctor says. But if you don't, allow me to recommend Chapter 7, which discusses injuries and injury prevention.

Self-discipline and focus: Bye bye space cadet

Mastering martial arts techniques leads to self-discipline and focus — both can benefit you in other areas of your life. You must regularly practice. You must repeat techniques thousands of times to master them. You must develop intense focus to do what you didn't think you could accomplish before, such as breaking boards with your bare hands.

Check your worries at the door: Stress-Relief

An intensely physical workout is stress relieving. You leave all your outside worries at the door. In the training hall, your only worry is to do the best you can (and to maybe avoid that jump-spinning-wheel kick coming at your head at 70 miles an hour).

It's just a darn good time!

One final benefit of martial arts training that's often overlooked is camaraderie. You train with interesting people from all walks of life. You root for each other as you master techniques, teach each other, and compete against each other. Almost all my closest friends are martial artists, and they come from diverse backgrounds. You find that you can share interests with people who are older than you, as well as those who are younger than you. You may enjoy having 10-year-olds cheer you on, as much as you enjoy cheering them on.

Preconditioning Your Mind and Body

So you're raring to go. Hold on there, cowboy. You have to do a couple of things first, such as choose a martial arts style (see Chapter 3) and a school or instructor (see Chapter 4). But even before you do that, you need to precondition your mind and body. That is, you need to get ready to get ready.

How do you get ready to get ready? First, you need to assess your physical condition. Your healthcare provider can help with this assessment. Although you can start learning martial arts no matter what condition you're in, it makes sense to spend a little time preparing your body for what lies ahead, especially if you spent most of the last ten years imitating a vegetable.

Work out (or at least get off the couch)

While you're choosing a martial arts style and school, you can start a light workout to help prepare yourself for your first training session. Because martial artists need to be flexible, you can do some light stretches a couple of times a day. Marital artists also need endurance. To help increase your endurance, you can start walking the dog every afternoon. Be sure to walk briskly or run. The dog will love it!

You can also focus on fixing potential problem areas. If you have problems with your knees, for instance, you can spend some time at the gym building your leg muscles to help strengthen those knees.

Condition your mind

Preconditioning your mind doesn't require as much physical effort as preconditioning your body, but it can be just as important. You're on the right track because you picked up *Martial Arts For Dummies.* You can also find other reference books on any of the specific martial arts that interest you. You can rent a couple of Bruce Lee movies to get you in the mood for practicing martial arts. Stop by a martial arts school and watch a class. Find someone who is a martial artist and interview her. Ask her what you can expect from training.

You can also think about what you want to get from your training. If you know your goals ahead of time, you'll be more likely to achieve them. If you want to lose weight and get in shape, for instance, you may have to make some changes to your diet as well as starting a martial arts class. But always approach your martial arts experience with an open mind. It's what you don't expect that's often the most rewarding aspect of martial arts training.

By giving yourself the opportunity to precondition your mind and body, you can be better prepared for the challenges of martial arts training. You may be less likely to suffer from burnout and injury if you spend some time getting ready to get ready. You'll also feel more confident about tackling the challenges of martial arts if you've walked around the blocks a couple of times before learning how to do a flying side kick.

Chapter 2

Martial Arts Culture

In This Chapter

▶ Understanding martial arts motifs

▶ Cultivating a martial arts mindset

▶ Discovering martial arts philosophy

*O*ver the centuries, martial artists have developed a culture that non-martial artists can find confusing and even intimidating. In this chapter, I describe martial arts culture, philosophy, and why martial artists are so fond of dragons. Along the way, I dispel a few myths.

It's important to remember that martial arts training focuses on the *martial* — this means that martial arts instructors are interested in making warriors. This training may require the occasional knuckle pushup for a rule infraction or standing at attention for 15 minutes just because the instructor told you to. A martial arts training session isn't your basic aerobics class. If it does resemble your basic aerobics class, you may not be learning the full potential of the art you're being taught.

But there's more to being a martial artist than obeying the instructor and learning physical techniques. You have to learn mental mindsets, and you have to exert excellent control over your emotions. These skills are taught as part of martial arts training, and you should expect to be challenged to develop them.

Martial Arts Wildlife

You've probably noticed by now that martial artists are fixated on dragons and tigers. Practically every other school is called "White Tiger Something" or "Dragonfire Something Else." What's *that* about?

This attraction to and celebration of dragons, tigers, and other wildlife comes from ancient Chinese martial artists.

Lions and tigers and bears, oh my!

The tiger, once a feared predator, was hunted in southern China for many years. Martial artists appreciate its qualities of cunning and alertness, along with its surprise attack capabilities.

The dragon is a mythical creature that's believed to have special qualities, including fearlessness and almost complete invincibility. The dragon is one of the twelve signs on the Chinese zodiac. Martial artists like to emulate the strength and fierceness of the dragon; some believe that the dragon is a source of wisdom and insight.

The monkey, so similar to humans and yet so different, is credited with inspiring many martial arts masters to incorporate monkeylike movements into their techniques. The most famous of these martial arts techniques is Monkey Style Kung Fu, founded by Kou Tse. Different aspects of Monkey Style include the Drunken Monkey, Lost Monkey, and Stone Monkey.

Finally, the lion is celebrated as a hunter who dominates his surroundings. During the Chinese New Year, some martial arts schools perform lion dances in parades, manipulating a huge papier-mâché lion head and fabric body. For Chinese martial arts schools, the lion represents the "soul" or "heart" of a school.

And that's not all . . .

Although other animals are also celebrated for the characteristics they bring to martial arts — everything from the praying mantis to the crane has been studied — the contributions of the lion, tiger, dragon, and monkey are the most well-known.

Over the years, other martial arts have adopted these Chinese animals by embracing their qualities and attempting to emulate them. That's why the picture of a dragon is stenciled on the front door of your school, even if you're not practicing a Chinese martial art.

Coffee, Chi, or Me?

In addition to their quest to be as invincible as the neighborhood dragon, martial artists also attempt to build character. Building character requires an understanding of certain innate qualities all humans share, a belief in martial arts philosophy, and the cultivation of certain martial arts mindsets.

The martial artist is usually introduced to the concept of chi early in training. *Chi* is simply the life force and inner energy that all creatures possess. The ability to focus on and harness this inner energy improves a martial artist's warrior skills as well as his ability to handle problems and stresses that arise in everyday life. Using chi can make you stronger than mere muscle mass ever will.

Chi, pronounced *key* or *chee,* depending on whether you're in a Japanese or Chinese martial art, is also spelled *ki* and *qi.* They all mean the same thing: life force.

Chi is creative and active. It exists in the abdomen and is tapped into through breathing techniques, focus and concentration, and by using the shout, *kiai* (also called *kihop*).

Yin-Yang and You

The concept of yin-yang is fundamental to most Eastern philosophy. This is the idea that the world is made of conflicting yet harmonious elements that wouldn't exist without one another. The concept of hot can't exist without the concept of cold; day does not exist without night; soft wouldn't be without hard. You can extrapolate from there. Understanding how yin-yang works helps the martial artist achieve correct balance in her life and in her warrior skills.

Yin-yang is also called *ura-omate, in-yo, am-duong,* and *um-yang,* depending on the martial art.

The eternal conflict: Not "Tastes great" versus "Less filling"

The concept of yin-yang helps the martial artist understand that everything has its place in the universe, and that everything is necessary, even your boss. The apparent conflict between two elements (for instance, you and your boss) is just the nature of the universe. By living a harmonious, balanced life, you reduce the conflict between these elements while accepting that such a conflict simply exists.

Yin refers to the elements in the universe that are considered destructive, passive, and feminine. (Early martial arts philosophers hadn't yet been introduced to feminism when they came up with this idea.) *Yang* refers to the elements in the universe that are considered constructive, active, and of course, masculine.

Walking the balance beam

To achieve a balance of yin-yang, you have to practice moderation in all things. This is called "following the Middle Way." It's harder than it first appears, but you can do it.

The Middle Way is the road politicians take when they don't want to annoy any of their supporters. It can work for you, too. Instead of living in one extreme or the other — total deprivation or complete hedonism — you find a middle path, one of moderation, where you don't do everything you want and to heck with the consequences; nor do you delude yourself into thinking that sleeping in a cave somehow makes you a better person than those of who are so soft that they use a mattress.

Character Building Beliefs: Resolute in Five Respects

Now the hard part. You can learn all the warrior techniques you want, but if you don't build strong character, it won't mean anything. Mastering a side kick is easier than learning how to control your road rage when the idiot in the Lexus in front of you deserves to be tailgated for at least six miles.

But you have to learn to "master" yourself (control yourself) if you want to become a martial artist. It's hard work, but you won't be alone. Everyone from the kid in class next to you to the instructor in the front of the room is trying to become a better person. Fortunately, a set of rules is also available that you can follow to help you learn to master yourself and to become a better person.

Guidelines called "Resolute in Five Respects" are taught in Japanese martial arts. They help you understand loyalty and perseverance. Even if you're not a student of a Japanese martial art, you can learn from these guidelines.

Resolution #1: You must believe in the philosophy of your school

Being uncertain about your school and instructor can undermine your training. Be sure that you feel comfortable with your school and your teacher before you commit to training. After you've committed, you have to give it your all.

Resolution #2: You must stay fit, regardless of circumstances

Finding excuses for not continuing your training or skipping practice "just this once" is too easy. When you commit to training, you commit to training forever. Even if time, money, or motivation becomes a problem, you must still continue training. You may just have to modify your approach.

Resolution #3: You must commit to mastering the martial art

Some people start off in Tae Kwon Do, decide after three months that it doesn't hold the answer to everything, and then start training in Kung Fu, only to decide six weeks later that they can't really defend themselves with Kung Fu and that maybe Muay Thai is the best style.

This is no way to become a martial artist. Instead, make a serious choice about the martial art that you want to learn and then stick with it until you achieve mastery (or at least until you earn your black belt). Only then can you truly decide if you need to learn more about other martial arts to make up for any skills or techniques your style may be lacking.

Resolution #4: You must be willing to endure hard training

If being a martial artist were easy, every one would be a black belt. Training is hard for a reason: it's supposed to make you a warrior. To that end, now and then, you have to be willing to train hard. This hard training helps you understand that you have greater abilities and resources than you thought you had. It makes you stronger and more confident. So don't slack off in class, even if you can or if no one notices. Hard training makes you a warrior and also firms up your glutes nicely.

Common sense must accompany the willingness to commit to hard training must be accompanied. Occasionally, I hear stories about people forced to train barefoot for two hours in 16 inches of snow and wonder what made them think they wouldn't get frostbite. Hard training doesn't include the loss of your toes.

Resolution #5: You must do your best in competition

Notice that the resolution doesn't say, "You must do your best in competition if you decide to compete." It says you must compete, and you must also do your best. Competition requires physical and mental preparation and training, and it forces you to confront and overcome your fears and anxieties in an environment that's safer than your average corner street fight.

Not all martial arts value competition. Some discourage it, saying that the only competition a martial artist needs is herself. If competition isn't considered important to your style, you can learn other, equally valuable guidelines, to help you become a better person. No approach is completely right or wrong for everyone, but after you choose a teacher and a martial art, you should be willing to follow the approach that's taught.

Funakoshi Gichin, the founder of modern Karate, modified "Resolute in Five Respects" to apply directly to Karate training. He taught that you must be serious about training, avoid ego, be self-aware, concern yourself with training rather than theory, and be ethically responsible in all areas of life.

The Five Tenets of Tae Kwon Do

In Korean martial arts, practitioners follow the Five Tenets, which are intended to build character. To understand Tae Kwon Do, an individual must understand how the Five Tenets are used in everyday life.

Tenet #1: Courtesy

Courtesy means bowing to your senior belts and the instructor. It requires acting in a respectful manner at all times. Not only must others be treated with respect, but the art itself must also be treated with respect.

Tenet #2: Integrity

Integrity requires a commitment to ethical and honest behavior in all aspects of one's life, even when it's not easy or convenient. In class, you train hard and with your greatest effort, even if no one is looking. Instead of offering excuses, you hold yourself responsible for your actions and their consequences.

Tenet #3: Perseverance

The willingness to keep trying even when something seems impossible to do is essential to martial arts success. Otherwise, we'd all take one look at the jump-spinning-wheel kick and say, "Nah, that'll never happen." Perseverance means that even though it may take weeks, months, or even years to reach your goals, you still keep trying, without letting discouragement or frustration stop you.

One of the common sayings in martial arts is, "If you don't fall down now and then, you're not trying hard enough." The thing is, we mean this literally: You should actually fall down, skinning your knee if possible, when you're reaching for that seemingly impossible new skill.

Tenet #4: Self-Control

Having control over your mind and body requires discipline and focus. When you have control, you use reason and judgment to make decisions, rather than responding to fear and anger. Self-control helps you make healthier choices and lead a less stressful life.

Tenet #5: Indomitable Spirit

Sometimes called *winning spirit,* indomitable spirit means having the right attitude whether you win or lose. Maintaining a positive, optimistic perspective allows you to remain focused and undiscouraged even if you fail.

Indomitable spirit and perseverance are related: Perseverance is the action, and indomitable spirit is the attitude.

Chinese Martial Arts and Tao

Chinese martial arts require humility, focus, and self-discipline. In Chinese martial arts, the Taoist philosophy underlies all that the martial artist is taught.

Tao who?

Taoism is essentially the belief that two worlds exist — the physical world and the spiritual world. People in the physical world can occasionally experience the spiritual world; this contact can be sought through the use of meditation techniques.

A Taoist lives simply and seeks *enlightenment* or a true understanding of both the physical world and the spiritual world. The Tao is the underlying principle of life as well as the process of achieving harmony. According to the *Tao Te Ching*, an important book of Tao, "The Tao that can be talked about isn't the true Tao." This makes it a bit hard to describe what the Tao is.

The Tao of washing dishes

When you perform a skill in harmony with its nature, you're practicing Tao. Any skill from washing dishes to performing archery can be done to seek enlightenment. Thus, a Chinese martial artist pursues Tao through the practice of technical, harmonious skills.

Practitioners of Chinese martial arts believe that personal fulfillment is achieved by living in a moderate, natural way, not at the expense of others, including the environment that surrounds us.

The Tao ethical tradition

During ancient times, the Chinese monks who practiced T'ai Chi and Kung Fu, as well as other, more esoteric, arts, developed an elaborate set of ethical and moral codes that they felt should be practiced by all civilized people. These guidelines included kindness towards others, respect for the elderly, and loyalty to family. Those who didn't abide by the rules could be severely punished. The power of these monks and the respect they commanded was such that even the emperor obeyed them.

In modern times, practitioners of Chinese martial arts are taught the following principles:

- Cultivate self-discipline
- Show kindness
- Help others
- Seek the truth
- Become educated
- Remain healthy
- Pursue spirituality
- Protect the weak

The Tao and the warrior arts

The skills a martial artist learns while training in a Chinese martial art are intended to be used only in pursuit of the art's modern principles. Therefore, one's intentions are an important aspect of training.

Martial Arts Mindsets

To succeed in martial arts — indeed, to succeed in life — you must cultivate certain mental mindsets that can help you get through any difficulty you may face.

You don't just show up in class one day and decide, "Today, I'm going to learn fudoshin." Instead, you learn fudoshin through a long series of lessons that begin the first day that you change into your martial arts uniform and step onto the mat. But unless you understand what mindset you're trying to cultivate and why it's important, you'll just be out there kicking and punching without any greater learning going on.

The terms used in the following sections are Japanese, but each martial art style uses a different name for the mental mindsets you need to develop. Some may simply call a mindset *focus* or *concentration*. But be assured that, whatever name a mental mindset goes by, it isn't simple or easy to develop. It requires dedication, time, and a willingness to learn.

Fudoshin

Fudoshin is the ability to remain calm and detached when confronted with a threat or difficulty. Sometimes, the threat or difficulty is an armed bandit, and sometimes, it's your boss laying people off again.

The famous Japanese swordsman Miyamoto Musashi named this concept as essential for all warriors to learn if they hoped to win in battle. Our battles may not be physical confrontations between sword-wielding warlords, but they're stressful encounters that often leave people feeling as though they didn't respond in the best way possible — or even appropriately.

Dispel fear, panic, and anger

If you have fudoshin, you react to a threat or difficulty with a clear, open mind. You use reason and thought to decide on an appropriate response, rather than simply reacting out of fear, panic, or anger. No one makes good choices when acting out of fear, panic, or anger.

Feel your emotions, but control them

To develop fudoshin, you must learn to control your emotions. This doesn't mean that you can't feel your emotions, it just means that you must set them aside while you determine the most reasonable course of action.

Sometimes, the most reasonable course of action must be decided on in a split second, which is why it's important to keep your mind calm and detached at all times, not just during training sessions or when you remember to.

Choose control rather than panic or anger

Control over your emotions comes from a conscious decision. To practice this control, the next time someone cuts you off in traffic, instead of inventing a new swear word, take a deep breath and don't say or think anything at all. Simply continue driving as if nothing frustrating has happened. In just a few seconds, your mind will be calm and clear, and you will feel as if nothing has happened. Instead of all that anger coursing through your veins, you'll feel relaxed.

Then decide what to do. You may not need to do anything. But if you do decide that you must do something, such as report the person's reckless driving, the action that you take will be sensible, logical, and well-thought-out instead of irrational and violent. The consequences of your actions will be easier to anticipate, and you'll find yourself a calmer, less stressed person in all areas of your life.

Muscle memory is developed by repeating an action so many times that your muscles automatically remember how to perform the action without any conscious thought on your part. Martial artist, Tae Kwon Do teacher, and social worker Carol Stambaugh takes this concept one step further and uses the term *emotional muscle memory* to talk about practicing what to do if you're afraid. She says that by putting yourself in scary situations — such as by competing at a tournament — you can train yourself to perform despite your fear. Then, if you *are* ever confronted by a crazed mugger on the street, your *emotional muscle memory* will kick in, and you'll remember what to do even though you're afraid.

Heijo-Shin

While having fudoshin helps you react appropriately, developing intense focus, or *heijo-shin,* gives you the tools that you need to actually overcome the threat or difficulty. If you have a calm mind but don't focus on solving the problem at hand, you can still find yourself in a great deal of trouble.

Why you need intense focus

The guy sitting next to you at the local bar takes offense at something you said about the President. (Believe me, it could happen.) Because you cultivated fudoshin, you don't panic when he throws a punch. Instead, your clear, calm mind tells you to block the punch. But the bartender is yelling something at you and because you didn't learn heijo-shin in class this week, you turn to see what he wants and . . . BAM! Now you have a black eye to explain to your wife.

However, if you had heijo-shin, you would have ignored whatever the bartender was saying until you had dealt with the immediate problem and blocked the punch that was coming. Then you would have turned to the bartender and discovered that he was yelling, "Watch out!"

Banish confusion, doubt, and indecision

Without focus, confusion and doubt can creep in, paralyzing you and making it difficult for you to take action. Without focus, you're easily distracted. You won't be able to solve Problem A before you solve Problem B. *With* focus, you can solve Problem A first and then get to work on Problem B.

Remaining alert and ready

Being alert and ready at all times is an essential part of maintaining intense focus. If you're unaware of what's happening around you, you can't act quickly and decisively; you'll be too busy trying to figure out what the heck is going on. If you're alert and ready, you're less likely to be afraid, surprised, or indecisive.

Heijo-shin is best achieved through committed training in a martial art and through the cultivation of chi and fudoshin. It can also be developed by learning to be aware of your surroundings and by following through when you make a decision to do something.

Kokoro

Fudoshin and heijo-shin are necessary mental mindsets. They can help the martial artist meet and triumph over challenges and tests of all kinds. But having these mental attributes is meaningless if you don't also have *kokoro*, which is heart or warrior spirit.

A person with mediocre technical skills but great heart often defeats a more technically skilled person who has no heart. You can have great talent, but without heart, you will fail.

To develop kokoro, you must care about what you're doing. You must be committed to training in, learning, and mastering your martial art to the best of your abilities. You must always give your best effort. A person who does this has heart. Kokoro develops when you persevere and maintain indomitable spirit no matter what the situation. With it, you can do anything.

Chapter 3

Choosing a Style

In This Chapter

▶ Learning about martial arts styles

▶ Identifying styles available in your area

▶ Comparing your abilities to the demands

▶ Observing classes and techniques

▶ Talking to students and teachers

*F*irst things first. You may be ready to start training in a martial art today, but before you can begin, you have to decide *which* martial art to practice. You have many to choose from, and all claim to be the best.

Although trying out a couple of styles before deciding what's right for you is okay, most martial artists discourage the cafeteria approach to learning martial arts. ("I think I'll have a little Karate for an appetizer, then maybe some Jujutsu as the main course; for dessert, I think I'll go for the Aikido.")

Most instructors feel that you need to be well grounded in one style before you start experimenting with others to decide what they can add to your repertoire. Otherwise, you become a dabbler and never achieve true competence, let alone mastery, in any martial art.

It can take months, even years, to be well grounded, so choosing the right style (and the right school) from the beginning is best. The wrong style or the wrong school can discourage your enthusiasm for martial arts, and that's no way to become a warrior.

How do you choose a particular style? If you grew up watching David Carradine in *Kung Fu* and have spent your whole life dreaming of becoming a Kung Fu master, then you know what to do: Go directly to the nearest Kung Fu school and sign up.

There. That was easy.

Unfortunately, for most people, it won't be as easy as that. Maybe you only have a vague sense of what various martial arts are about. Or maybe you're interested in Escrima, Karate, *and* T'ai Chi. You may be able to learn them all some day but not all at the same time. You have to choose one to start with. So which one shall it be?

How Do You Pronounce That Again? Discovering Martial Arts Styles

If you think that a Drunken Monkey (see Chapter 15) is an inebriated primate and not a martial art, you need to do some homework. Chapter 1 gives a brief discussion of the various martial arts that are popular today. It's a good place to start on your quest for the perfect martial art for you. You can also turn to Part III, where you'll find a more in-depth profile of ten of the most popular martial arts. This section should help you begin to understand what's out there and what to expect. But that's not all. You have plenty more to research before you declare that you're going to be the next Olympic gold medal *Judoka* (person who practices Judo).

The public library is the place to be

Hit the library and check out books on various styles. You'll find martial arts encyclopedias, histories, how-to books, and more.

Some of the best martial arts books were written by yours truly, but some other writers have had a word or two to say, as well. Dig into books by Bruce Lee, Donn Draeger, and Hee Il Cho, for starters.

Plenty of martial arts magazines also cover the most popular martial arts. These periodicals are worth a look to get an idea of what practitioners of various martial arts are concerned with. They include profiles of martial artists, how-to pieces, the latest fitness and nutrition research, and historical information about martial arts-related items.

You can get a good laugh looking at the classified ads ("Dim Mak Death Touch in Ten Easy Steps," and "How to Be a Babe Magnet in Less than 30 Minutes a Day") in these magazines, but please don't take them seriously.

Some of the best martial arts magazines are *Black Belt, Tae Kwon Do Times,* and *Martial Arts and Combat Sports.*

Let's go surfing now

The World Wide Web has thousands of martial arts sites. You could spend so much time surfing that you would never actually get around to training. Just type in words like *martial arts* or *Karate,* and off you go. You'll find informational Web sites, the official Web sites of martial arts organizations, home pages of amateur martial artists, and more.

It almost goes without saying, but if the Web site features scantily clad women warriors, it's probably not a legitimate martial arts Web site. You know what it is, so try not to fall for it.

Make it a blockbuster night

Rent a couple of videos to see the martial arts in action. Sure, you can rent *The Karate Kid,* or a couple of Jackie Chan flicks, but after you're done with them, pop in a *how-to* video. How-to videos are available on every martial art and every aspect of martial arts training. These videos will help you get a sense of what techniques the different styles use, how they're performed, and why they are used.

Try to get your hands on a couple of Ultimate Fighting Championship videos. These are mixed martial arts tournaments (the Karate guys fight the Aikido guys), so they're not anything like what you'll experience at the corner martial arts studio, but they do give you a taste of what no-holds-barred fighting is about.

All Around the Town

To develop all the techniques of a martial art, you have to train under an instructor. All the books and videos in the world don't make up for having an instructor show you exactly how your foot should look when you're doing a roundhouse kick. For this reason, you need to join a martial arts school or club. More on choosing the right martial arts school and instructor follows in Chapter 4

But before you get your heart set on Muay Thai kickboxing, you need to find out if there's a school nearby. Otherwise, you'll just be disappointed. You need to see what types of martial arts are available in your area before making a decision.

Perhaps the easiest way to find out what schools are in your area is to turn to your local phone directory. Also, check the directory for any nearby cities or towns that are within a reasonable driving distance. For most people, a half-hour drive is about all they're willing to do regularly for their training. If you have to drive two hours both ways, you'll probably have a tough time sticking to a training schedule.

Some people do have their hearts set on learning a certain style, and they're willing to travel considerable distances to do it. One Kung Fu practitioner travels an hour and a half each way; he goes to class once or twice a week and practices on his own the rest of the time. You can try it if you think that you'll only be satisfied with a certain style, and the closest school is located in another city.

Kick, Punch, or Grapple?

After you know what's available in your area, you have to decide if you'd rather kick and punch your way to better health or grapple your way there. The young and flexible often choose a style that emphasizes high kicks, speed, and power. If you're older and less flexible, you shouldn't shy away from choosing such a style, but you should be aware that other styles might complement your needs and abilities better. See Part III for more information on the various martial arts styles.

T'ai Chi is an excellent choice for older students or those with joint problems. Muay Thai is probably not right for you if you have a serious medical condition. See Part III for specific information on the types of techniques each style demands.

To find out more about martial arts styles, ask around. You may be surprised at how many people have trained in a martial art or know someone who has. Of course, you need to take what you hear with a large dose of salt, because someone who has trained in Aikido for two months may feel that he knows everything about his martial art . . . but he doesn't. Still, if your neighbor, who's your age and dress size, loves her Muay Thai class, maybe you can learn to love it, too.

Join a chat group on the World Wide Web to learn more about martial arts styles, especially if you don't know anyone who is already in the martial arts. Be wary, of course. You have no way of verifying what anyone tells you. But martial artists will usually be happy to tell you honestly what you can expect from the style, or styles, they practice.

Watching and Analyzing Classes

Watch practitioners from the various styles before making a choice. Actually go to a school and watch a class rather than rely on what you see on television. What you see on television and in the movies bears absolutely no relationship to real martial arts.

Before you go to watch a class, call the school to find out about class times and get permission to watch. If the instructor refuses to let you watch a class, it is probably not a good sign. Skip that school.

As you watch, try to make sense of what you're seeing. Are there many basic body-conditioning exercises? Do the techniques require the flexibility of a 6-year-old? Are allowances made for people of differing abilities?

Hey, I can do that!

As you watch classes, check out the techniques that the students are using. Can you imagine performing those techniques yourself? This doesn't mean that you have to be able to do those techniques now. (One of the joys of martial arts training is finding out how to do what you didn't know you could do.) Still, it should be within the realm of possibility for you.

Bear in mind that if you have a medical condition or a disability, the instructor should be able to modify the techniques for you. By visiting several schools, however, you should be able find out which martial art can be most easily adapted to your needs.

White belts as role models

Pay special attention to what the beginners are doing. They're the ones with the white belts and the slightly clueless expressions. They're doing what you'll be doing if you sign up. Does it look like fun? Does it look *possible*?

Look at the advanced students to see what you'll be expected to do in the future. Don't let the advanced techniques intimidate you too much, though. You'll have plenty of time to learn how to do the techniques as you get promoted through the ranks.

Don't worry too much about what the future holds. Focus on what a beginner is expected to do. When I was an innocent white belt, I watched a first-degree black belt attempt to break a concrete block as part of his promotion test. He was a blacksmith, about a foot taller and a hundred pounds heavier than I was, and when he hit the block, *it didn't break.* He scraped his knuckles in the attempt and started to bleed, at which point I would have given up. He didn't. He hit the block again. This time it broke. I said, "Only a total idiot would do that," and decided that I would never test for my first-degree black belt. Of course, when it came my turn to test several years later, I had lost enough brain cells to qualify as an idiot, and I happily broke whatever they put in front of me.

Interviewing Students and Instructors

Arrange to speak to the head instructors of the various martial arts styles that appeal most to you, as well as to a few students at each school. This can help you to narrow down your choices.

Grill the instructor (gently)

Ask the head instructor about the martial art she teaches. What does she like most about it? What does she think is the greatest benefit of training in her martial art?

Although beginners often focus on the differences between martial arts, more experienced martial artists often see the similarities. Don't be surprised, then, if the instructor isn't comfortable telling you how her martial art style is "better" than another martial art. Instead, ask specific questions about the style.

Focus on getting answers to questions that are related to your practicing that specific martial art style, such as, "Do people my age tend to do well?" Or, "If I have physical limitations, does this style accommodate for that?" Or even, "If I haven't been athletic in the past, can I still do well in this martial art?"

Many martial arts instructors have day jobs; they teach because they love it, not because it allows them to buy a new Mercedes every year. Try to be considerate of their time and patience.

Talk to students

Although the head instructor can tell you much about a martial art style, she doesn't make any money by trying to talk people out of joining the school. (Although this is one of the few businesses that I know of where instructors will do just that.) Also, the head instructor has probably been teaching for a long, long time and may not remember exactly what it was like to be a beginner. For these reasons, it can be helpful to talk to students in various martial arts styles to get another point of view.

You can ask students how they got started, why they chose their particular style, and what they like about it. You can also ask what piece of advice they wished that they would have heard already when they started. This reveals plenty about the martial art — and the student.

You can also look around and see if any of the students are like you — are they your age, are they the same gender, or are they of the same physical condition. This more objective information can tell you plenty about a style and a school.

Don't Stop Now!

Be sure to visit several training halls (another name for a school) that teach different martial arts styles. Compare what you've seen from one style to another. Keep in mind that, even within one style, differences exist.

For instance, in the striking styles, such as Tae Kwon Do and Karate, the physical contact allowed during sparring varies. Some schools are no contact. With the *no-contact* schools, you risk less injury, but the fighting situation doesn't resemble reality very closely. Some styles allow light contact. The *light-contact* styles help you learn how to hit another person, which is more fun than you'd think, and also help you to develop good physical control. Some styles encourage *full contact,* where you blast away at each other as hard as you can. The full-contact styles more closely resemble an actual fighting situation, but they also increase the risk of injury. You have to decide which approach is appropriate for you.

Don't just take the head instructor's word for the amount of contact allowed in a school. Watching sparring sessions and talking to students will give you a better idea of what actually happens on the mat.

The Chosen Style

If you follow all the advice that I list in this chapter faithfully, you should be able to decide on a martial arts style that seems right for you. You may think that selecting a style is the last step before you put on your *dobo* (martial arts uniform), but it's not. You also have to choose a school, and that's no small task. Chapter 4 helps you decide which training hall to grace with your presence.

Often, schools in the same style emphasize different aspects of the martial arts. One Karate school may be no-contact, and another may be full-contact. One Tae Kwon Do school may be traditional, and another may be more sport-oriented. How do you know which approach is right for you? It helps to know your goals (what you want to achieve from training) and your expectations (do you want the whole wear-a-uniform, bow-to-the-head-instructor treatment, or would you prefer a more casual approach?) Choosing the right school is discussed more in-depth in Chapter 4.

Chapter 4

Choosing a School or Instructor

- -

In This Chapter

▶ Finding a high-quality school and a good instructor

▶ Avoiding gender bias

▶ Looking over a prospective school from stem to stern

▶ Asking the right questions

▶ Considering costs

- -

Choosing the right martial arts school and instructor is the most important decision that you can make in your martial arts career — not only for reasons of safety and cost but also because many students give up on martial arts unnecessarily. Unfortunately, they choose the wrong school at the beginning of their adventure, and it robs them of their enthusiasm.

Don't let this happen to you. Spend some time researching the possibilities and get enough information to make the right decision for you. And don't forget, what's the right decision for you isn't necessarily the right decision for that fella who works across the hall.

Keep in mind that if you choose a particular style, such as Hapkido (see Chapter 20), yet feel dissatisfied with the only school that offers Hapkido classes in your city, you're much better off choosing a different style. Learning a different style and thus attending a different school is far more beneficial than sticking with your original style decision and ending up in the wrong school.

First of all, understand that you can pick from many options for martial arts training:

✔ Sign up at a traditional school, called a *dojo* in Japanese and a *dojang* in Korean.

✔ Work in a small group setting at the home of a free-spirit instructor. (Bruce Lee taught small groups of people in his backyard.)

✔ Take classes through the local parks and recreation program or at the local Y.

✔ Take classes at a nearby university or community college.

✔ Join a martial arts club consisting of like-minded martial artists.

All these possibilities have benefits and drawbacks, and you have to weigh them. Spend some time visiting various schools and talking to instructors. This can help you to make a good match. But before you do any of that, you need a basic understanding of what makes a good martial arts school and what makes a good martial arts instructor.

Locating a Good School

A school consists of not only a physical setting — the training hall where you actually work out — but it also consists of instructors and other students. I describe what makes a good instructor in "The nitty-gritty details" section, later in this chapter, but keep in mind that you can't have a good school with a bad instructor.

What makes a school good depends on many factors, and some of them have to do with you. If you want to immerse yourself in the philosophy and culture of martial arts, and you sign up at a sport-oriented school, you'll be unhappy no matter how "good" the school is. Thus, you need to have some understanding of your martial arts goals to decide what school is good for you.

Fundamentals that all good schools share

All good schools have certain fundamentals in common:

✔ The training area is large enough for the students to perform their techniques without running into each other.

✔ It's neat and well kept.

✔ Equipment is appropriate to the martial art and in good condition. It may not be brand new, but the equipment is well cared for.

✔ The changing area for men is separate from the women's area.

✔ Instructors encourage courtesy, respect, and discipline, such that students feel safe during their workout.

✔ At least some feeling of camaraderie is shared among students.

✔ Students of all levels of experience, all ages, shapes, colors, and sizes, and both genders are accommodated.

The martial arts are open to all people, regardless of shape, size, gender, ability, ethnicity, sexual orientation, religious background, or favorite rock star, and you'll probably have more success if you find a school that's truly inclusive. Play close attention to this as you make your choice.

Differences in types of schools

- **Traditional schools** operate year-round with full schedules of classes that may include advanced classes as well as classes for

  - Adults
  - Beginners
  - Children
  - Women only

  Classes may vary in size and quality, and traditional school classes are usually the most expensive option.

- **Chain martial arts schools** operate just like McDonald's franchises, but this doesn't mean that anything is necessarily wrong with them. Be aware, however, that some of them produce black belts by the bushel, which isn't always a good thing.

- **Independent instructors** don't operate out of a school. They may have small groups of people come to their home, a nearby park, or in the case of one martial artist, a local parking lot. These people often have day jobs, but some of the most gifted teachers choose to teach this way, selecting only a handful of eager students to spend time with. What they charge their students varies.

- **Parks and recreation programs** and **YMCA or YWCA Programs** usually offer short-term class sessions, often for periods of six to eight weeks. Classes meet once or twice a week in the basement of a community building or perhaps in a high school gym. The cost is low, but you can only train during a limited time. After one session ends, you may have to wait a week or two for the next session to start.

- **University and community college** classes meet on a semester basis. If they're offered for credit and you're not a student, you're allowed to take the class only if room is available after all the students have signed up. The price can vary, but the quality of instruction is usually good.

  Less emphasis is placed on the spiritual and philosophical aspects of martial arts because these programs are usually part of the physical education department.

✔ **Martial arts clubs** are informal groups of like-minded martial artists who may meet a few evenings a week at a donated space. They're usually nonprofit, and the senior member usually conducts the classes. A small membership fee may be charged, especially if the club must rent space. Quality varies, and clubs can come and go pretty quickly.

Going for your goals

Because a school that may be right for somebody else may be absolutely wrong for you, you need to identify, at least minimally, what your most pressing martial arts goals are.

The serious martial artist who intends to work out for two hours out of six days a week won't be satisfied with a parks and recreation program that meets only once a week. On the other hand, a person who wants to work out a couple of times a week to get in shape probably doesn't want a school that's highly competitive and tournament-oriented.

To determine what your beginning martial arts goals are, ask yourself these questions:

✔ What do I hope to achieve through martial arts training?

✔ How much time do I have to devote to the effort?

✔ What aspect of the martial arts interests me the most? The sport aspect, the culture and philosophy, the fitness and conditioning, or the self-defense?

✔ Am I interested in competition? Do I want a school that emphasizes tournament participation?

✔ Do I envision myself earning my black belt in a few years of dedicated practice or am I really more interested in getting in better shape?

After you answer these questions, you're in a position to better evaluate the schools in your area.

Your martial arts goals can change. Many people start training in martial arts just to get in shape, and then they realize that they really want to go for their black belt. Some people who are only motivated by a desire to earn a black belt never make it past the first few months of training. So keep in mind that your present goals are simply a place to start rather than a destination that can't change.

Finding a Good Instructor

A school can be safe, clean, and reasonably priced, but if the instructor isn't any good, you may as well save your time and money. Choosing a school with good teachers is essential to martial arts success. So what makes a good teacher?

Who teaches what and when

First, recognize that especially at larger schools, a variety of instructors may be teaching. If at all possible, you should meet most or all of them before signing up. You don't want to meet Ms. Smith, the greatest instructor of all time, sign up for a class, and then discover that Mr. Jones, a total jerk, actually teaches the class that you signed up for.

The head instructor's role

The head instructor, who is usually but not always the owner of the school, sets the tone for the entire school. She has usually trained the other instructors, and she supervises them.

The use of assistant instructors isn't good or bad in and of itself. What is important is that the head instructor should still be actively teaching. This keeps the quality of the school and the teaching high. If the head instructor is 80 years old, however, bear in mind that the title is probably a courtesy title, and someone else is actually the head instructor. *That* person should be actively teaching.

The nitty-gritty details

When selecting an instructor, ask if you can observe the instructor's class before signing up. Pay particular attention to nuances. Do men and women work together or are they segregated? In mixed-age classes, are adult women always paired with children, or are adult men and women paired with children equally? The bottom line is that a good martial arts instructor:

- **Insists on a certain amount of respect and courtesy.** This helps enforce discipline, which can be difficult to maintain in a school, but discipline is essential to safety.
- **Takes his teaching seriously.** If all the students are joking and laughing all the time, they probably aren't working hard enough, and the teacher probably isn't serious enough.

- **Motivates students to work harder, but without ridiculing any of them.** He pushes you to your limits but never beyond; he encourages you to work hard, which may make your muscles sore, but he'll never work you in such a way that any damage is done.

- **Demonstrates a technique, explains it, and moves about the room correcting students' techniques.** A teacher who stands at the front of the room barking out commands may be *leading* a class, but he isn't *teaching* it.

The Gender-Neutral Zone: Finding a Female-Friendly School

More and more women sign up for martial arts lessons every year, but some of them quit because of sexism in the training hall. Sexism can still be a problem in some martial arts schools because, generally, only few women (as compared to the numbers of men) fill the training ranks. The fact that the number of female participants is low perpetuates the sexism, and the sexism perpetuates the low numbers of women who participate. It's a vicious cycle. However, the situation is improving as more and more women participate in all kinds of sports, so if you're a woman thinking about becoming a warrior, by all means do it!

For women, finding a school that makes them feel welcome is important. For men, choosing a school that emphasizes everyone's ability to succeed is surely healthier than succumbing to a macho need to prove that testosterone is cooler than estrogen.

A female-friendly school doesn't necessarily offer women-only classes or advertise that it's female-friendly, but it does make students of either gender feel welcome.

Female students

A school that has many female students is probably female-friendly, and a school that has zero female students may be sexist — the complete lack of women is probably a warning. It at least should serve as a signal for you to investigate further. Unlike other sports, nowhere near half — more like 15 to 25 percent — of all martial artists are women, so don't expect to see a 50/50 ratio. Some of the black belts in the school should be women. Again, don't expect to see a 50/50 ratio yet, but a substantial proportion of black belts should be women. If female black belts are nowhere to be found, or if only a few women are black belts, it may be because women feel forced to drop out of the school owing to gender bias.

Female instructors

Female-friendly schools have female instructors. If the head instructor is male and he's the only instructor, he should at least expect the same of male and female students. At the end of class, if everyone is supposed to do 50 pushups, then *everyone* should do 50 pushups (or at least get as close as possible). If a person testing for black belt is supposed to break four boards, then a person should have to break four boards, whether he's a man or she's a woman.

If the head instructor has assistant instructors, some of them should be women. Just because a teacher is a woman doesn't make her a good teacher, of course, but it does mean that the head instructor feels that women can succeed in the martial arts just as men can.

Partnering with prejudices

In a female-friendly school, women aren't paired solely with women or with children for drills and sparring. Everyone should partner with people of different ages, genders, and abilities. When choosing partners for drills, the head instructor may occasionally take height, weight, skill, and age into consideration but shouldn't take gender into consideration.

Condescending to the "weaker" sex

Nothing irritates female martial artists more than expectations that differ for men and women. In a female-friendly school, the rules are the same for all students. The same expectations should be in place for all students, regardless of gender. If special considerations must be made, they should be made based on age, skill level, or physical disability, not gender.

Visiting Schools

You may have visited several schools when you were choosing a martial arts style. Now is the time to go back to your final few choices, make additional observations, and ask more questions. Be sure to go at a time when a class is in session so that you can see how a typical training session is conducted.

Ask for a schedule of classes and make sure that at least several classes are scheduled each week at times that are convenient for you. The best school in the world won't help you become a better martial artist if all the classes are held while you're at work.

Checking out the scenery

More and more martial arts schools are finding homes in fitness centers. This can seem impressive: All those shiny weight machines and perky front desk clerks can make you think a school is better than it is. Don't be distracted by a showy exterior. Some of the best schools look like they've seen better days.

That said, the school should be in good condition, equipment should be appropriate to the martial art, and it should also be in good shape. The workout area should be clean, uncluttered and well-lit. The floor should be suitable for the workout. (For example, a concrete garage floor is murder on your joints.)

The school should have mirrors on the walls, so students can see what they're doing and correct their technique. Mats should be available for throwing and grappling (wrestling) techniques. For striking styles, plenty of padded targets should be available, including a heavy bag.

Choosing the right size

As you observe a class in session, see if enough space is available in the room for everyone to perform the techniques adequately. Cramped quarters make for a frustrating experience. Find out how many students are active in the school and what the average class size is.

Calculate the student-to-teacher ratio. In a larger school, a class may have a lead instructor calling out the commands, and several assistant instructors demonstrating the techniques and correcting students' mistakes. More than 10 or 15 students per instructor can be awkward.

Although some large schools manage to instruct everyone quite well even with large student-to-teacher ratios, you're more likely to get the attention that you need to succeed in a school with a smaller student-to-teacher ratio.

A smaller school may mean that you get more individual attention. However, if the school is too small to support the instructor, and she has a day job, the day job may interfere with the instructor's ability to teach well. Also, a school may be small because the head instructor annoys all the prospective students and drives them off. On the other hand, the instructor may be deliberately keeping the school small in order to produce a handful of well-trained martial artists rather than a big bushel of mediocre black belts.

A larger school may mean a more successful teacher. In a larger school, you can work with a diversity of people of different backgrounds and skill levels, thus contributing to your success as a martial artist. You may get a chance to help teach (and thus learn more) sooner than at a smaller school. But you may not get as much individualized attention as at a smaller school, and you may feel frustrated that you don't get the training that you need to succeed.

Ask the head instructor to describe the pros and cons of the size of his school. This can help you to determine if the school is being kept small deliberately (rather than because the instructor is bad) and if a large school can still offer you the attention that you need to master the martial art.

Do you prefer formal or laid-back?

Some people find the traditional martial arts appealing. They want a special uniform to wear, an atmosphere of strict discipline during training sessions, and an instructor to make them do 50 pushups for talking in class.

For other people, this is the kiss of death. Anything that rigid would make them run screaming for the exits within the first ten minutes.

You probably know what kind of person you are — laid-back or formal. (I prefer to use the word *formal* rather than *anal-retentive* because I have a preference for formal structure.) Even so, it helps to pay attention to formality and structure in the classroom before making a decision. You may find that while you prefer a laid-back approach at home, you want formality and discipline from your martial arts school.

Watch what the students do in the training hall. Do they bow to the instructors and senior students? Do they work quietly before and after class, or do they laugh and joke? What is the level of discipline? Must everyone remain quiet while class is in session or are questions or quiet conversation allowed?

Look more closely. Are children allowed to run around, or are they expected to sit or practice quietly? Are the students especially courteous to each other? Is each class taught in the same general way? How important is consistency among classes and instructors to you?

After you have the answers to these questions, you can analyze the results easily. If you think students should be allowed to ask questions during class, for example, don't sign up at a school where this is forbidden.

If you're not sure what you think after watching a class, ask if you can take an introductory lesson. Most schools allow you to do this so that you can get a sense of what training at the school is like.

Comparing yourself to others

Notice the students. Are some of them your age? Are students of a variety of fitness levels? Does your fitness level appear to be represented? If you're a woman, do you see other women in class? If you're thinking about signing up Little Joe for his eighth birthday, do you see other Little Joes in class?

Interviewing Instructors

After a school has made the cut — it offers the martial art style that you want to practice, you've watched a class or two, the way that the classes are run appeals to you, and you noticed several other 40-something men with a slight tendency toward beer belly like the one you have are in class — it's time to get down to business. This means interviewing instructors with an eye toward signing up at a specific school.

Start with the head instructor because she sets the tone for the whole school. Then ask to meet assistant instructors, especially those who teach the classes that you would take if you signed up at this school.

Although you have specific questions to ask the instructor, you can get a feel for what she's like just in a general conversation. Impatient, arrogant, or distracted head instructors aren't the best teachers.

Instructor qualifications

After you ask any questions about the style that you may have, ask what the head instructor's experience is. How many years has he been teaching? Where did he train? What teachers did he train under? Ask the same questions about the assistant instructors.

If the school and the instructor are all that you dreamed about and more, you still need to check references before signing on. If the head instructor tells you, "I taught for Kim Lee in Detroit for ten years before moving here to open my own school," you should call Kim Lee to make certain this is true and also to verify that the instructor wasn't tossed out of Kim Lee's under a cloud.

You can ask for the school's affiliations. Most good martial arts schools are members of at least one or two martial arts organizations or associations that are meant to keep standards high. Usually, you'll see certificates of membership on the walls of the school (or the instructor's office) but you can ask if in doubt.

Don't forget to ask for the translation, too. If the instructors says, "I'm a member of the KMAIA," it won't help you much unless you also know this is the Korean Martial Arts Instructors Association.

Some of these organizations are bogus, so don't put too much stock in affiliations. But an instructor who bothers to join professional organizations may be better than one who doesn't.

Also check the Better Business Bureau and the local chamber of commerce. Speak with current members and find out how long the school has been in business. Reference checks can help to ensure that the school is safe and well run.

Finally, ask the instructor what she thinks is most important about her martial art style and her school. Ask the head instructor what the main purpose of the school is. If the instructor has nothing to say, that's not a good sign. If the instructor tries to convince you that the school is right for everyone, no matter what their goals are, that's also not a good sign.

On the other hand, if she says that the purpose of her school is to help students become stronger and more confident, then that would be a good answer. If you asked her if she thought her school and approach was right for everyone, and she said, "We try to accommodate for people's different needs, but sometimes, people have goals and expectations that we can't help them with," then that's a good answer, too.

Injuries occur in the martial arts. A good instructor tries to minimize them. Ask the instructor what the most serious injury has been in his class and what he does to keep injuries under control.

Competition: Thumbs up or thumbs down?

Find out whether other martial arts experts are ever invited to the school for seminars or workshops, and whether tournament competition is encouraged or discouraged. If tournament competition is encouraged, then find out how important it is to the school.

Tournament competition is exhilarating, liberating, and empowering, and it can be tons of fun. Therefore, it can be a good idea to choose a school that routinely hosts tournaments and sends students to tournaments. However, a school that focuses only on this may neglect other important aspects of the martial arts. Winning really isn't everything.

Achieving rank

Ask how long it takes to earn a black belt with consistent effort and attendance. If the answer is six months, the school is a diploma-mill and not worth your time. If the answer is "Never" or "12 years," you may be dealing with a teacher who thinks that no one will ever be good enough to wear the belt that he has reverently tied around his waist, and that's nonsense. It usually takes three to five years of consistent effort to earn a black belt in a martial art, although this can vary.

Paying a Pretty Penny

Training in the martial arts requires an investment of time, energy, and money. People starting out sometimes don't realize how *much* money until it's too late. Although it can seem crass, you need to ask questions about costs and compare what you'll be expected to spend with how much you have in your wallet.

Find out how classes are paid for. Schools take different approaches. Some ask for annual tuition, due in one big lump sum when you sign up. Others ask for monthly payments, like a health club might. Still others may ask for a per-class payment. Make sure that you understand what you get for your money. If you pay tuition upfront, what happens if you have to move halfway across the country? Can you attend unlimited classes or only one or two per week? If you pay per-class, is the fee still due if you don't attend class one session?

Expect to pay between $30 and $70 per month on tuition. In big cities, it may be at the higher end of the scale, as it is for well-known instructors. Private lessons are higher and may run closer to $100 an hour, but these aren't necessary for most martial artists.

Ask if you can get a discount for paying several months or a year in advance. Ask about introductory offers or free lessons before you sign up. Some schools have promotions at different times of the year ("Sign up now and get a free uniform.") If no promotion is currently on offer, ask if one is coming up soon.

To compare different answers, determine how many classes that you think you can attend each week and the length of each class. Determine the approximate cost per lesson for each school to obtain an adequate comparison.

Most martial arts instructors help you to devise a payment plan if you can't pay according to their set schedule. For example, if an instructor usually asks for all the tuition upfront, he may agree to accept monthly payments for a slightly larger total (to make up for any risks he takes for not making you pay all at once).

In addition to tuition, you have to purchase equipment and pay for promotion tests. Ask how often promotion tests are given and find out how much they cost. For lower belts (nonblack belts), promotion tests, depending on the style, may be offered once a year or as often as four or six times a year. The cost is usually from $25 to $70. Black belt tests can cost $100 to $200 and are offered less frequently.

Equipping Yourself

After you decide on a martial art style and school, you need to equip yourself. This can be an expensive proposition, so start out with just the basics — the must-haves — and as you continue training, acquire the additional items that you need.

Check with your instructor regarding your equipment needs. She may own a pro shop where you can purchase your equipment. (It's always courteous to do this.) If not, see Appendix B in the back of this book for information on finding supplies.

Depending on the martial arts style, you can expect to spend $30 to $100 for a uniform. Safety equipment, which varies according to style from simple chest protectors to full body armor, can cost between $50 and $200. Practice weapons (for training) and live weapons (for competition) can cost upwards from $30.

Chapter 5

Go Get 'Em: Goals and Ranking Systems

In This Chapter

▶ Aiming for near- and far-sighted targets

▶ Making the necessary moves to hit a bull's-eye

▶ Understanding belt ranks and their colors

▶ Going through the paces for a promotion

You've started out on an incredible martial arts journey that, with commitment, passion, and a bit of luck, you'll be on for the rest of your life. Maybe you're thinking that it would help to know where you're going and how you're going to get there.

You're right. It would help. And that's what this chapter is about: planning and setting martial arts goals and finding out how to achieve those goals.

When you first set out, you're a mere beginner in training. You stand at the back of the class, and the belt on your uniform is white. You feel, look, and act totally clueless. You feel as though your belt is working its way loose from around your waist, and you don't want it to slide down your hips toward your knees. So your main goal in class is not to lose your belt. This isn't much of a goal but holding onto your belt is a start.

Have a senior student show you how to tie your belt, which stays up if you tie a square knot.

Being a beginner can be disconcerting, especially to martial arts students who've had success in other areas of their lives. Enjoy this time while it lasts, however, because pretty soon, the expectations are going to be much higher than keeping your belt on.

Setting Martial Arts Goals

As soon as you learn to keep your belt on, you need new goals. But you're a beginner, and setting goals is hard to do. How can you set a goal when you don't know what your goals should be?

The answer becomes clearer as you continue to train. Talk with your instructor, learn the techniques, and watch your fellow students to get an inkling of what's important for success in your martial art.

Think about what made you start training in martial arts. Was it because you wanted to become stronger and lose a little weight? Did you want to spend more time with your kid, a veritable ninja? These can form the basic goals that you set.

As you continue to train, your goals may change and develop. This is okay. Getting frustrated and giving up before achieving your goals, however, is not okay.

Setting goals works better if you can use objective measurements, but in the martial arts, this is sometimes difficult. Measure progress creatively. Don't be afraid to use technology — such as video cameras — to help you measure your achievements.

Having goals not only helps you to achieve, it gives you a reason to get off the couch and go to class when you don't feel that motivated. You can simply say to yourself, "I'll never earn my black belt sitting here," and off you go. Without such as goal, it can be hard to convince your behind to get up off the couch.

Long-term and short-term goals

One of the goals that you may have as a martial artist is to earn your black belt. Later in the chapter, belt ranks and promotion tests are covered more thoroughly, but for now, suffice it to say that if you've never set foot inside a training hall before, a black belt is a long-term goal.

If you haven't been physically active within memory, just making it through class may be a goal of yours. Because class only lasts an hour or two, this would be a short-term goal.

Early on, you should make some decisions about your martial arts goals. Although you don't want to have 97 goals (this makes it difficult to focus on achieving any one goal), you can have more than one goal. Having a mix of short-term and long-term goals works best.

For example, you may have a list of short-term goals that looks like this:

- ✔ Get through class tonight
- ✔ Memorize my first *form* (also called *kata* or *hyung,* a precise pattern of specific martial arts movements) by Friday

You may also have a list of long-term goals as follows:

- ✔ Increase my strength by 50 percent in the next 12 months
- ✔ Lose 15 pounds in the next six months
- ✔ Earn my black belt before I'm 40

Setting goals that are attainable is important. If you've never trained in Karate before, you're not going to earn your black belt in the next 12 months. (And if you did, it wouldn't be worth much!) Although your goals should be attainable, you can (and should) still set goals that are difficult to achieve.

Not reaching your goal exactly when you said that you were going to doesn't mean that you failed. Setbacks happen. They don't have to be permanent. Revise your goals, set a new deadline, and get cracking.

Sharing your goals with others

Make certain that your goals meet the standards listed in the "Long-term and short-term goals" section that precedes this section. Talking about your goals with other martial artists, including your instructor and the students that you admire and respect is a good idea. They can often help you set realistic goals while helping you to understand what's necessary to achieve those goals. Also, after they know what your goals are, they'll be eager to help you achieve them.

People are flattered when you ask them for their advice. So don't be shy about consulting your instructor and senior students as you set your goals. Be open-minded but don't assume that just because they have more experience than you do that they're right and you're wrong.

Planning the Steps to Reach Your Goals

Whew! You finally did it! You came up with a list of several short- and long-term goals that meet all the criteria of good goal setting. You've asked your instructor for advice, and with her input, you polished your list. You're practically a black belt now, right? Well, maybe not exactly . . .

After you decide what your goals are, you're not through. You need to figure out how to achieve your goals. This is an essential element of goal setting that often gets overlooked. But if you don't do it, success is practically impossible.

In order to achieve those goals, you need to determine what steps that you'll take to reach them. For example, you can't just decide to lose weight without thinking about how weight loss is achieved.

Considering how goals are reached

The first goal is to make it through class tonight. That may seem simple, but you can still plan steps to make it easier.

You need to think about how making it through class is achieved. You may realize that you need fuel to make it through. Eat a small snack an hour or two beforehand to make sure that your workout is fueled, and drink plenty of fluids before you leave the house so that you don't run out of steam part of the way through.

You may also find, for example, that the instructor's comments are confusing, which makes you feel like throwing in the towel. So during class, prepare and plan to focus on what the teacher is saying so that you don't get confused.

Finally, you may remember that breathing correctly helps to keep your energy from stalling. So you breathe with each technique as you do it so that you don't exhaust all your energy. Before you know it, you made it through class, and you've achieved your first goal.

Breaking down every goal: Forms

All goals can be broken down this way. Take a look at the second goal, memorizing your first form. Consider what you're going to need to accomplish. A *form* is a pattern of specific movements incorporating martial arts techniques. The techniques in the form are always done in the same sequence (sort of like a traditional dance). To be successful, you need to understand that a form is not open to negotiation (the techniques can't be changed), but it can be open to interpretation. (The way that you do a side kick will be a little different from the way the next person does a side kick.)

First, you're going to need someone to demonstrate the form to you. As the instructor or senior students does this, you can ask questions about what you see so that you're not confused when it comes time for you to try. Then, with the instructor's help, you can break down the form into its basic parts. Maybe the footwork forms a certain pattern that you can easily remember. Maybe the techniques follow a certain sequence, such as a punch follows every block. Then, with the instructor's guidance, perform the form several times, asking for help if you get stuck or listening to the instructor's comments as you do the movements.

Finally, keep the memory fresh. As soon as you get home from class, practice the form in your living room. As soon as you get up in the morning, practice it again. When you go to class in the evening, ask a senior student to watch you do your form and ask him to correct any mistakes you may make. Before you know it, it's Friday night, and you've memorized your form!

Planning for the long term

While short-term goals may require only a few steps, long-term goals require more in-depth planning, which is an important part of the process because it may cause you to reconsider your goals or to decide that one goal is more important than another. Determine what's important before you spend much time and energy in pursuit of a goal that you find isn't important after all.

Determining the steps needed to reach a long-term goal is sometimes difficult to do by yourself. After all, if you're not a black belt yet, you may not know everything that's involved to become a black belt. Always ask for advice. Your instructor and the senior students recognize how important it is to have goals; they'll be pleased to help you learn what's necessary to achieve them.

Setting markers toward your goal

In order to plan for a long-term goal, you need to set markers to measure your progress. If you want to lose 15 pounds in six months, for example, your markers would be losing about a pound each week. If several weeks went by without your losing a pound, you would need to reconsider your strategy and revise it so that you start losing about a pound a week.

Meeting your markers

After the markers are in place, identifying the specific steps needed to reach them is easier. If you need to lose a pound a week and you know that a pound consists of about 3,500 calories, then you need to determine what steps you'll take to reduce your calorie intake and increase your energy expenditure to reach 3,500 calories per week. How you manage this is up to you. You can walk the treadmill for an hour and 15 minutes every day and expend 3,500 calories that way, you can cut 500 calories from your daily calorie intake, or you can do some combination of calorie-cutting and exercise.

Assessing your progress routinely

As you progress toward your goal, take routine measurements of your achievements. If you're trying to lose weight, step on the scale once a week to see if your approach is working. If it isn't, consider your options. Have you failed to cut back your calorie intake? Would it be smarter to exercise more and diet a bit less?

Don't overdo it on the assessment. If you're trying to lose 15 pounds, don't weigh yourself everyday. You'll just get frustrated and feel like you're not making progress. Instead, each time that you reach one of the markers you set, do a brief assessment and make any adjustments that you need.

Trying the quarterly approach

For some long-term goals with many steps needed to reach them, using the quarterly approach can make the whole process seem less intimidating.

Determine what your long-term goal is. Say that you want a black belt. From talking with your instructor, you know that if you commit to training, you can test for your black belt in about three years. To be ready for this, break the next three years down into quarters. At 4 quarters per year and with three years to prepare, you have 12 quarters total. Check out the following quarterly plan for the first 4 quarters:

- ✔ **Quarter 1:** Go to Karate class four times per week. Practice each technique at least ten times per day. Memorize the names of instructors and senior students. Memorize first form. (For more on forms, see the "Breaking down every goal: Forms" section, earlier in this chapter.)

- ✔ **Quarter 2:** In addition to continuing with your Quarter 1 plans, cut back on fried foods and alcohol. Begin a diet that's lower in fat and higher in carbohydrates. Memorize second form and continue practicing first form.

- ✔ **Quarter 3:** In addition to your Quarters 1 and 2 plans, begin strength training with weights. Do flexibility training every day to prevent loss of flexibility owing to weight training. Test for orange belt.

- ✔ **Quarter 4:** In addition to your Quarters 1, 2, and 3 plans, consult with your instructor about progress and learn about areas needing improvement.

Don't forget that you'll have intermediate belt ranks to achieve before you're ready to test for your black belt. (More on this in the next section, "I Have a Black Belt . . . and Green Suspenders: The Ranking System.") Factor these belt ranks into your plan. If you don't achieve them on target, reassess your plan.

I Have a Black Belt . . . and Green Suspenders: The Ranking System

If you don't know much about martial arts, the meaning of belt ranks can be a bit confusing. You know that a black belt designates the most skill, and you have the idea that you earn other colored belts as you progress, but that's the extent of your knowledge.

You're not alone. Most beginning martial artists are a bit obsessive about rank, and how it's achieved, and who has what. After you've been a black belt for a while (and you will be!), rank becomes less important to you, and you measure yourself by what you give back to the art, what kind of students you've taught, and other intangibles.

But for your first few years of training, belt-ranking can help you to determine your progress toward your goals. If you don't seem to be promoting as frequently as other students are, you may need to recommit to your training. If you fail a test, you may need to assess what went wrong and what areas of your training need work. Belt rank tests serve as excellent markers on your way to a black belt. If you're not progressing through the ranks as you'd expect, it's time to have a serious talk with your instructor.

Belt-ranking systems are the invention of the modern-day martial artists. In the past, a student took many years to learn a master's system. When the master was satisfied that the student had learned all he could, he was awarded a teaching certificate. Belts were used to keep one's robe closed.

White-belt wannabe

In almost every martial art, the merest beginner wears a white belt to symbolize his innocence and lack of knowledge. As the beginner learns and practices the techniques, he becomes eligible to earn higher and higher ranks or to "promote" through the system.

Instead of being called "a student with a white belt," you'll usually just be called "a white belt." If an instructor wants you to do something, he may say, "White belt, close the door." It's just a shorthand method of communicating. And, by the way, you'll want to say, "Yes sir!" and then run and close the door.

The blue-belt blues

As you progress through the ranks, you'll reach an intermediate level where you know many, if not most, of the techniques, yet you won't have enough experience to be anywhere near mastery. You'll be wearing a blue belt (or a green belt or a purple belt), a color that signifies that you're no longer a white belt. You know you've made some progress. But you may feel you're not making enough progress. Many students hit a plateau at this point, become frustrated when they don't make much progress, and then drop out. Don't let this happen to you! Be prepared, and work through it.

I can't count the number of people I know who earned intermediate belts in Tae Kwon Do — even many who were brown belts, the rank just before black belt — then hit a plateau but didn't grit their teeth and stay with it. Whenever I meet these people again, they tell me, "If only I'd stayed with it for another month or two, I could have earned my black belt." The moral of the story is to stay with it even when you hit the rough spots. That's part of the training.

Black-belt beginners

What do I mean, black belt beginners? Isn't a black belt someone who has mastered the art? The answer is yes and no. A person who has earned a black belt has trained in a martial art with dedication and commitment for several years. She has learned most of the techniques and may be quite expert at the system but not yet a master. It takes, literally, a lifetime to master a martial art. The black belt is simply a recognition that a person is dedicated to a martial art.

The black belt rank is divided into degrees with the higher number being the more experienced. Thus, a third-degree black belt has more experience and a higher rank than a first-degree black belt.

In some systems, the black belt is actually a white belt. That is, the most experienced martial artists and the least experienced martial artists wear the same symbol. This reinforces the idea that the master is also a beginner in some ways, that he has come full circle, and that the beginner has the seeds of the master in her already.

Ranking systems

Each martial arts style has a different ranking system, but most styles recognize at least one beginner rank, one intermediate rank, and one advanced rank. In some styles, rank can only be achieved through competition; you must defeat a higher-ranking student in order to achieve that rank. This is uncommon. Usually, a promotion test is given, and the student demonstrates proficiency in the techniques of a given level in order to promote to the next level. At the higher ranks, technical skill is less important to promotion than a martial artist's contribution to the art. Even if you can't perform a triple-spinning-double-roundhouse kick, your commitment to the art is the measure of your mastery. If you teach others, for example, you're giving back to the art even if someday all your students are more technically proficient than you are. If you promote the martial arts through living a life of integrity and honesty, that's more important then whether you can break three concrete blocks with a single punch. When you're older and less able to perform difficult, athletic feats, your successes will be based on how you encourage others to achieve and how you represent the art in the world outside the training hall.

Promotion opportunities are given at the discretion of your teacher. If she decides that you aren't ready to test for the next belt level, you must abide by the decision.

Demotions, though rare, can occur when a student fails to adhere to the standards of a school, such as by using the techniques to attack instead of in self-defense. After a grave offense, such as a felony, membership in a school and all ranks earned can be revoked.

The kyu/dan system

The most common ranking system is the *class/degree* or *kyu/dan* system. The nonblack belt students are ranked by *kyu* (class); the black belts are ranked according to *dan* (degree). Different schools award different color belts for each class; sometimes a stripe is added to a belt to distinguish between various classes. The basic principle is that the darker the color of the belt, the higher the rank.

Some of the common belt colors used to indicate different classes are

- 10th class: white belt
- 9th class: white, yellow, orange
- 8th class: white, yellow, orange
- 7th class: white, yellow, orange, green
- 6th class: yellow, green, blue
- 5th class: yellow, green, blue
- 4th class: yellow, green, blue, brown
- 3rd class: green, brown, red
- 2nd class: brown or red
- 1st class: brown or red

Nonblack belt classes may be as many as 15 or as few as 2. In general, the black belt has 9 or 10 grades/degrees with the higher ranks achieved only by the founder of the martial art and a few masters with extensive experience who have contributed greatly to the art.

Testing 1, 2, 3 . . . Testing 1, 2, 3 . . .

In most modern martial arts, in order to earn a higher belt rank, you must take a test. Unlike testing in geometry class, looking at your neighbor's paper won't help you here. That's why you need to be prepared before you test.

Depending on your style, you may be eligible to test for rank every few months or only once a year. Black belts test much less often than colored belts. The higher a degree the black belt is testing for, the longer she must wait between tests. We usually don't feel too bad about this.

In almost all schools, testing costs money. Be sure that you understand this expense up front. Also, don't be surprised if that new blue belt costs you $35 when you know that little bit of material couldn't possibly wholesale for more than a buck fifty. Your instructor has to eat, too.

Just use your common sense and don't get taken advantage of. Rank promotion may cost as much as $50 for nonblack belts. So if your instructor insists on charging $1,000 for that blue belt, you may ask yourself if you're getting true value for your money.

Although some schools allow informal testing, where an instructor watches you perform your techniques, asks you a few questions about the martial art, and then gives you a brand new belt, most require more formal rank promotion testing.

Usually, groups of students at about the same level (for example, all beginners or all intermediate students) are tested at the same time. A panel of judges observes them and determines whether they're proficient in the techniques taught at their level. Each person is judged individually although everyone takes the test at the same time.

A senior student or instructor leads the students through the test. Often, the test is simply a shortened, fast-pace version of a regular training session.

You should be wringing wet and exhausted after you finish a promotion test. If someone asked you to demonstrate a kick, you wouldn't have the energy to do it. That's the kind of energy and enthusiasm the judges appreciate.

What the judges are looking for

Skill isn't the only criterion. Judges also take into consideration what you're capable of. (So age and any physical disability are taken into account.) Your effort, the courtesy that you show toward others, and your overall attitude also count for a great deal.

Even if you fail to demonstrate proficiency with a certain technique, you can still pass as long as you persevered, showed a winning spirit, and in general, appeared to be a credit to your school. By the same token, someone who could do all the techniques easily but was rude to the judges may not pass.

A student may be passed "with reservation," which means that the student is awarded the higher rank but must work on certain aspects of his training before the next test. In general, a student isn't given two "with reservation" promotions in a row. He won't be passed the second time.

Preparing for your ordeal by fire

A rank promotion test is less intimidating if you know what to expect. Therefore, if you can watch one before it's your turn, take the opportunity to do so. Also, ask the instructor and other students what you'll be expected to do for your test.

For the most part, you need to know how to do the techniques that you've been taught so far, you should be able to demonstrate all the forms (also known as *kata* or *hyung*) that you've been shown, even those you learned for previous belt ranks, and you should be able to perform mock combat drills similar to the ones that you might do in class. (For more on forms, see the "Breaking down every goal: Forms" section, earlier in this chapter.) You may also be expected to know some terminology, such as the Japanese and English names for your techniques. You may be quizzed on aspects of martial arts culture, such as why one bows to senior belts.

What's expected of you at your test is usually quite clear. Now and then, something unusual will be thrown in just to see how you react. Just do your best. Prepare for what you know is coming, and expect a little something no one told you about, such as board-breaking, conditioning exercises, and concentration drills.

Often, your focus and concentration is judged at a promotion test. Practice for this by performing your forms with your eyes closed or oriented in a different direction from usual. You'll be surprised at how much concentration this takes, but when you're asked to do it at your test, you'll be ready.

Coming out with flying colors

On test day, be sure to arrive with plenty of time to spare before you're scheduled to be judged. Eat a small snack, such as an apple or a bowl of oatmeal, an hour or two before your test. If you'd rather not eat anything, drink a few ounces of juice to give you a bit of energy without making you sluggish. Drink plenty of water beforehand.

Stop drinking water about twenty minutes or so before your test. You're going to be nervous, and your kidneys are going to be nervous. Enough said.

To help focus and to keep a calm mind, find a quiet corner and do some meditating and a few deep-breathing exercises. A few minutes before your test, do some light warming up and stretching. You'll get a huge surge of adrenaline when the test starts, and you don't want to overstrain cold muscles when that adrenaline hits. When the test starts, concentrate on doing your best and showing warrior spirit. You'll do fine!

If you make a mistake during the test, just fix it and go on. Many times, a judge won't even notice it if you appear confident. If the judge does notice, he'll give you credit for not getting distracted or flustered by making a mistake.

Chapter 6

Clothes, Shoes, and Equipment

. . . .

In This Chapter

▶ Learning what to wear and how to wear it

▶ Discovering equipment and what it might cost

▶ Finding what's appropriate for your home-training space

▶ Protecting yourself and your sparring partner from injury

. . . .

Y ou decide to kick your way to better health. It can't be that complicated, right? Just throw on some workout togs and hit the training hall.

Well, not exactly. In *some* martial arts schools and styles, showing up in a spandex leotard or a muscle shirt and short shorts may be okay but not in many. Instead, you wear a uniform, called a *dobo, gi,* or *dobok,* depending on your style.

Putting the martial arts uniform on should be a ritual. While you're doing it, you should clear your mind and prepare for training.

Pajama Paradise

The uniform usually consists of loose-fitting trousers and a tunic top or a wrap-style top. The wrap-style top works like a bathrobe with one side covering the other side. Yes, you'll look like you're wearing pajamas, but that didn't stop Bruce Lee.

Women warriors, keep in mind that martial arts clothes are made with men in mind — sexist but true. That means that when you put a wrap-style top on, the left side goes over the right side — not the other way around. I wore my dobok the wrong way around for about three years before I detected the difference between what I was doing and what everyone else was doing.

The top is closed with a belt that indicates the rank that you have so far achieved. (See Chapter 5 for more information on belts, ranks, and other martial arts achievements.)

The uniform is usually purchased through the school. The instructor will often have a special name and logo silk-screened on the top, and he would like everyone to wear the same outfit when training. If your instructor doesn't provide a special uniform, he'll explain how and where you can purchase one, what color it should be, what material it should be made from, and may even suggest a manufacturer.

Using regular workout clothes

In Jeet Kune Do and related styles, you may be encouraged to wear regular workout clothes or even street clothes. So asking your instructor about attire (and taking a peek at your new classmates) makes sense before you shell out for the kind of outfit that you really can't wear anywhere else.

When you're training at home, you can choose your workout clothes, but do give some thought to wearing traditional attire, at least occasionally. It makes you feel like a martial artist. And that's why you're studying the martial arts, isn't it?

Finding a uniform: Plain or with sprinkles?

If you do need a traditional uniform, choose a plain white one. Okay, okay, in some styles, you'll wear a *black hakama,* which is similar to Samurai dress — with loose, flowing trousers that look like a long skirt — but even so, make sure that it's plain. Avoid the blue satin version until you've achieved some training in martial arts. (You'll need the training because of the amount of trouble that people will give you for wearing a blue satin uniform.)

Where to shop

Your instructor may provide you with a uniform as part of your tuition or for a small additional fee. If not, you can purchase most martial arts uniforms and equipment at martial arts supply stores (most cities have one) or sporting goods stores. See Appendix B at the end of this book for mail order and online merchants.

Purchasing uniforms, equipment, and supplies from your instructor (if she sells them) is good courtesy.

What that uniform may cost

A uniform costs from $35 to more than $100, but you should be able to start with one at the cheaper end of the spectrum. You may want to have more than one outfit, especially if you train frequently, because if you don't have more than one, it's always in the laundry when you're getting ready to go to class.

How to take care of your uniform

Your uniform should always be clean and pressed. After all, you're representing yourself, your instructor, and your art. Do a good job of it.

Some schools have rules about wearing your uniform outside of class. The rule is, don't do it! This prevents people from challenging you on the street: "Hey! There's a guy wearing pajamas! Let's see if he can really kick our butts!"

The uniform or a set of basic workout clothes is all you really need to get started. The splints and bandages don't come until later.

Something's Afoot: Martial Arts Shoes

Most martial arts are practiced barefoot. This is to harden your feet and prepare them for fire walking and performing gymnastic feats on broken glass. (Just kidding.) Actually, working out without shoes does toughen your feet. Your first martial arts trophy will be a couple of blisters on the soles of your feet, but safety is an important reason for going shoeless. When you kick your partner in the head while wearing Army boots, it annoys your partner.

You can purchase special lightweight martial arts shoes that have a pivot point beneath the ball of your foot, so you can do your techniques without spraining your ankle. They're useful for practicing outdoors or on hard floors. People in grappling styles may do well with boxing or wrestling shoes, which add extra stability to the ankles.

Special shoes run from $50 to $100, but you can always wear your old sneakers.

The Right Rigging

If you like sports paraphernalia, you came to the right sport. Although you only need a minimal amount of gear, some cool, new gadget is always being marketed that'll catch your eye.

Sparring equipment

In general, you'll need some protective equipment for sparring styles, such as Karate and Tae Kwon Do, but you don't need it right away because you won't be expected to bring it on the first day of training.

In fact, a couple of months may pass before the instructor ever says, "Bow to your partner. Begin!" This is because you have to learn the basic techniques of the art before you can use them in mock combat.

- ✔ **Full-body armor:** Some martial arts styles consist of practitioners hitting each other sharply with sticks, wooden swords, and other solid implements. They have developed full-body protective equipment to keep from permanently maiming one another. Sets of full-body armor may cost a few hundred dollars. Your instructor can help you find the right style and fit.

- ✔ **Headgear:** Your sparring equipment may include headgear to protect your face, skull, and not incidentally, your brain. These are usually made of foam and may have a face mask or clear plastic shield (to keep your nose in the shape and condition that it's currently in).

Some styles don't use headgear because of the contention that it causes people to hit each other harder. I've sparred with headgear and without, and I have to agree, people do hit each other harder when they're wearing more safety gear. But I like to thank my brain for all it's done for me, and one way that I can do that is to wear headgear.

- ✔ **Mouthguard:** A mouthguard is essential. It protects your teeth and mouth from expensive dental surgery. Not bad for a hunk of plastic that'll set you back about five bucks. You can get custom dental guards for about $200 if you turn pro or decide to try your hand at the next Ultimate Fighting Championships. (In which case, you obviously haven't been wearing your headgear).

- ✔ **Chest Protector:** In some schools, you're required to wear a chest protector that extends from your neck to mid thigh. Although cumbersome, this will prevent broken ribs and mangled spleens. Some women wear small, light chest protectors that slip inside their bra to prevent damage to their breasts. Chest protectors run from $50 to $75.

- ✔ **Groin Protector:** This little device ensures a man's future fertility and prevents severe pain and emotional distress. A plastic cup slips into a jock-strap. A must for men. Different versions of groin protectors are available for women, but I don't know any women who use them. About $15.

- ✔ **Sparring Gloves:** Gloves protect your hands and your partner's face when you hit him hard. These come in a variety of styles, but a foam version that slips over the back of your hand and secures at the wrist is the most popular. Expect to spend $25 to $40 or more.

You can use protective gear when working out on the heavy bag, too. *Handwraps* resemble those elastic bandages that you wear when you sprain your ankle. They protect your hands and stabilize your wrist to prevent it from rolling over when you punch. Wraps cost between $5 and $15. Plus you have to figure out how to put them on — a good exercise in spatial relations. *Bag gloves* are also used to punch the heavy bag. They protect your hands, stabilize your wrists, and can be purchased in a variety of sizes. They cost about $50. They don't require superior spatial relations to use.

✔ **Foot protectors:** These aren't really intended to protect your feet. They're to protect your partner should you hit a little harder than you meant to. Two popular versions exist, a foam version that slips over your foot, covering the sides, heel and top, and a padded version that covers the instep and the shin. These run from $30 to $50.

✔ **Shin protectors:** These protectors slip on your leg and cover the bony part of your shin, guarding against painful bruises when someone's elbow blocks your roundhouse kick. You'll spend about $30.

✔ **Forearm protectors:** These padded protectors slip over your forearms to protect them the way a shin protector guards your leg. They're not commonly used and run about $30.

Before investing in any equipment, ask your instructor what you need, when you'll need it, and how to use it. This ensures you that you don't waste time and money on things that you don't need.

Weapons

In some styles, you train with weapons, such as *nunchuks* (flails), *tonfa* (a short stick with a handle), and *bo* (staff). To train effectively, you'll need to invest in practice weapons.

Foam-covered escrima sticks (hardwood fighting sticks used by Escrimadors) prevent you from whacking your partner too hard; foam-covered nunchuks prevent personal concussions. Bokken, wooden swords, prevent pesky bleeding when you're practicing Kendo (sword art).

You may also have to invest in regular weapons for competitions and demonstrations. Expect to spend anywhere from $25 to hundreds of dollars on weapons. The good thing is, though, that you don't have to spend more than a few dollars at first. Only if you're truly interested in pursuing traditional weapons practice will you have to invest more. (For more information on weapons, see Chapter 12.)

Grasshopper's Home Gym

Eventually, most martial artists set up a corner of the basement for practicing martial arts. Some martial artists do the majority of their training at home and need to set up a reasonable facsimile of a training hall.

How should you get started? First, you'll need a clear space, preferably about eight square feet. If you don't have this much room, smaller will also work, but you may have to modify your workout a bit.

If space is a problem, you can do supplemental training, such as weight lifting, in small places.

Try not to choose an area with a concrete or wood floor. Hard surfaces mean a total knee replacement down the road. If you have to work out on a hard surface, a wood floor is better than a concrete floor. At least put some mats or carpet squares down, and don't do so many flying side kicks. And watch those Judo throws!

Outfit your space with a mirror — a couple of mirrors if you can — so that you can see what you're doing. Otherwise, you'll never master that fierce warrior expression that you've been working on.

Decide what you want to accomplish during your home workouts. If you want to build strength, you can purchase a good set of free weights for $100. If you want to increase flexibility, you just need clear floor space for stretching exercises. Other equipment that will round out your workout include the following:

✔ **Heavy Bag:** The heavy bag is a must, even for people who practice grappling arts. Because it is the general size and weight of a person, kicking and punching it is similar to kicking and punching a person. Grapplers can use it to build strength and timing. Try breaking the balance of a heavy bag, and you'll see what I mean. Working with it improves coordination, strength, and stamina. The traditional heavy bag is made of canvas and is filled with sand (or foam) and hangs from a ceiling joist. Because it hangs, when you hit it, it moves. So you have to anticipate where it's going and if it's going to come back and smack you in the hip. But a hanging heavy bag is not the only option.

You can get a freestanding heavy bag if you think the landlord will object to your screwing an eye bolt into the ceiling. These freestanding bags are made of foam with a base that you fill with water. Although they don't swing around like traditional heavy bags (which tests your reflexes and timing), they're good for smaller spaces. (You don't have to worry about the heavy bag smacking into the stereo cabinet. It's not going anywhere.) Heavy bags run from $100 to $250.

You can get little vinyl heavy bags that you fill with water and air for the kids. They'll get a kick out of kicking alongside you! About $15.

The canvas on traditional bags rips up your equipment, so opt for vinyl instead. (You can get leather if you're the kind of person who drives a BMW.)

✔ **Bags, Bags and More Bags:** *Speed bags* make you develop a rhythm in order to strike the bag as it moves back and forth. *Double end bags* make you respond to the movement of the bag in a broken rhythm. The *tear drop bag,* about 36 inches long, is fuller at the bottom than the top, and is great for perfecting knee strikes. The *banana bag* is longer and thinner than a traditional heavy bag and is used to develop knee and shin strikes. Expect to spend between $50 and $150.

✔ **Striking Pads:** These come in a variety of shapes and sizes. *Focus mitts* are small, about 12 inches square. A partner moves it around as you try to strike it. *Kicking targets* and *Muay Thai pads* are quite a bit larger, with more padding. A partner holds it as you work on kicking with power. *Makiwara boards* or *striking posts* condition your hands and help you master punching techniques. *Blocking pads* are soft rectangular pads attached to a stick; your partner strikes at you with the pad, and you block or evade the strike. Striking pads can set you back $20 to $50 each.

✔ **Miscellaneous Equipment:** If you use grappling techniques or throws, invest in a good set of *tatami* mats (about $50). A *jump rope* can improve your endurance (if you use it). About $15; get one in the right weight and length (or borrow your daughter's). A weighted *medicine ball* improves your upper body strength when you throw it around ($35).

Great gizmos

Even if you don't set up your own home-training center, you may not be able to live without some pieces of equipment:

✔ A *rebreakable board* (made of hard plastic and costing $50) prevents you from deforesting the Amazon on your way to earning your black belt because you can reuse it in place of pine boards.

✔ How about a *stretching machine*? Just attach your legs to the frame, crank the handle, and voilà! Instant flexibility for $150 to $500.

✔ *Wing Chun Dummy* and related items resemble humans with more or less realistic arms, legs, and torso and costs $100 to $300. One version even lights up if you strike in a vulnerable target area.

Pick up a martial arts magazine, such as *Martial Arts and Combat Sports* or *Black Belt,* for some great finds in the ad pages!

Chapter 7

Playing It Safe and Avoiding Injury

- -

In This Chapter

▶ Coming at it from the right perspective

▶ Discovering how to deal with physical contact

▶ Speaking up when your partner doesn't do right

▶ Preventing painful injuries with simple techniques

- -

*N*ow you're set. You have your *dobok* (uniform), your sparring equipment, and your rebreakable board. (Made of hard plastic, a *rebreakable board* is reusable.) You have an instructor and a school, and the babysitter is due at 6 p.m. You're ready for anything . . . or at least for martial arts class.

You *are* ready . . . if you have the right attitude.

Attitude? I'll Give You Attitude!

There are two kinds of people: sane people and martial artists.

This can create a bit of a problem when a sane person decides to become a martial artist. A transition takes place during which the formerly sane person tries desperately to cling to the last vestiges of normal, appropriate behavior; his fellow martial artists' gung-ho exhortations are slightly bewildering.

Accomplished martial artists display tenacity, focus, and determination, which can come in handy in daily life, such as when Wal-Mart is having a sale. To the innocent bystander, these qualities may be misinterpreted as aggressive, cocky, or arrogant. However, this isn't the martial artist's intention. Pure and simple self-confidence, which comes with martial arts training, sometimes seems to be other than what it is.

Martial artists know the value of humility. Everyone has fallen on his behind performing a technique. If you haven't, you weren't trying hard enough.

Suffice it to say that to an inexperienced beginner, the world of martial arts — inhabited as it is by brash and confident martial artists — can be confusing and a bit frightening. But with the right attitude — an open mind, willingness to try, and the commitment to persevere — anyone can succeed in martial arts. To find out more about developing the right mental attitude, see Chapters 8 and 11.

Unnecessary Roughness

For many people, one of the most frightening aspects of training in the martial arts is that other people have the opportunity to hit you, throw you, or strike you with a large wooden sword. For many others, one of the most frightening aspects of training in the martial arts is that you have the opportunity to hit, throw, or strike other people with a large wooden sword.

For example, I was so afraid of hitting other people that I couldn't spar when I first began training. Fortunately, a wonderful black belt, Jeanne Heitzman, took me aside and made me hit her repeatedly until it no longer bothered me to do so. Of course, my mother isn't so sure that this is an improvement.

Either way, striking or getting struck, the idea of physical contact — especially hard physical contact — is scary. That's why it's important that your first experiences in martial arts are safe and well planned.

I'll have light contact, please

In most schools, beginners aren't allowed to jump right in and start fighting, and the reason is safety. Besides not knowing the techniques, beginners don't know their own strength and abilities. Until beginners learn to control their bodies, it's best for all concerned that mock combat sessions take place with *no contact*.

Advanced martial artists agree that the most dangerous martial artists are those in the early intermediate stages of training. They know just enough to be able to perform the techniques, but they lack the hesitancy and caution of beginners and the finesse and control of more advanced martial artists. After the beginner has learned some of the basic techniques using no contact, it's time to move on to light contact. In the grappling arts, *light contact* means running through the throwing techniques without using full power to perform them or full power to stop them. In the striking arts, it means sparring at such a distance and with such control that the kicks and punches touch the partner's uniform but are no harder than a light touch.

Using a light touch requires a great deal of control. Smacking everyone as hard as you can is much easier. (Well, it's much easier on you; the partners who you're smacking may have something to say about how easy it is.) Control is a product of strength, timing, experience, judgment, and flexibility, so it takes some time to acquire. Good martial artists always have control over their bodies and can go as hard or as gentle as you tell them to.

It's not sparring if you don't bruise

For many people, light contact is sufficient for all their needs, but for a few hardcore martial artists, light contact isn't enough. They want to push it, fight closer to the edge, and perform at a riskier level. They want to know that if they miss that block, they're going to know that they missed that block. This gives a sense of realism to their practice. They're not happy unless they can show their bumps and bruises to all their friends and co-workers.

Don't attempt heavy contact until you're well advanced in the study of a martial art and then only with the permission of your partner. You can't just nail him with a side kick to the ribs and then ask, "Okay to go a little harder today?" when he's rolling on the floor in agony.

Full contact is slightly different from heavy contact. In *heavy contact,* people might strike with enough force to leave a bruise. The goal of full contact is to knock out the opponent. Obviously, full-contact martial arts are reserved for professionals and for the odd mugger who needs to be taught a lesson.

Safe sparring

Feeling safe while learning a martial art is important. Partners should respect your wishes if you ask for lighter contact or slower techniques.

Sparring between unequal partners

Often, partners of unequal size, very different ages, or ranks are paired together. In this case, the stronger or taller partner should accommodate the size-impaired partner; the adult should accommodate the child (or the teenager for the old-timer); and the higher-ranking student should see to it that the practice goes at the pace that the lower-ranking student prefers. Of course, the size-impaired student, the child (or the old-timer), or the lower-ranking student should speak up if this doesn't happen.

Tattling is indeed honorable

If any student repeatedly ignores your requests for lighter contact (or any similar request), report it immediately to the head instructor. If someone is causing you problems, he's most likely causing similar problems with other students. You can always refuse to work with a partner who you feel is unsafe at any speed.

Higher-ranking students sometimes forget how intimidating it is to start training in the martial arts. They soon forget that they had fears and anxieties, too. So a gentle reminder is usually all it takes.

By gradually increasing the amount of contact you experience, you learn to overcome any fears that you have about getting hit or hitting other people. Soon, you'll be thumping on people with joy and abandon, hardly believing that you ever felt timid or afraid. But remember, when it's your turn to teach the beginner, how intimidated or frightened you may have felt in your early days of training.

By helping to keep the school environment safe and nonthreatening, you're doing your part to promote martial arts for everyone.

Injury Prevention

You may think that getting kicked in the head while practicing a step-sparring combination is your greatest risk for injury in the martial arts, but that isn't the case. In fact, the martial arts are remarkably safe, considering that the goal of training is to be able to defeat another warrior in armed or unarmed combat.

In fact, the most common injuries sustained in martial arts are similar to those sustained by tennis players and rollerbladers — strains, sprains, bumps, and bruises. To avoid injury, you need to treat your body right, and you need to practice safely.

Watching like a hawk

In the training hall, you must always be alert and aware of what's going on around you. This is doubly true if the training hall allows children to participate. The partners sparring next to you may run into you if you're not careful. If you turn your head to talk to someone while picking up equipment off the floor, you may smack into someone's jump-spinning-wheel kick, or it might smack into you. Remember that all around you, people are practicing throws, pins, punches, and kicks, and some of them aren't good at it.

Don't be a sitting duck

Walk around other students, not between or behind them. Never turn your back when you're performing drills. If you must stop what you're doing during a drill or a sparring match, look your partner in the eye, hold both hands up in front of your chest, step back slightly and say, "Time out!" Wait until the other person has acknowledged you before you bend over to fix your foot protector (see Chapter 6) or pick up the mouthguard that you dropped. Otherwise, you may get a nasty surprise right between your eyes.

I can't count the number of people who have been brained by an incoming technique because they forgot to warn their partner that they were going to fix their footgear. *Never* bend over, turn around, or look away when working with a partner until the partner knows what you intend to do.

Always clarify the ground rules when working with partners. Often the instructor does this for everyone. If not, it's up to you.

Never assume that another student or partner will do things the way that you think they should be done. And never assume that the other person is responsible for your safety.

Control, control, control!

Never forget that you must exercise control over your body and other people's when it's in your power to do so. For example, when you're practicing throwing techniques, you have several choices in how you complete the technique. You can hold the partner's uniform as you take her down, releasing her as she reaches the mat, or you can simply drop her to the floor. The first option is the safer. The second option should be reserved for a real-life assailant — *not* your training partners.

Don't forget that people sometimes do the unexpected. For example, sometimes a beginner darts between two partners who are working, not realizing how dangerous it is to go between rather than around people. Your quick reactions are essential to maintaining safety. Not to mention that the beginner might find getting flattened by your inadvertent ax kick a trifle discouraging.

Wearing armor

Wear protective gear when practicing drills or engaged in mock combat (sparring). Men should wear groin protectors at all times, even when hanging out with other martial artists at the local bar. (Martial artists love to horse around in ways that can be exceedingly painful.) All martial artists should wear mouthguards. Try to get one that allows you to breathe while it's in your mouth. Optional, but still important, is being able to swallow with the mouthguard in place.

Headgear, chest protectors, hand and foot protectors, and even full-body armor (see Chapter 6) may be required in some schools. A teacher requires certain kinds of equipment for a reason, and generally it's in your best interest to follow along.

Always bring your equipment with you to class. It isn't going to do you much good sitting on the floor by the front door.

Make certain that your equipment fits correctly. If your headgear is too large, a kick can spin it around your head, and that won't help your chances of victory (not to mention the likelihood of getting clobbered).

Protective equipment must be replaced periodically. In general, if you use it several times a week, you'll probably have to replace it every year. If you don't use it that often, you can go a little longer before replacing it. Immediately replace any equipment that's torn, has loose straps, or no longer fits correctly.

Treating your body right

When you start training in the martial arts, you start asking your body to do what you never envisioned back when your body was comfortably ensconced, couch potatoesque, on the recliner in front of the TV.

It's no wonder, then, that beginners often develop injuries that could have been prevented if only they had realized what they were asking their bodies to do.

In order for your body to perform well, it needs to be fed, watered, and rested appropriately. This means nutritious meals with plenty of fruits and vegetables and not so many French fries. It means about a gallon of water every day. (The 48-ounce burst-your-bladder Slurpee from 7-11 doesn't count.) And it means eight hours of shuteye every night. Otherwise, your body can't cope with the demands that you make on it, and it will rebel, usually by coming down with a really violent case of the flu.

To fuel a workout without weighing yourself down with a meal, try drinking a few ounces of juice a few minutes before class. This is a great pick-me-up for people who rush to class right after work and don't have time to eat and digest a meal.

Understanding common injuries

Martial artists suffer the same injuries as other athletes suffer, except that they're prouder of their injuries. Common injuries include overuse injuries, hyperextension injuries, dislocation injuries, broken bones, strains, sprains, cuts, and bruises. In many cases, the injury could be prevented.

There's nothing to be proud of when you injure yourself! It just means you've been stupid. And it also means that you have to stop training or reduce training until you're fully recovered. Take steps to prevent injuries and enjoy a pain-free martial arts career.

Overuse injuries

Overuse injuries occur when you use a certain part of your body repeatedly, subjecting it to special stress, especially when it hasn't been used this way before. Tendonitis and bursitis are common overuse injuries. The irritated and inflamed tissue becomes quite painful.

Overuse injuries are frequent among beginners who jump right in training five days a week after months of merely getting off the sofa to find the remote.

Hyperextension and dislocation injuries

Hyperextension injuries occur when a joint is forced past its normal range of motion. A *dislocation* occurs when a bone is moved out of its usual position in a joint, sometimes causing damage to the surrounding tissue. Both of these injuries can occur when martial artists perform their techniques incorrectly.

Broken bones

Broken bones occur as the result of a one-time accident or over time after repeated stress (stress fracture). In the first instance, performing techniques correctly generally reduces the risk of fracture. In the second instance, a stress fracture is similar to an overuse injury and is more likely to occur when a beginner doesn't understand that the body has limits.

Strains and sprains

Strains and sprains occur when a body part is forced to move in a direction or to a degree that it does not ordinarily do. These are often the result of incorrect technique.

Bruises and cuts

Bruises and cuts are generally the result of direct impact from a partner. They can be avoided by wearing safety equipment and by agreeing on a reasonable level of contact with partners.

Taking simple precautions

Although most martial artists have a catalog of injuries that they're more than happy to share with you (I have three broken bones, two blown out knees . . .), many — probably most — injuries can be avoided with simple precautions.

Warming up and stretching

Cold muscles are more susceptible to injury than warm muscles. Warm up and stretch before each training session, and cool down afterward. This helps to prevent strains and sprains that occur when you try to kick head high on muscles stretched only chest high.

Stretching also increases flexibility, which allows you to do techniques correctly, without strain.

Building strength

Often, joints are unstable and prone to injury. Building the surrounding muscles can strengthen them. For example, strengthening the hamstring and quadriceps muscles can prevent knee injuries. A few minutes of weight lifting a few days a week can reduce your risk of injury significantly.

Performing techniques correctly

If you don't perform techniques correctly, you put plenty of stress on your body. For example, to do a side kick, you must pivot on the ball of your foot to position your body correctly for the strike. If you don't pivot, you strain your knee and your hip and force these joints into an awkward position. It's only a matter of time, then, until a sprain or even a dislocation occurs. Do the techniques exactly as you're taught, and not only will you become an excellent martial artist, but you'll avoid injury as well!

Part II
Walking the Walk and Talking the Talk

The 5th Wave   By Rich Tennant

CHO'S KARATE SCHOOL

CLASSES TODAY

In this part . . .

This part shows you what it takes to succeed in martial arts. You can find out how to get the most from your training, defend yourself against an attacker, use traditional weapons, and kick butt at competitions. It also shows you how to incorporate your martial arts knowledge in your everyday life. You'll discover how to balance your mind with your body and your spirit, and you'll understand how to use your martial arts outside the training hall even if you never kick anybody. So let's get started!

Chapter 8

Getting the Most from Your Training

In This Chapter

▶ Cultivating the right attitude

▶ Seeing how persistence pays off

▶ Discovering the benefits of living right

▶ Learning how to condition for strength and flexibility

Y ou can't succeed as a martial artist if you never get up off the sofa. You also have to quit eating all those crispy crunchies. It's true: Learning how to do a jump-spinning-wheel kick requires some personal sacrifice. (But just think, you'll learn how to do a jump-spinning-wheel kick.)

A Martial Artist in Training

Think of yourself as being in training, just like any other athlete, even though the intensity ebbs and flows. Your training may be more intense at times, such as when you prepare for the upcoming tournament that pits you against your arch-rival: the pencil pusher whose office sits right next to the water fountain. And at other times, your training is less intense, such as during that three-week, around-the-world cruise. But you'll make better health choices if you keep the mindset that you're always in training.

Training consistently

Only by training hard and often can you achieve the greatest benefits from martial arts. This means working out at least three times a week. If you practice your techniques only once or twice a week, you won't gain any ground. You'll be lucky simply to remember the techniques, let alone get better at them.

If you haven't been physically active in the past, start slowly and build up. Don't start working out suddenly for three hours a day, six days a week unless you're hoping for a hospital stay. Start with a reasonable workout for your physical condition and do the workout three days a week. Never add more than a 10 percent increase to your physical activity in any one week until you're completely up to speed.

Attend training sessions faithfully and consistently. Mark upcoming classes or at-home sessions on your calendar and attend those classes and workout sessions as if they were any other appointment. Don't attend class five days a week one week and one day the next week. This is a great way to abuse your body. Instead, look at your schedule and determine the best time and days for your training and commit to training at that time and on those days. The key to success is planning for it.

Research shows that it takes about six weeks for any new program to become a habit. So if you can stick with your training program for just six weeks, you'll make it a habit — hopefully, one that's lifelong.

Developing the right attitude

Succeeding in martial arts is more a matter of attitude than aptitude. I should know. My instructor used to say that he wanted to make a video of martial arts bloopers with me as the star.

Nonetheless, I succeeded where many others with greater physical ability dropped out. Partly, this is because I had no life and preferred to hit the training hall rather than watch another rerun of *Friends*. But mostly, I succeeded because I found martial arts so exciting that I didn't want to stop.

Open mind, shut mouth

The right attitude is a combination of an open mind and a passion for martial arts, what might be known as having "heart." An open mind is drained of all preconceived notions, allowing you to accept new ideas. If you decide that you'll never be able to do that jump-spinning-wheel kick, then voilà! You'll never be able to do that jump-spinning-wheel kick. But if you keep an open mind about it, then someday you *will* do that kick.

When an instructor is demonstrating a technique or a partner is explaining why your fighting strategy stinks, keep your mouth closed. Listen to what the person is saying. You may learn something. Even if you don't agree, simply say, "Yes, sir," or "Thank you, ma'am." You don't have to argue about every point, at least not until you've let the other party have their say.

Martial artists love to argue about everything from whose street-fighting style is most effective to who is the better martial artist, Jean Claude van Damme or Steven Seagal. You, too, can enjoy these arguments but save them for *after* your training session ends.

Pass the humility, please

Keeping an open mind requires a little humility. It means accepting that you *don't* know it all and maybe never will. The best martial artists don't spend much time bragging about how they can whup up on muggers. Instead, they seem calm, tranquil, and willing to learn from whomever can teach them.

Heart trumps all

Along with keeping your mind open and your mouth shut, you have to have heart. You must love what you're doing, be committed to it, and feel passionate about it. This is what makes you get up off the floor after you've fallen down for the fourth time trying to perform a hip throw. Long after the 20-year-old hardbody has abandoned the attempt in favor of skiing, you'll be mastering the techniques that'll knock him off his skis.

Showing your excitement about martial arts is okay. You don't need to act like an untrained puppy, but you can share your excitement without looking like an idiot. Fellow students appreciate it, and it gives an added intensity to your training.

Persistence pays off

To master the techniques of martial arts, you have to be persistent. No one ever got the front kick right on the first try. No one even gets it right on the tenth try. In fact, it takes thousands of repetitions to develop the muscle memory that you need to fire off each technique without thinking about it.

Thinking about each technique as you do it interferes with your ability to perform the technique quickly and accurately. Timing is everything in martial arts. Learn to rely on your body instincts, which are developed through repetitive practice.

Because truly learning a technique takes thousands of repetitions, practicing a kick or throw only a few times each day means it will literally be years before you master it. Commit to performing your techniques repeatedly every day, so that you achieve mastery sooner.

Having the heart to keep going even when you fail requires courage. And that's something that you can learn in your martial arts training. Your instructor and fellow martial artists can encourage you to keep trying even if you don't think that you'll ever succeed.

It took me ten years to master the jump-spinning-wheel kick. Surely, you'll figure it out much sooner than that.

Perfect practice makes perfect

Okay, so you probably heard this more times than you can count. But I'll say it anyway: It isn't practice that makes perfect; it's *perfect* practice that makes perfect.

Think about it this way: If it takes 2,000 repetitions for your body to "remember" how to do the front kick, and 1,500 of those repetitions are sloppy, what's your body going to remember? Your body will remember how to do sloppy front kicks. This is *not* the result you want to achieve.

So part of having the right attitude toward training is making a perpetual commitment to practicing as perfectly as possible. You can actually do more harm by practicing sloppy techniques than if you had simply skipped practice for the day. Your intention during each training session should be to perform each technique as perfectly as possible.

Sloppy practice can also be hard on your body. For example, for certain kicks, you're supposed to pivot on the ball of your foot. If you don't bother to do this, you can strain your knees and hips, causing overuse injuries, sprains, and strains. Always perform the techniques correctly and to the best of your abilities.

Treating yourself right

Too often, martial art students push themselves in training without giving adequate attention to fueling their bodies right. Without good nutrition, you won't achieve the optimum benefit from martial arts practice. And trust me, French fries aren't optimum fuel for your body.

You are what you eat

In the distant past, humans were hunter-gatherers, hunting large animals for their meat, and gathering fruits and grains. But because of our busy modern schedules, people have become grabber-stuffers — grabbing whatever's available and stuffing it in their mouths. This isn't an adequate diet, especially for an athlete. But choosing, preparing, and eating a healthy diet doesn't have to be hard, and you don't have to eat tofu or sprouts. That is, unless you want to.

Your mama was right when she told you to eat your vegetables. If you emphasize carbohydrates and protein and de-emphasize fats and sweets, you're on the right track. (Consult mama for further details.)

If you're single-handedly keeping the neighborhood burger franchise in business, there's still hope for you. Changing your eating habits doesn't mean boring yourself to death with salads and raw fruit. Changing your habits simply means making better choices: Skip the fries and order a diet drink or iced tea instead of a sugary beverage. Plan so that you don't have to stop at the burger joint for lunch every day. Bring your lunch to work or visit the sub shop next door instead.

You'll find, after you start eating better, that you have more energy throughout the day, and you won't tire so quickly during your workout. You won't feel sluggish and slow. The better that you perform, the more that you'll want to keep eating right. After the first few weeks, you may be surprised at how easy it is to stay on track with your new eating plan. Instead of craving sugary snacks and high-calorie colas, you'll *want* to eat fruit and sip water. Even mama would be proud.

Eating a big meal before you work out can slow you down because your energy is directed toward digesting the food rather than fending off front kicks. Eat a small, sensible snack (say, an apple or a bagel) about an hour before class. If you're rushed, a few ounces of juice just before class fuels your workout and won't slow you down.

Water: Not just for fish

Along with eating right, you'll want to stay hydrated, which means drinking water and plenty of it. You can drink other beverages if you want, but they don't count toward your water total. Bring water with you everywhere — keep a glass on your desk at all times, bring a water bottle in the car with you, and fill up the 32-ounce Big Gulp with water instead of pop when you stop to gas up the car. Try to down at least eight 8-ounce glasses of water a day. More if you can.

You may drink other beverages as long as you don't use them as substitutes. Don't forget that other beverages may quench your thirst, thus making it more difficult for you to drink as much water as you need to. Always think of drinking water first and use other beverages as "treats."

Your body can thank you for keeping it hydrated, but if you're not used to drinking this much water everyday, your body can take a few days to adapt. In the meantime, be sure to know where the bathroom is located in each building that you enter. I promise that you *will* stop needing to visit the urinal every 30 minutes eventually.

Consult your local RD

If you're having trouble sticking to a good diet, or if you're a hardcore martial artist intent on getting the most from your body, a consultation with a registered dietician may be in order. The RD can help you understand how to plan nutritious meals and can offer tips on how to avoid common pitfalls, such as fending off the temptation to eat every chocolate pie between here and Pittsburgh when you're traveling.

Be suspicious of supplements

Most martial artists don't need to take supplements, such as protein compounds, vitamins, and related items as long as they eat right. And eating right is better for your body (not to mention less expensive) than indulging in supplements. Although some promise to make you stronger, firmer, and fitter with just a pill a day, be wary of such claims. In reality, the only way to get stronger, firmer, and fitter is to work your body harder than you have in the past.

Steer clear of supplements until and unless you know that one is right for you based on solid evidence (rather than the claims of the personal trainer who's trying to sell the supplement to you). Check with your doctor or a registered dietician if you feel frustrated with your physical progress and are considering how supplements may work for you. Chances are that the doctor or RD could help you structure a meal plan that can do all the work that a supplement would, without any of the drawbacks. And supplements do have drawbacks: They can be expensive, difficult to use, and hard to find. Some supplements are also dangerous under certain conditions.

Consulting with your doctor before taking supplements can help you rule out physical problems that should be treated. For example, being tired all the time could be a sign of anemia, a fairly common medical problem that can be treated with diet and medication.

Some supplements are actually dangerous for you to take, especially if you have a pre-existing medical condition. Proceed with all possible caution before deciding that supplements are right for you and be sure to consult with your doctor first.

Good night, sleep tight

In addition to eating right and drinking enough water, you need to give your body enough rest so that it can heal from the stresses of the day. Your body gets stressed when your boss yells at you, when you work out hard, and when you sit at a computer screen for eight hours running without moving. It deserves a break. Make sure it gets that break. Give it a good rest on a comfortable mattress in a well-ventilated area. If the dogs insist on sleeping with you, make them sleep at the foot of the bed. (Don't, however, require this of your spouse.)

Everyone needs a minimum of eight hours of sleep daily. Captains of industry often comment on how they sleep only four or five hours each night, as if only sloths need more. Captains of industry also suffer heart attacks, ulcers, and mental disorders that may have been prevented if they'd had eight hours of shut-eye.

Supplemental Training

"What's that?" you say. Supplemental training? In addition to the five times a week that I work out at the Karate studio? Don't you know that I have a job to go to and a family that likes to see me now and then?

Of course, I know all this. I have a job and a family, too, and sometimes, they wish they'd never heard of martial arts. (Well, my job *is* martial arts, so really, just my family and friends get a little bored with it.)

But supplemental training *can* jump-start your martial arts training. Here's how: Martial arts training emphasizes learning and applying the techniques of martial arts. You may do certain body-conditioning exercises as part of your workout session, but the main focus is on skill building. This means that working on bodybuilding is up to you.

Doing additional workouts of different kinds can enhance your martial arts performance in such a way that simply going to a martial arts class may not be able to.

Cardiovascular training

In order to build your endurance and improve your level of health and fitness, you need to do some form of *cardiovascular* (also known as *aerobic*) training at least three hours per week. Cardiovascular refers to your heart and blood vessels. (Thus, a cardiovascular workout strengthens your heart.) *Aerobic* (in this case) refers to strenuous physical exercises that temporarily increases your heart rate and respiration. Aerobic workouts (also called cardiovascular training) improve your overall fitness and burn fat. Cardiovascular training should be spread out over the week instead of all in one three-hour lump on Saturday morning. (Doing all your training once a week can turn you into a lump if you're not careful.)

Almost any type of aerobic training works well with martial arts. You can bike, run, or swim. You can take an aerobics class or hit the stair climber at the gym. Any of these approaches improves your fitness and helps you lose weight. Most people find that combining more than one fitness activity makes the process of getting and staying fit more enjoyable. So one day, they take a brisk walk with the dogs, and the next day they go biking with the kids.

You should shoot for a minimum of 30 minutes of aerobic exercise three times a week. That's 30 minutes of elevated heart and respiration rate — *not* ten minutes of stretching, a walk around the block, and a lengthy chat with your next-door neighbor — although you should always stretch before any workout.

Keeping that old ticker ticking

Aerobic training consists of doing an activity that keeps your heart rate *(pulse)* at its *target rate* for at least 30 minutes at a time. To determine your target rate, subtract your age from 220 (your maximum heart rate). Multiply that number by .70, which is 70 percent of your maximum heart rate. This is the low end of your target heart rate, and should be what you aim for when you begin cardiovascular training. As your stamina improves, increase your target rate slowly to 90 percent of your maximum heart rate. Just subtract your age from 220 and multiply the result by .90, but you knew that. You don't ever want to work so hard that you meet or exceed your maximum heart rate. Dire results follow.

You can purchase a heart-rate monitor to help you keep tabs on how your heart is doing while you're working out. Some can be worn like watches; others you slip over your finger during training. Some cardiovascular workout machines have heart-rate monitors built in. A less effective method (but still reasonably reliable if you don't have a heart rate monitor readily available) is simply to press your fingers against your wrist and count the number of heartbeats in 10 seconds and then multiply by six. Or count the number of heartbeats in six seconds and multiply by 10. This will give you a rough idea of your heart rate. *Never* take your pulse by pressing your fingers against the blood vessels in your neck. Although the pulse is strong there, pressing on the blood vessel can restrict blood flow to your brain, causing you to faint. Bad idea.

Work up to an hour a session four or more times per week. Listen to your body, and don't overdo it. Give yourself at least one day off per week to allow your body time to rest.

Cardiovascular training can get you through tough martial arts training sessions and help you to reach a greater level of achievement in your martial arts training by developing your energy and stamina.

In training, you'll often be asked to "dig deep," which means to keep going even if you think you're too tired to manage it. By going beyond what's easy, you build strength and endurance, and dig your well (of energy and strength) deeper. So what seemed hard today won't seem hard the next time that you do it if you keep digging deep.

You can make cardiovascular training an easy part of your martial arts workout by doing it just before class, then going to class warmed up and ready. The first few sessions are more difficult than usual because you already used up some of your energy, but you'll be surprised at how quickly your body adapts.

Conditioning for flexibility

In all martial arts, flexibility is at least as important as strength. Maybe you're doing Tae Kwon Do (Chapter 16) and want to kick head high. (Hey, that's a noble goal.) Without adequate flexibility, that can only remain a dream. Or maybe you practice Aikido (Chapter 18) and know that your arm locks and hip throws would be easier and more effective if you had more mobility in your joints.

You need to train your body to be flexible just as you train it to be strong. Fortunately, flexibility exercises can be done anywhere. Almost any stretching exercise can improve your flexibility. See the "Simple stretches" section, later in this chapter, for a description of some stretching exercises.

You can also use martial arts techniques to improve your flexibility. For example, you can do a kick stretch, which is described in the section "Kick stretches" that follows. It helps to have a partner with these.

Whenever you do stretching exercises, remember to move smoothly into the stretch position and hold the stretch for at least ten seconds. Don't bounce. Bouncing can cause damage to your muscles and ligaments by over-stretching them. Besides, this isn't cheerleader tryouts. Stop if you feel pain. You should feel the stretch, however.

Kick stretches

1. **Position yourself near a wall for support.**

2. **Do a front kick using correct technique. Kick directly to the front, foot pointed, toes pulled back, striking with the ball of your foot.**

3. **Have your partner lift your leg as high as possible.**

4. **Tell your partner when to stop.**

   You should tell your partner to stop when you simply feel the stretch. Don't wait until it becomes painful because pain isn't good for stretching. If you feel any pain, stop stretching immediately. Pain is a signal that you could be pulling and damaging muscles, ligaments, and/or tendons.

5. **Have your partner hold the stretch for ten seconds. Then have your partner slowly release your leg.**

   As he does so, try to keep your leg in its stretched position. (Make certain your body is upright, and your leg is in a good front kick position with foot pointed and toes pulled back.) This builds muscle strength, which is necessary for strong kicks.

6. **Hold your leg without your partner's aid in its stretched position for ten seconds, then slowly lower it.**

7. **Relax and repeat on the other side.**

Any kick can be used to perform a kick stretch.

Simple stretches

- **Neck stretch:** When you're sitting at your computer all day, you can take a few minutes to stretch your neck muscles. First, try to touch your chin to your chest. Hold the position for 10 to 15 seconds. Then try to touch your left ear to your left shoulder. Hold the position for 10 or 15 seconds. Do the same for the right side. Then tilt your head back, so you're staring at the ceiling. Hold the stretch.

- **Shoulder stretch:** Holding your arm straight, horizontal to the floor, bring it across your chest until you feel the stretch in your shoulder. Use your opposite arm to push further. Hold the stretch. Relax, repeat, and then do the same for the opposite shoulder.

- **Back stretch:** While watching television or grading papers, sit on the floor with your legs spread apart in a V. Reach toward your left foot trying to get both hands around the sole of your foot. Don't bend your knee. Hold the stretch. Relax and repeat with the other side. Then stretch between your knees. Keeping your back straight, bend at the waist, trying to touch your chest to the floor. You can use your hands to help *pull* you forward. Hold the stretch and then relax.

  If this is stressful to your knees, bend one knee in while keeping the other leg straight, and then stretch toward the straight leg. For the stretch between your knees, simply bend both knees and try to touch your chest to your legs.

- **Hip stretch:** Standing, put your hand on a wall for support. Lift one knee up in front of you. Bring your knee up level with your hips, bent at a 90-degree angle, and your foot toward the floor. Make a half-circle around you, leading with your knee. The knee moves from the front, then out to the side, and toward the back. Repeat with the opposite leg.

  You can do countless stretches to increase your flexibility. Be on the lookout for them in magazine articles, books, and among your martial arts friends. Some stretches work better for you than others, and you'll want to vary your routine now and then to keep it from getting too monotonous.

You should do at least some stretching exercises for flexibility every day.

Speed training

No, speed training isn't finishing your workout as fast as you can. It's training designed to give your muscles explosive power and to narrow your reaction time.

In martial arts, timing is important. When you're sparring and you see an opening, you must strike immediately. If you intercept a punch, you have to time your interception to coincide with the strike. To improve your reaction time, you can do simple drills with partners.

The following sections, "Reaction drills" and "Explosive power drills," describe effective ways to improve your speed. Doing timing drills and explosive power drills every day is the best way to see the fastest improvement. If you can't do them each day, at least three times a week can help your speed. Making this a part of your martial arts workout — spending a few minutes after class to do it — is for the best. This lessens the burden of working it into your workout.

Reaction drills

In any martial art that includes mock combat, you can have your partner deliberately show an opening as you're sparring. You then try to take advantage of that opening by striking or throwing your partner. As your skill improves, the length of time that the opening stays open should decrease.

It should go without saying that if your partner wants to improve her reaction times, you will do the same for her.

Some martial artists show an "opening" when they're sparring with you as a way to set up a counterattack. If you take the bait, they immediately counter with the move they intended all along. As your skills improve, you'll be able to judge when an opening is a deliberate trap and when it's a mistake — an opportunity for you to take advantage of.

Another simple drill is to have a partner hold a target and call out, "Now!" as you wait in a fighting stance. Your goal is to strike as soon as you hear the command. Your partner can make things more difficult by calling out the type of strike, such as, "Side kick!"

A drill borrowed from boxing is to have your partner strike at you intermittently while you try to evade, block, or intercept the strike. Start in a relaxed, natural, and unguarded stance. As the strike comes, respond in the most appropriate way. For example, certain kicks can be intercepted with other kicks; certain punches can be avoided merely by moving your body. Some version of any of these drills can be used in any martial art.

Explosive power drills

Many martial arts techniques rely on speed for effectiveness. If you're too slow, the technique won't work. What's worse is you'll get hit. That'll motivate you to build speed.

More than simple speed, many techniques require explosive power — that is, the ability to go from standing to full speed as quickly as possible.

Speed is important, and a simple physics equation can demonstrate: Speed times mass equals momentum (or power). So if you're big but slow, and you're fighting against someone small but fast, your momentum or power may be equal.

This is one area where women and smaller people can compete equally with men and bigger people. The smaller your mass, the easier it is to get in motion. So smaller people can be quick, and this translates into power.

To acquire this skill, use *plyometric drills,* which are exercises designed to build explosive speed. Some of the games that you played as a kid, such as hopscotch, fall into this category. (See, training can be fun.) Think foot races: If you "explode" out of the blocks, you'll likely cross the finish line before your competitor does. A leapfrog race that requires springing up from a crouching position as quickly as possible also qualifies as a plyometric drill. Even jump rope can help you build explosive power. Just think of it: You can goof off with your kids and tell your martial arts buddies that you're in serious training.

Plyometric drills, such as hopscotch, foot races, leapfrog, and jump rope, are hard on your knees. You should be in pretty good shape before you attempt them. You may need to strengthen your quadriceps and hamstring muscles in order to protect your knees. If you have experienced knee trouble or find these drills leave your knees sore, avoid plyometric drills.

By combining reaction drills and explosive power drills, you can improve your speed considerably, and develop excellent timing and quick, agile techniques.

Strength-training techniques

Many martial artists know that building muscle mass increases the power of their techniques, but they often worry that building muscle means sacrificing flexibility — a reasonable worry. The more muscle mass that you build, the less flexibility that you have — unless you combine strength-training with flexibility-training.

You don't need to look like "Aaahnald" to be powerful. In fact, if you bulk up like the powerlifters on late night sports television, much of your flexibility will be lost. But you can have six-pack *abs* (abdominal muscles) and *biceps* (inner arm muscles) that can be found even without a flashlight and still maintain flexibility.

Shhh! Strength-training secrets

The secret to building strength without giving up flexibility is in how you work out. Essentially, the only way to build muscle mass is through resistance training. That is, you exert your muscle against something that resists it. To get the best effect, you work the muscle to failure — until it can't work anymore without a rest.

The more you pile on the resistance, the bigger your muscles get. To build huge muscles, you exert against plenty of resistance a few times. To define your muscles and build strength, you exert against a moderate amount of resistance more times.

Most martial artists choose to exert against a moderate amount of resistance. They won't bulk up so much and can still kick high while also kicking hard.

To build massive muscles, lift enough weight so that your muscle *fails* after three or four repetitions. Rest for a minute after one set of repetitions, and then do another set. To build strength and lean, defined muscles, lift enough weight so that your muscle *fails* after seven to ten reps. Do two or three sets of repetitions for each muscle group. If you lift more than ten reps, you're probably not lifting enough weight to do much good.

Don't forget to work into weight training just the way you work into aerobic training or Karate training — slow and easy at first, until you find out what your body can do. Consult with a personal trainer at a gym for a session or two to learn to lift weights correctly and to develop a good weight-lifting routine.

Hit the deck, soldier: Isometric training

Weight lifting is commonly thought of as the only way to build muscle, but it's not. Isometric training — that is, using your body weight as resistance, as in pushups — also builds muscle. Isometric training has some advantages: It's cheap, easy, and the muscle bulk that you can add doing it is limited.

Before you invest in a gym membership or lug home a pile of free weights so you can stub your toes on them in the basement, spend some time building strength through isometrics. When this is no longer challenging, go ahead and a spring for an in-home four-station weight machine.

Pushups

Pushups are the old isometric standby. You can do them anywhere. I know a former marine who used to do them next to her desk at work a couple of times a day. If anyone asks, just say that you're in training.

Basic pushups are straightforward. Stretch out on the floor with your palms flat on the floor, directly under your shoulders, and your toes supporting your legs. Push directly up, and then lower yourself to the ground without touching (see Figure 8-1). Repeat.

If even one pushup is too difficult to do, go ahead and rest on your knees instead of your toes. Gradually, you can build enough upper body strength, so you won't have to use this method. Don't be embarrassed if you have to resort to this — never trying to build your upper body strength is more embarrassing.

You can do variations on the basic pushup for laughs and to build different muscles:

- ✔ Place your hands close together under your sternum to work your *triceps* (the muscles on the back of your upper arm) a little more.

- ✔ Place your hands far apart to work your *deltoids* (shoulder muscles) more.

- ✔ And don't forget the old martial arts standby, *the knuckle pushup:* Instead of placing your palms on the floor, make your hands into fists and place your knuckles on the floor. Use only your hand's first two knuckles, unless you practice a style that permits you to punch with the last three knuckles of your hand. If you punch with the last three knuckles, do the exercise resting on the last three knuckles so as not to confuse yourself.

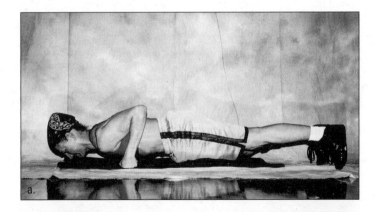

Figure 8-1:
A variation of the basic pushup: Placing your knuckles on the floor.

Crunches

Crunches work your abs in a way that no other exercise even comes close. Your abdominal area is your "base" and the spot where much of your power comes from, so it pays to have strong abs. Also, if someone hits you really hard in the abs and you don't flinch, they're suitably impressed.

As shown in Figure 8-2, the basic crunch requires you to do the following:

1. **Sit on the floor with your knees bent and your hands near your ears.**

   Don't lace your hands behind your neck as this can cause strain on your neck.

2. **Slowly bend forward, using your abdominal muscles.**

3. **Equally slowly, return to the starting position, keeping your shoulders off the floor.**

By moving slowly, you isolate the abdominal muscles, and you use your muscles, rather than momentum, to do the work.

The basic crunch has variations:

- ✔ Touching your left elbow to your right knee (and vice versa) can work your *obliques* (the muscles that run laterally on either side of your stomach).

- ✔ Lift your legs straight up in the air to form a 90-degree angle with the floor while doing a basic crunch to work your lower abs.

- ✔ Putting a free weight on your chest increases the amount of resistance. Cross your arms over your chest to hold onto the weight.

Rope up

Some people call this a pelvic-tilt crunch, but that's a mouthful. "Rope up" is easier to say. These exercises also work your abs, especially your upper abs, and to a smaller degree, your lower back (see Figure 8-3).

1. **Begin by stretching out on your back.**

2. **Lift your legs to a 90-degree angle to the floor.**

   Although Figure 8-3 depicts hands and arms flat on the floor, if you find that keeping your arms on the floor at your sides tempts you to use your arms to "help" you do the exercise, then cross your arms over your chest. That kind of help defeats the point of the exercise.

3. **Visualize a rope dangling from the ceiling to your ankles.**

4. **Lift your pelvis and legs straight up the rope.**

Figure 8-2:
To strength-
en your
abs, do
crunches.

Figure 8-3:
Rope ups:
Imagine
working
your legs
and feet up
a dangling
rope.

Move slowly in order to work your muscles and to prevent momentum from doing the work for you. (Momentum is a helpful guy, always willing to lend you a hand, but letting him do the job for you won't improve your strength.)

Wouldn't you know; this technique also has a variation. To work your upper abs more, tilt your legs toward your chest, keeping your knees straight. Then, instead of lifting directly up, lift your legs as if you were pushing at something behind your head. Avoid this technique if you have back trouble.

Boxer sit-ups

These exercises, shown in Figure 8-4, work your abs and, to a lesser degree, your leg muscles. You need a partner to do them correctly. If you can't find a partner, use a wooden chair . . . no, wait, wrong exercise.

1. **Have your partner stand with his feet spread about a foot apart.**

2. **Stretch out on the floor with your head between your partner's ankles.**

   If you find the exercise too difficult, grasp your partner's ankles for stability. This will make the exercise easier.

3. **Lift your legs up toward your partner.**

   He grasps your ankles and then throws them down toward the floor. Your job is to keep your legs from touching the floor, returning them to the starting position slowly and smoothly.

The variation to this exercise (you knew it was coming) is to have your partner throw your legs to one side and then to the other side rather than directly down. This works your oblique abs.

Stance training

One of the traditional strength-training methods deserving of mention is stance training, which is one of the best ways to build leg strength, at least as long as you don't blow out your knees doing it.

If you have knee trouble, this may not be the exercise for you. Use caution or skip it entirely.

1. **Select any stance that you've been taught.**

2. **Exaggerate the stance by bending your knees, lengthening your stride, or a similar method.**

3. **When you feel the stretch, hold your position for as long as you can.**

   Try to do it for 20 seconds at first, building gradually to a minute or more at a time.

When you're done, your muscles should be burning a bit, and you should feel like you worked your legs pretty good.

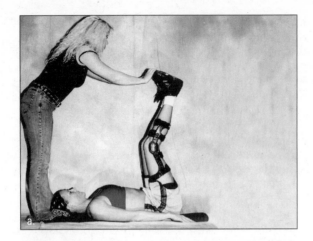

Figure 8-4:
Boxer sit-
ups work
the abs and
leg muscles.

Weight training

When you can do the isometric exercises easily and you still feel the need to increase your strength, move on to weight training. This requires a gym membership or an inexpensive set of free weights. Remember, you don't want to add too much bulk, or you'll reduce your flexibility. If you start weight training, increase the number of stretching and flexibility exercises that you do to counteract the effects of weight lifting.

Weight training can seem a bit complicated at first. Keep in mind that you tear down the muscles each time that you work them to failure, and they need time to heal. Therefore, never lift with the same set of muscles two days in a row. Weight training schedules can get pretty complicated, but if you do a simple workout twice a week — one day focusing on the upper body and one day focusing on the lower body — you'll do fine. It doesn't need to take more than 30 minutes or so after you get the hang of it.

The other consideration is whether to use free weights or machine weights. Each has its pros and cons. Free weights make you work both sides equally; on a weight machine, one side may be stronger than the other, and the machine would never know. Free weights work the smaller stabilizer muscles that may be missed if you do only weight machine workouts. But you're not likely to drop a weight machine on your foot. Weight machines are easy to use, and lifting incorrectly is harder on a weight machine.

Most martial artists find that a quick muscle-defining workout is best accomplished using a combination of free weights and machine weights. Biceps curls are most effective using free weights; leg curls can't be done without a machine.

To get started lifting weights, consult a couple of good weight-lifting books, such as *Weight Training For Dummies,* 2nd Edition, by Liz Neporent and Suzanne Schlosberg (Wiley Publishing, Inc.), and talk to a personal trainer at a nearby gym. You'll want to have expert instruction when you first begin so that you don't lift incorrectly and hurt yourself.

What's a weekend warrior to do?

So you want to be the best martial artist you can be, but with your schedule, you're lucky to get to class once or twice a week. What to do?

Easy. (You knew I'd say that.) Martial arts and supplemental training can be worked into even the busiest schedule. It just takes creativity. Stretch for flexibility during the workday while seated at your desk. Do leg stretches on the kitchen counter while talking on the phone, and lift weights for 15 minutes while you're waiting for the weather report during the evening newscast.

One martial artist does a mental walkthrough of all his techniques after he's in bed at night. This rehearsal keeps his techniques sharp even when he's busiest.

Many martial artists alternate cardiovascular exercises with weight training before their martial arts workout. They take a half-hour before class to lift or walk on the treadmill, then do class, hit the showers, and head home. You have no reason to spend more than a half-hour three or four days a week on supplemental training.

Consider any kind of sport or play "supplemental." For example, playing Horse with your teenage daughter counts. Depending on how you explode toward the basket, it may even be called a plyometric drill. (For more on plyometric drilling, see the "Explosive power drills" section, earlier in this chapter.) Work the drilling, stretching, and practicing technique into your everyday life, and you'll be rewarded with improved performance and lower stress levels.

Chapter 9

Protecting Yourself: Self-Defense Details

In This Chapter

▶ Defending yourself only when you have to

▶ Shouting to thwart an attacker

▶ Preparing for the worst-case scenario

▶ Discovering the three levels of self-defense

▶ Defending yourself from the most common attacks

*O*kay, so you signed up for lessons at the nearby Shotokan Karate school with visions of tying an attacker into knots without breaking a sweat. It can happen, right?

Simple self-defense is a primary reason for why people train in martial arts. A person can learn self-defense without training in the martial arts, and to some extent, a person can train in martial arts without *learning* self-defense (sad to say). Martial arts taught as sports generally lack a critical foundation in what works on the street; instead, they concentrate on what works in the ring, with its strict rules and time limits.

If learning self-defense skills is crucial to you, then make certain your instructor is qualified and is willing to teach these skills to you.

While each martial art (and each instructor) emphasizes different techniques and drills, almost all martial artists share a basic self-defense philosophy. This chapter describes that philosophy and offers some basic self-defense moves that almost anyone can use to fight off some common attacks.

The Philosophy of Self-Defense

The most important concept in self-defense is *defense*. All reputable martial arts instructors agree that what they teach should be used only to defend, never to attack. Someone else must make the first move. The first move doesn't have to be hitting you between the eyes with a beer bottle, but the attack must be something that justifiably threatens you or someone under your protection. It can be a statement: "I'm a-gonna shoot you with this here gun." Or it can be the windup to a punch.

Just walking away

When you feel threatened, the best response is simply to walk away. This prevents broken bones and nasty legal problems later. Many, many headaches could be prevented if people just walked away when they had the chance.

Using only the necessary amount of force

If someone shoves you in a crowded bar, you unload your fists of fury, and the poor slob winds up in the hospital, then you haven't done yourself any favors. You'll probably wind up in front of a judge explaining why what you did really isn't assault and battery.

The law — and common sense — says that you may meet a perceived threat with sufficient force to stop the threat, but that you can't use excessive or lethal force unless you have reason to believe your life (or the life of the person you're protecting) is at risk.

Disparity of power

Disparity of power is one handy legal guideline for determining how much force you can and should reasonably use against an attacker. Essentially, this means that if you're evenly matched with your attacker, you may not use excessive force to stop the attack. (That is, shooting someone who punches you in the nose is probably excessive force.)

If you and someone your size get into a shoving match outside the movie theater, the amount of force that you would be allowed to use to stop the fight is much less than if you faced multiple attackers or if one attacker were armed with any type of weapon. A woman attacked by a man is generally considered to have a power disparity and may use greater force to stop the attack.

The law varies from place to place. In some locales, using deadly force against someone who enters your home uninvited is permissible, regardless of that person's intentions and whether he is armed. However, not all municipalities agree. So be sure you understand what constitutes acceptable force in your area before you have to find out the hard way.

See, isn't it just easier to walk away if you can?

Fighting only for what's worth fighting for

One definition of obsessive-compulsive behavior is treating all things equally and giving the same emotional weight to everything that happens. Thus, losing a dime and losing your girlfriend both make you equally angry. This, of course, is ridiculous, as most people can plainly see, but you'd be surprised at how often otherwise intelligent individuals fail to distinguish between what's worth fighting over and what's not worth a whistle. Like an obsessive-compulsive, they weigh all things equally: a panhandler demanding ten bucks, a purse-snatcher grabbing a pocketbook, and a serial murderer wielding a knife.

Remember, only certain things are worth fighting for. You are worth fighting for. Your kids are worth fighting for. Maybe your dog. But not the ten bucks in your wallet or even your car. Get your priorities straight and commit to physical self-defense only when you must.

Keep in mind that anytime physical violence erupts, someone can wind up seriously injured or dead. Knowing what the future holds is impossible. That's why never resorting to physical violence except as a last resort is so important. If you must use physical violence, then use only the amount needed to end the threat.

De-escalating a potential conflict

Anytime two or more people start pawing the ground around each other, knowing what can happen next isn't possible. Often, what happens is that a fight escalates from words to deeds until someone draws blood and/or the police arrive.

Your goal should always be to de-escalate tension. Instead of responding to an insult with an insult, just keep your mouth shut. Walk away. Let someone else set the heckler straight and get a busted nose for his efforts.

In some schools, students are trained to block punches while saying, "I don't want to fight." This is intended to defuse tension in a fight or potential fight. It helps remind you that even if your adrenaline is pumping, you don't *have* to hit anyone.

Kiai!

One of the most powerful tools a martial artist has is her *kiai* (*kihop,* shout). In fact, the Department of Justice crime statistics show that frequently an attack can be stopped if the intended victims screams or shouts. Not only can this alert others that a crime is taking place, but it can surprise the attacker, allowing a few precious moments for you to escape.

Knowing your attacker

A common failing in many self-defense programs is that they assume your attacker is going to be some strange psychotic mugger who jumps out at you from behind the bushes. In that case, you may feel free to jab him in the eyes with your house key. Unfortunately, however, the victim of an attack usually knows the attacker. (This is especially true when the victim is a woman.) Therefore, learning self-defense techniques that you can use on people you know and maybe love is important because you can stop an attack without maiming the attacker for life. (More on that later.)

First, stop the attack. Then decide what you're going to do about the attacker and his place in your life. You may need legal, psychological, or spiritual counseling to do this. But remember, you're worth defending, so stop the attack before you worry about what's going to happen next.

If you've been the victim of domestic violence, acquaintance violence, or fear that you may be in the future, think through a plan for how to handle the situation should it arise. Where would you go for help, who can you call on, and how can you get there? You don't have to be helpless. Domestic violence is a more complicated issue than can be dealt with here. But martial arts training can often empower women enough to get out of an abusive relationship.

If your son's football coach grabs you with evil intent in mind, your first reaction isn't necessarily to knee the idiot in the groin. Your first reaction may be, "I can't believe this is happening to me!" During that moment of disorientation and disbelief, the attacker can take advantage, and you can find yourself unable to defend yourself adequately.

For this reason, you must practice self-defense techniques with people you know, you must role-play possible self-defense scenarios, and you must always remember that when you see a punch coming, it doesn't matter who's throwing it. Your reaction should be the same: Block the punch and counter if necessary.

The kiai also helps you focus your energy and concentrate on the task at hand. This is why you see martial artists using the kiai just as they break a board with their foot, and why they use the kiai in sparring when they're committing to a strike that they expect to score a point with. So if you use the shout when someone threatens you, it focuses your adrenaline and energy on the task at hand, which is to get away from the attacker.

Practice a good strong kiai that comes from your abdomen, where your *chi* is located. For self-defense purposes, turn the kiai into a strong, "No!" Most self-defense experts advise yelling, "No!" if you're under attack, because people are more likely to respond to that cry than to a person yelling "Help!" or "Rape!"

A good strong "No!" can surprise an attacker. It can also stop an acquaintance or friend from hurting you. Sadly, many times a victim knows his attacker. Make your feelings clear about any unwanted physical contact, and you may prevent it. If the "No!" isn't enough, then have a good knee strike to the groin in reserve.

Stand and deliver

The most important aspect of self-defense is to act confidently. This means different things at different stages of the self-defense process. When you're simply walking downtown to get to your office, if you move confidently, without hesitation, as if you know what you're doing and where you're going (even if you don't), you make an unattractive target for an attacker. Instead, she's going to look for the person who doesn't seem to know what he's doing, and who would therefore be easier to victimize.

One of the benefits of training in the martial arts is that it often gives you a feeling of confidence even in unfamiliar surroundings. People can sense your confidence and are more likely to leave you alone. Confidence also means having belief in your ability to defend yourself and those under your protection. This confidence comes through practice over a long period of time.

Even the best, most confident martial artists know that they can't defeat every possible attacker. But they're confident that they can handle most situations. They also know that they'll leave bruises even if they aren't ultimately successful in fending off an attack.

Finally, confidence is essential when you choose to respond to a threat physically. If you decide to punch, kick, or throw the attacker, then you must be committed to the punch, kick, or throw. If you decide to stop an attack, then you must stop the attack. You must finish the fight even if it takes longer than you expected and even if your hand hurts because you just broke your knuckle. If you're not willing to commit to finishing the fight, then you should *never* respond physically to a threat.

Over the years, I've read many self-defense books and talked to many self-defense instructors who say something like, "In the case of rape, women who fight back get hurt more than women who don't fight back." Of course, no statistical evidence is available to back this claim up. But the fact that people said it and believed it always struck me as odd, because it assumed that getting raped wasn't getting hurt, and it assumed that women who fight back never win. Nothing could be further from the truth. In fact, women who fight back are able to fend off an attack the *majority* of the time. So even if they have some bruises to show for it, they know they have prevented a far worse injury physically, mentally, and emotionally, and they have the satisfaction of knowing that they won the war.

Preparation and Planning

Thinking about self-defense shouldn't be something that you do once a week during self-defense training at the *dojo* (martial arts training space). It shouldn't be something that you do while taking a two-week, self-defense course, and then never think of again. Self-defense is an ongoing process.

The key to successful self-defense is preparation and planning. If you practice self-defense techniques, for example, you'll have much better luck using them than if you don't practice.

When you practice self-defense techniques, tweak them to fit your own circumstances. Some techniques don't work well when a short person tries to use them against a tall person. An older person with less agility may need to modify techniques that were originally intended for a teeny-bopper.

Consider places where you can be attacked. What would you do if you were attacked in the parking lot at work? Where is the nearest phone or source of help? Where should you run? This doesn't have to be a scary or boring exercise. Think of yourself as a spy scoping out the possibilities. Practice your techniques in the type of clothing that you wear frequently. Can you perform kicks in high heels and a suit? Can you perform throws in your skin-tight blue jeans? I don't advocate changing your wardrobe for the sake of self-defense, but I do suggest finding techniques that work if you attempt them in your everyday clothes.

Practice training outside on hard surfaces with your shoes and street clothes on. You may be surprised at how difficult some techniques are to do. Better to know this ahead of time.

Be aware of implements that can be used as weapons. For example, you can use the letter opener as a knife if you must. You can throw your coffee mug at someone. (This is most effective if it has hot coffee in it.) Your awareness not only increases your options, but it also helps you see what in the environment can be used against *you*. Then you can think of ways to defend against it.

Simple Precautions

When I was young and single, I lived by a list of rules that were meant to keep me safe: no going out after dark; no answering the phone after 10 p.m.; and no letting on that I lived alone. One day, I realized the muggers were having all the fun.

Shortly after that, I realized that I was in more danger from people who knew me than from strangers on the street. And the people who knew me knew that I lived alone, and staying off the streets after dark wouldn't help much if one of them had malignant designs on me. All they had to do was come to my front door, and I'd let them in.

Although I refuse to live by all the restrictions that supposedly make people safe, some people feel more comfortable doing so. No one has the right to tell you how to live, so you choose what to incorporate into your life in order to feel safe.

Instead of restricting my movements and living in fear all the time, I learned how to use general martial arts concepts to stay safer.

Choosing your friends wisely

Most victims know their attackers. Therefore, it makes sense to choose your friends wisely. Many people defeat the purpose of expensive burglar alarm systems by befriending the wrong people. Obviously, you can't always know whom to trust, but victims often fail to heed the warning signs. People who are unkind to animals, who admit to being unable to control their violent tempers, who drink, or who take drugs should be handled with extreme caution.

Also be careful of friends or acquaintances you don't really know. Sometimes, people forget that they don't know a person very well. Get to know people better before allowing them access to your personal life. Just because you met someone at your sister's party doesn't mean anyone can vouch for him.

This is another good reason why you should know who your children's friends are. Not only do they influence the decisions that your children make, their friends can also be dangerous to them in other ways. Their friends can even be dangerous to you! If that doesn't scare you enough to start asking your Johnny where he's going and whom he's going to be with, nothing will.

Being aware

Awareness is key. If you know what's going on around you, you're less likely to be surprised by an attack. Pay attention to what you see and hear. Look around. Know what's happening behind you as well as what's happening in front of you.

You may not know what's happening around you because the situation is confusing. Stop and get your bearings before continuing into the confusion. The neck that you save may be your own.

Listening to intuition

Now and then, you may feel threatened without understanding exactly why you feel that way. It can be the way someone is looking at you, or maybe the horror movie music playing in the background is too eerie for your ears. Whatever it is, respect your feelings. This basic animal response to your surroundings is often called *intuition* and should be respected. Just as the herd of gazelles doesn't stand around arguing when one of them catches a whiff of the lion, you shouldn't stand around talking yourself out of it when *you* catch a whiff of the lion.

You can cultivate your intuition by practicing awareness. Pay careful attention to your surroundings, to the people near you, and the like. Make it a habit to notice everything. Quiz yourself: Take a glance at your surroundings, then ask yourself how many people are there, what are they doing, maybe even what are they wearing? Heightened awareness feeds directly into intuition.

Don't risk your safety because you're afraid of offending someone else. If you don't want to get on the elevator with what is apparently the local chapter of Hell's Angels, then don't. Take the stairs or wait for the next car.

Anticipating danger

Learn to think like a criminal. This is more fun than it sounds. Consider how you could attack a person if you were so inclined. Then use the information for your own safety.

For example, many people routinely look in the backseat of the car before they get in. This is a good precaution, it's easy to do, and it doesn't interfere with living your life. But how many people think about looking *under* the car? That's where I'd hide. (Okay, so maybe I'm weird.)

If I were a criminal looking out for a victim in the parking lot at the mall, I'd pick the man rummaging around in his coat looking for his car keys, while juggling three packages, and talking on his cellphone.

On a downtown sidewalk, if I wanted to mug someone, I'd casually stand in a doorway or an entrance to an alley as if I were waiting for a friend. Then I'd grab the person who walked nearest to me (unless it was a wino) by the elbow, pull him into the alley, steal his wallet, and walk briskly away.

This scenario setting can help you incorporate simple precautions into your life. For example, glance under the car or at least be aware that a criminal can hide there. Don't be distracted when you're going to and from places. If you need to talk on the phone, find a quiet bench in the food court and call. Get your keys out before you leave the front door. Walk in the center of the sidewalk so that you don't get pulled into an alley.

Responding quickly

If you sense a threat — or are confronted by a bat-wielding maniac — respond immediately. Leave the room, get off the road, walk into the nearest lighted shop, and do whatever is necessary to respond to the threat. If you feel uncertain, you act uncertain, and are more likely to become a victim. This doesn't mean that the first time that you don't like the way that the bartender looks at you, you should leap over the bar, and punch her in the nose. But it does mean that if you don't like the way the bartender looks at you, maybe you should find a new bar.

You may feel awkward about responding to a perceived threat. Unless you actually physically attack a person who means you no harm, you don't have a reason to feel awkward. Instead, feel good that you avoided a potentially dangerous situation and accept that you won't always know whether the threat was real.

Beginner paranoia occurs when a person begins training in the martial arts and with a sudden burst of confidence in his abilities starts looking for trouble or sees it everywhere. Paranoia is an ineffective form of self-defense, so remember to use reason and judgment as well as relying on emotional intuition.

While these simple changes can help keep you safe, they don't restrict your activities, change your life, or make you feel like the lunatics are running the asylum. They are ways that you can take control over your safety and live with less fear.

The Three Levels of Self-Defense

If a physical confrontation is so threatening that you can't walk away from it, then you have to respond. But someone grabbing your sleeve to set you straight about who's the best quarterback in NFL history requires different treatment from someone who drags you into a deserted alley when you're walking home from a friend's house late at night. The following list presents, in order of escalation, the three levels of self-defense:

- ✔ **Escape:** The person who disagrees with you about quarterback rankings grabs your sleeve; you pull your arm free and the threat is over. You can walk (or maybe run) away if needed.

- ✔ **Control:** You stop the attack and control the person through a joint lock or similar technique. This method is used for a more serious attack or when the escape technique isn't enough. The benefit to it is that you don't inflict permanent damage; any pain the attacker feels is only temporary. The first and second levels of self-defense are especially appropriate when you know the attacker and don't necessarily want to cripple him for life.

- ✔ **Counterattack:** You stop the attack and counterattack with a devastating series of techniques intended to immobilize the attacker. This level is used for the most serious physical threats or for when you tried another approach and the attacker continues the attack.

Of course, you don't have to go through each level to stop a single attack. You choose the method (escaping, controlling, or counterattacking) that seems most in line with the actual level of threat. At the same time, you must always understand that the stakes can get higher. You may think that all you have to do is pull your arm away from the sleeve-grabber, but you may have to counterattack. Always react to the situation; don't be taken by surprise or assume that you can end an encounter easily.

Basic Self-Defense Techniques

The following sections show basic self-defense techniques that you can easily learn to use against common attacks. Each defense has three variations: escape, control, or counterattack as described in the preceding section, "The Three Levels of Self-Defense," so you can use each defense appropriately, depending on the circumstances of the attack. For example, if you're attacked in a wide-open space with a police station only a half-block away, you may use the escape level of defending yourself from someone grabbing your wrist. However, if someone much larger and stronger than yourself grabs your wrist in a dark cul-de-sac with no visible escape route, then at least go for the control method if not the counterattack.

Whenever possible, walking away is the best defense. And don't forget to *kiai* or shout when you defend yourself. (See the "Kiai!" section, earlier in this chapter.) You may be able to scare off an attacker or at least summon help.

The basic techniques offered in this chapter have been effective against common attacks. They assume that your attacker is unarmed and that only one individual is attacking you. They don't require the use of any weapon, although they can be used in addition to a weapon.

Learning empty-handed self-defense against multiple attackers and against an attacker with a weapon is quite difficult and requires special training. Many self-defense instructors offer courses for advanced students who have already mastered basic self-defense techniques. It would be inappropriate to suggest that you can easily learn these techniques by reading a book.

The wrist-grab defense

Pretend that an attacker has grabbed your wrist, maybe getting ready to drag you off somewhere that you don't want to go. (See Figure 9-1.)

Figure 9-1:
Getting out of the wrist grab.

Escape

Make a fist and twist your wrist so that your wristbone is near the attacker's thumb and pinkie finger. This is the weakest point of the grab. Pull your hand free, making sure not to hit yourself with your own fist.

Control

With your free hand, grasp the attacker's hand in the fleshy spot between the thumb and index finger. Jam your thumb next to the attacker's thumb and peel his hand off of yours. Continue twisting your attacker's hand and wrist to control him. After your trapped hand is free, use it to assist with the wristlock or to block any attempted punch the attacker may make with his free hand.

Counterattack

Make a fist and twist your wrist so that your wristbone is near the attacker's thumb and pinkie finger. Pull your hand free (as in the previous "Escape" section, earlier in this chapter). Then, with the same hand, slam the back of your fist into the attacker's nose or throat. Follow up with additional techniques (kicks, punches, and throws) as necessary.

The double-wrist grab defense

Pretend that an attacker has grabbed both your wrists. (See Figure 9-2.)

Figure 9-2:
Breaking
free from
the double-
wrist grab.

Escape

Keeping your hand rigid and your fingers together, sharply strike the attacker's opposite arm near the wrist with the heel of your hand. This is known as a *palm strike*. With your now-freed hand, perform a palm strike on the attacker's other arm. Run away.

Control

Keeping your hand rigid and your fingers together, sharply strike the attacker's opposite arm near the wrist with the heel of your hand (known as a *palm strike*). With your now-free hand, grasp the attacker's other hand in the fleshy spot between the thumb and index finger. Jam your thumb next to the attacker's thumb and peel his hand off from around your wrist. Continue twisting your attacker's hand and wrist to control him. (This technique is similar to the control method in the "The wrist-grab defense" section, earlier in this chapter.)

Counterattack

Step back and deliver a kick to the attacker's groin or midsection with as much power as you can. The kick can be delivered after using the escape method or can be performed while the attacker holds your wrists. Be prepared to follow up with additional techniques.

The shoulder- or sleeve-grab defense

Imagine that an attacker has grabbed your shoulder, your upper arm, or your sleeve near your shoulder. Grabbing any lower on the arm should be treated the same as a wrist grab. (For more on the wrist grab, see "The wrist-grab defense" section, earlier in this chapter.)

Escape

Stepping toward the attacker, with your free hand, perform a palm strike on the attacker's arm near the wrist to free yourself. Pull away from the attacker with your trapped arm as you strike.

Control

Swing your trapped arm up, reach over your attacker's grabbing arm, and hold it tightly between your body and your upper arm. With your hand or forearm, push up on the attacker's elbow joint (or as near the joint as possible) to control him.

Counterattack

Swing your trapped arm up, reach over your attacker's grabbing arm, and hold it tightly between your body and your upper arm, as shown in Figure 9-3. With the attacker's arm trapped, kick to his now-exposed ribs. Be prepared to follow up with additional techniques as necessary.

Figure 9-3:
Self-
defense
from a grab
to the
shoulder.

The shirt- or lapel-grab defense

Imagine that an attacker has grabbed the front of your shirt.

Escape

With your opposite hand, grab the opponent's hand, placing your fingers under his hand near the pinkie finger, and placing your thumb on the fleshy part of the attacker's hand between his thumb and forefinger. Dig in with your fingernails. With a sharp twist, peel the attacker's hand from your shirt (see Figure 9-4).

Control

With your opposite hand, grab the opponent's hand, placing your fingers under his hand near the pinkie finger and your thumb on the fleshy part of the attacker's hand between his thumb and forefinger. Dig in with your fingernails. With a sharp twist, peel the attacker's hand from your shirt. Keep hold of the attacker's hand and continue to twist, using both hands if necessary or using one hand to twist and the other hand to block any potential attacks. Increase the twisting pressure to control the attacker.

Figure 9-4:
The shirt-grab defense: Dig in with your fingernails and twist the attacker's hand.

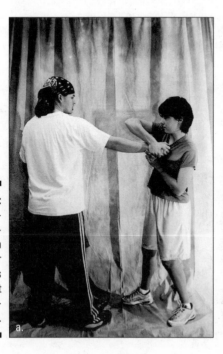
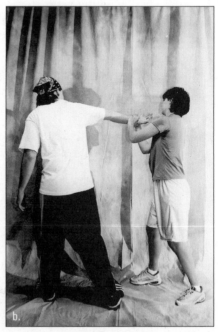

Counterattack

With your opposite hand, grab the opponent's hand, placing your fingers under his hand near the pinkie finger and your thumb on the fleshy part of the attacker's hand between his thumb and forefinger. Dig in with your fingernails. With a sharp twist, peel the attacker's hand from your shirt. Kick his groin or *solar plexus* (the torso just below the sternum), or punch his nose or solar plexus. Keep your guard up to defend against a potential attack from the attacker's free hand and prepare to deliver more kicks or punches as needed.

Defending yourself in a chokehold from the front

Pretend that an attacker has grabbed the front of your throat with both hands and is choking you (see Figures 9-5).

A chokehold is a serious threat. Do not hesitate to counterattack immediately, rather than attempting an escape or control technique.

Figure 9-5: Getting out of a front chokehold.

a.

b.

Escape

Raise one of your arms, bending your elbow so that your upper arm is perpendicular to the floor. Turning in the direction opposite the lifted arm, swing your arm against the attacker's arms, breaking his grip. Run away.

Control

Raise your left arm, bending your elbow so that your upper arm is perpendicular to the floor. Keep this arm in this position. Raise your right arm, bending your elbow so your upper arm is perpendicular to the floor. Turning toward the left, swing your arm against the attacker's arms, breaking his grip. Trap the attacker's arms between your left arm and your body. You can also use the upper part of your right arm to secure the trap.

The opposite arm can be used, too, in which case you would trap the attacker's arms between your right arm and body, securing with your left arm if necessary.

Counterattack

Raise your left arm, bending your elbow so that your upper arm is perpendicular to the floor. Keep this arm in this position. Raise your right arm, bending your elbow so your upper arm is perpendicular to the floor. Turning toward the left, swing your arm against the attacker's arms, breaking their grip. Trap the attacker's arms between your left arm and your body. You can also use the upper part of your right arm to secure the trap. With your right fist, strike the attacker's temple, nose, or throat or kick your attacker's groin or solar plexus. Be prepared to continue striking to subdue the attacker.

Defending yourself in a chokehold from behind

Suppose that an attacker has grabbed you with one arm from behind, with his elbow at your throat, as shown in Figure 9-6.

A chokehold is a serious threat. Don't hesitate to counterattack immediately, rather than attempting an escape or control technique.

Escape

Turn your head so that your throat is in the crook of the attacker's arm. This allows you breathing space and can help reduce panic. Grab the hand, wrist, or forearm of the arm that's around your throat with one or both of your hands. Pull the attacker's arm out away from your neck while simultaneously turning in the same direction that you're pulling. If this doesn't loosen the attacker's grip enough to allow escape, then supplement by driving your elbow into the attacker's solar plexus (the torso, just below the sternum).

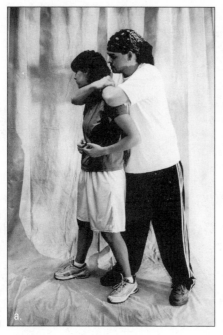 

Figure 9-6:
Defending
yourself in a
chokehold
that comes
from behind.

Control

Turn your head so that your throat is in the crook of the attacker's arm. This allows you breathing space and can help reduce panic. Grab the hand, wrist, or forearm of the arm that's around your throat with one or both of your hands. Pull the attacker's arm out away from your neck while simultaneously turning in the same direction that you're pulling. If this doesn't loosen the attacker's grip enough to allow escape, then supplement by driving your elbow into the attacker's solar plexus. With one hand, retain your grip on the attacker's wrist or forearm. Place your other hand under the attacker's elbow. Push down with your hand that's on the attacker's wrist or forearm while pushing up with the hand that's on the attacker's elbow. Increase the pressure of both hands to control the attacker.

Counterattack

Turn your head so that your throat is in the crook of the attacker's arm. This allows you breathing space and can help reduce panic. Reach back to the attacker's shoulder (of the arm that's performing the chokehold) with one or both hands and pull the attacker toward you. Using your hip for leverage, force the attacker off balance and throw him over your hip. Stomp or kick the attacker if needed.

If you can't gain sufficient leverage, such as if your attacker is much taller than you, use elbow strikes to loosen the attacker's grip, claw at his face with your hands, stomp on his instep with as much force as possible, or bite the arm that's around your throat.

Biting should only be used as a last resort; the attacker may have a communicable disease that you can contract by drawing blood.

As the attacker's grip loosens, continue performing elbow strikes, kicks, or stomps. Prepare to continue the counterattack as needed.

Defending yourself while seated

An attack may occur while you're seated, such as on a subway, waiting on a bench for the bus, or a similar seated situation. A common method of attack is for someone to grab your shirt from behind while you're seated in order to throw you to the ground or to take away your possessions. Often, you can use the same self-defense techniques that you can use while standing, as shown in Figure 9-7. If possible, move to a standing position as you're performing the self-defense techniques in order to equalize the playing field and to make your escape.

Figure 9-7: Disabling an attacker from a seated position.

Keep in mind that you can't see this attacker, so you don't know if he's armed. Your best bet is to move swiftly and escape before he can react.

Shout as you move to attract attention to your predicament and to throw the attacker off balance.

Escape

Lift your arm nearest the attacker's grab. Bend your elbow and make a knife hand by holding your fingers close together and keeping your hand tight. Strike the attacker's wrist or arm with the edge of your hand and your forearm while simultaneously turning toward the attacker. You should end this escape technique on your feet with your hands up to guard.

Control

Lift your arm nearest the attacker's grab and bend your elbow. Holding your fingers close together and keeping your hand tight, move your hand to strike the attacker's wrist while turning toward the attacker. When your hand strikes his wrist, grab the wrist instead of forcing it away. Rise to a standing position. With your other hand, grab the attacker's arm just above the elbow. Exert downward pressure with one hand while pushing up with the other in order to control the attacker.

Counterattack

Lift your arm nearest the attacker's grab. Bend your elbow and make a *knife hand* by holding your fingers close together and keeping your hand tight. Move your hand to strike the attacker's wrist while turning toward the attacker. When your hand strikes his wrist, grab the wrist instead of forcing it away. Rise to a standing position. Kick the attacker's now exposed ribs, or using your free hand, strike his temple, nose, or throat (whatever is exposed) using a palm strike, the back of your fist, or a punch. Continue your counterattack until the threat has been defused.

Defending yourself while prone

You may be attacked while you're sleeping, or you may be grabbed and thrown to the ground. This attacker may try to rape you or to subdue you in order to steal from you or commit some other crime. He may attempt to choke you or may intend to tie you up. (Watch out for friends bearing duct tape.) See Figure 9-8 to get an idea of what this looks like.

You must get out of this situation before you're rendered helpless. This means striking out in a counterattack from the outset.

If you're on your stomach, do your best to turn over or get to your feet so that you can at least see what you're dealing with. Try elbow strikes to the attacker's solar plexus (the torso just below the sternum), head butts to his nose, and mule kicks with your heels into any part of his body that you can strike. After you create an opening, you can deliver more effective kicks and strikes and then get away.

If you're on your back, your goal is to get to your feet and get away. If you can roll the attacker off you, do so. Otherwise, try gouging his eyes with your thumbs and scratching at his face with your fingernails. If you wear jewelry, such as a wedding ring, use it to scratch his face. You may not be able to simply push the attacker away, but short repeated jabs can be effective. Knee him in the groin. Twist your upper and lower body to loosen his grip. Follow up with whatever strikes you can manage in your position.

Remember, you can always bite your attacker, which can effectively disorient him enough to let you get free or deliver a strong technique. However, be aware that an attacker may have a communicable disease that you can contract by drawing his blood.

Figure 9-8:
Counter-
attacking is
your only
defense
from a prone
position.

Chapter 10

Preparing for Competition without Losing Your Head (Literally)

In This Chapter

▶ Understanding the joys of organized competition

▶ Discovering what happens at a tournament

▶ Finding a competition to suit you

▶ Getting yourself ready for the big day

Many martial arts styles encourage participation in organized competition. Participating in tournaments allows you to hone your skills, pit your techniques against other people at your level, and learn new ways to embarrass yourself (just kidding).

Some styles of martial arts, such as traditional Aikido (Chapter 18), frown on students participating in organized competition. Even the founder of Judo (Chapter 17) strongly discouraged competition, saying that the purpose of the art was to help each individual develop to the best of her abilities — not to compare herself to people with different gifts. (The irony is that Judo is almost entirely sport and competition oriented today.) If this is the viewpoint of your style or instructor, respect it. Don't compete without your instructor's approval; this is dishonorable. Instead, ask you instructor to help you hone your skills in a noncompetitive way.

Making an Idiot of Yourself and Why You Should Risk It

So you belong to a school that allows and even encourages students to enter competitions, but you're not sure if you should do it. Many martial artists shy away from organized competition because they're afraid of making fools of themselves. This is for good reason. Falling down while attempting the jump-spinning-wheel kick in the (relative) privacy of your instructor's training hall is one thing, but doing it in front of a panel of judges and two thousand spectators is another matter altogether. But you should risk it anyway.

Getting the hang of it

The purpose of entering competitions isn't to garner fame, glory, and an action-movie contract, but wouldn't it be nice? The purpose is to help you develop your martial arts skills.

Training for competition gives a little extra kick to your ordinary workouts. Knowing that you're going to go head-to-head with others at your rank can give you the extra incentive that you need to really get those kicks head high or to really sharpen those throws.

Naturally, if you're going to be performing forms for judges or sparring other competitors, you want to do your best. So spend extra time working on areas that may be weak ahead of time. You can set goals and challenge yourself to achieve certain results in time for the competition.

Finding out who's doing what

Martial artists are successful so long as they achieve to the best of their own abilities — no matter what the other guys are doing. Spending too much time comparing yourself to others is counterproductive; however, an occasional glimpse of what the other guys are up to can be healthy.

Competition helps everyone become better, and constantly pushes the envelope of what people can do. At one regional tournament, a competitor did a double-jump-spinning-wheel kick through a board, breaking off one third of the board on the first kick and another third of the board on the second kick. No one had seen this particular board break before. But at the *next* regional tournament, everyone was doing that board-breaking kick or some variation of it.

No one — even the pros — makes much money competing in martial arts tournaments, but entering and doing well in competition can add luster to your credentials as a teacher or coach. So a tournament is worth the investment even if the medals that you receive aren't worth more than a buck-fifty each.

Winning isn't the only thing (really)

Although you try to do your best in competition, winning the gold isn't the most important thing. Think of it like the Olympics: You win just by being there. If you did your work and trained especially for the competition, you're in better shape than you were before. You had a chance to see what other martial artists are up to, and you practiced performing while nervous. So enjoy the experience whether you win or lose.

Beating the jitters

Participating in competition is nerve-racking: You fork over a bunch of money, stand around in your uniform for a couple of hours, then suddenly have to perform your techniques in front of a group of judges who don't appear to be even looking at you, and then stand around some more to see how you did. If you enter more than one event, this process occurs repeatedly. Competing is enough to turn you into a couch potato.

So why do it? Nerve-racking competition is good for you. (Bet your mother never told you that.) You're a martial artist. You're learning skills that you hope you can use one day should a mugger grab you and drag you down an alley. Now *that* can make you nervous. If you never practice your techniques when you're nervous, then when the time comes for you to use your skills in real life, you may not know what to do.

Although you have no guarantees, if you practice your techniques while you're nervous, you're much more likely to remember what to do when faced with a real assault than if you never practice your techniques outside the training hall.

 Donald Booth, founder of New Horizons Black Belt Academy of Tae Kwon Do, tells all his students that participating in competition is "good stress." If you practice performing under "good stress," then you're more likely to be able to perform under "bad stress" (such as when someone is attacking you).

Tournament Events

Martial arts competitions are divided into events, such as forms (Chapter 5), sparring (Chapter 7), and breaking (Chapter 1). You can enter as many or as few events as you like.

Forms competition

Forms competition simply requires you to perform a *form* — a prearranged pattern of techniques — (see Chapter 5) in front of judges. Select a form that showcases your skills and abilities the best. You're judged on criteria, such as grace, control, power, and agility.

If you make a mistake during the performance of your form, continue doing the form as if you had made no mistake. Some judges won't even catch it, and the others may admire your poise. Do each technique with confidence, even if it's the wrong technique.

In forms competition among multiple styles, judging is generally divided into *hard style* and *soft style*. Hard-style martial arts are those that focus on direct, linear strikes, using many kicks and punches. Soft-style martial arts are those that focus on redirecting the attacker's energy, using circular movements, deflections, and joint manipulation. Thus, Karate and Tae Kwon Do (hard style) practitioners would compete against one another, while Kung Fu (soft style) practitioners would compete separately. (See Chapter 14 for information on Karate, Chapter 16 for the details of Tae Kwon Do, and Chapter 15 for more on Kung Fu.)

In some tournaments, competitors may do weapons forms or musical forms (forms set to music) or team forms.

Judging

In general, a panel of five judges scores the form on a ranking of one to ten, ten being highest. Sometimes, more judges or fewer judges are used, and sometimes, the high and low scores are discarded to get a better average score.

Judges look for confidence, grace, agility, and power. In weapons forms, they look to see if you handle the weapon skillfully and if you incorporate it effectively into the form. In musical forms, showmanship and harmony of the form and music are considered. In team forms, synchronicity is also judged.

Sparring competitions: Mock combat

Sparring competitions pit competitors one-on-one with each other. Rules vary widely according to style, sanctioning organization, and even the organizer's whim. Some general guidelines follow:

Judo

In Judo competition, the participants begin in a standing position, perform appropriate courtesies, then grasp each other's uniforms, and begin. The object is to throw the opponent to the mat and pin him.

Judo competition has no rounds. National contest matches last from six to ten minutes. Olympic competition can last 15 to 20 minutes. If a competitor scores *ippon* (a full point), the match ends, and she wins.

Judging

A referee, two judges, and a scorekeeper are required. The referee controls the match and makes calls although the judges can disagree. Majority rules. If a tie results, the judges confer and declare one of the participants the winner.

Ippon is awarded if the opponent is thrown squarely on her back with considerable power. It can also be earned by immobilizing an opponent for at least 30 seconds or by applying a chokehold or an arm lock until the opponent surrenders. Half points are also awarded for techniques that don't meet all the criteria for an ippon. Half points can be added together to make a full point. Two other scores are also given:

- ✔ **Yuko:** less than a half point
- ✔ **Koka:** less than a yuko

These two scores accumulate throughout a contest but don't add up to ippon.

Penalties

Penalties are assessed as points awarded to the other competitor, so you can win a Judo match even if you never throw your opponent — if your opponent gets penalized enough.

Karate

Karate sparring is generally no contact. Competitors of equal rank and in the same weight class strike and block with hands and legs until a blow comes extremely close to a target area on the opponent's body. The following are some variations in Karate competitions that include contact:

- ✔ **Semicontact Karate:** Light contact is allowed, and participants wear protective equipment. In general, these matches are judged according to the accumulated point system in two-minute rounds. Heavy contact can be grounds for disqualification.

✔ **Professional Karate:** Full-contact Karate is fought to the knockout. In most cases, full-contact kickboxing has replaced full-contact Karate tournaments.

Judging

In traditional Karate, if the strike is correctly executed and it's not blocked, a full point is awarded. A technique, if not correctly executed or if partially blocked, may still be awarded a half point. The winner is the first person to gain a full point. This system is rarely used in modern competition.

Accumulated point sparring is more common. In this case, a full point is awarded for a correctly executed, unblocked technique. No point is awarded for an incorrect or blocked technique. A bout lasts between two and three minutes. Whoever has accumulated the most points at the end of that time wins.

In black belt grand championships, which are matches between the winners of all black belt weight divisions to determine the single-best fighter, each match usually has two rounds with a one-minute rest in between.

Penalties

A competitor is usually given several warnings before a foul is called against him. A *foul* requires a point deduction or a forfeit of the match. Fouls include too much contact and striking below the target area. They may be given if a competitor repeatedly steps outside the ring or turns away to avoid an attack. Figure 10-1 shows the various target areas.

In some Karate matches that end in ties, the person who can break the most boards is declared the winner.

Team competition

In international tournaments, teams of participants compete. Five people comprise a team, and the team that accumulates the most points wins. In the case of a tie, one contestant is chosen from each team, and they fight a title bout.

Kung Fu

Sparring can be done with and without weapons. Because of the vast variation of Kung Fu styles, only general notes about sparring competitions can be given in this book. Specific rules are determined and posted ahead of time. Frequently, rules similar to no-contact Karate are followed. Contact the tournament organizer to learn the details and to find out what to expect.

Judging

Four judges and one chief judge decide the score of each competitor. The number of referees varies.

Target Areas

Muay Thai,
Tae Kwon Do:
side of head

High section

Muay Thai, Karate
Tae Kwon Do: front
and sides of chest
above belt and
below neck

Middle section

Muay Thai: shin

Low section

Figure 10-1:
Target
areas.

Muay Thai

Muay Thai kickboxing matches consist of five three-minute rounds with two-minute breaks in between. Competitors strike the head, body, and legs. Some throws, joint locks (manipulating the joints and immobilizing the limbs), and holds can be used. Elbow strikes are generally illegal, and the groin is generally an illegal target area. Muay Thai fights can be fought to the knockout.

Judging

Two judges and a referee award a decision in the case of no knockout. Points are awarded for any legal attack.

Penalties

Competitors can be disqualified for rules infractions, usually for using illegal techniques.

Tae Kwon Do

Tae Kwon Do matches are similar to Karate matches, with two- or three-minute rounds. Points are awarded when a correctly executed technique strikes the target unblocked. A blow must cause a visible shock to count. All matches are semicontact, and protective equipment is worn.

Legal target areas are the front of the body from the waist to the base of the neck (not the throat). Kicks to the sides of the head are allowed, but hand techniques to the head are *not* allowed.

Judging

All competitions require a referee and four or five judges. Now and then, the judges score the match independently; at other times, they must agree (by majority) that a point was scored.

Knockdowns and knockouts score the most points. Foot techniques score higher than hand techniques, jumping techniques score higher than standing techniques, and a kick to the head is scored higher than a kick to the body. These guidelines are used to determine the better fighter.

Penalties

Fouls are called when someone steps out of bounds on purpose (to avoid an attack), for turning away, throwing an opponent, and similar infractions. Penalties result in point deductions.

Escrima

Competitors use escrima sticks (see Chapter 19) to strike target areas, each other's sticks or legal targets on the body. They wear padded armor and headgear for protection. Matches usually run two minutes and are governed by guidelines similar to those used in other martial arts.

Judging

One center-ring judge and four corner judges determine when a point is earned. The person with the highest number of points wins the match.

Penalties

Penalties are assessed for striking illegal target areas.

Breaking contests

Breaking contests are generally limited to Tae Kwon Do and some Karate tournaments. Each participant is given a specified number of one-inch thick boards to break using a variety of techniques. Lower-ranking students attempt to break fewer boards than higher-ranking students.

Competitors choose which techniques they use to break their boards. Generally, competitors have two tries to break each board.

Block or tile breaking is also done, but this is rare in competition.

Judging

Board-breaking is judged by a panel of judges who award scores (usually one to ten) based on the difficulty of the techniques attempted, correct execution of the techniques, and the number of boards broken. In the case of a tie, the referee may determine what technique the competitors must use to break the tie-breaking board.

Although difficulty of technique is an important factor in judging board-breaking competitions, you can't win if your boards don't break. Therefore, choose techniques that you *know* you can break the boards with.

What to Expect When You're Expecting to Compete

Before you enter a competition, you should have some idea of what to expect. It helps to talk with veteran tournament-goers to get information on what happens. Also, talk with your instructor to learn what's expected of *you* (such as proper etiquette and representing the school honorably).

Always get your instructor's permission before entering tournaments. An instructor may guide you away from certain tournaments that you may not be prepared for. She can help you find good, well-run tournaments to slake your competitive fire.

Not all tournament competitors are 20-year-old fitness freaks. In fact, one woman likely to make the women's Tae Kwon Do team for the 2004 Olympics is 57 years old.

On the day of the contest . . .

Generally, you arrive the morning of the competition (or a day or so before if the tournament is being held in a distant city). If you haven't already paid your registration fee, you'll do so now. This can range from about $10 per event to hundreds of dollars for prestigious national and international competitions. Some martial artists are able to attract sponsors to help defray these costs.

You must bring your own uniform and equipment with you. The judge or referee may examine them to make certain that your uniform and equipment conforms to guidelines. If you don't have certain required pieces of equipment (such as groin protectors for men), you may be prohibited from participating until you can supply the required equipment. Don't count on there being a pro shop at the tournament venue.

Spectators are always welcome at martial arts tournaments. Most are kid-friendly, so bring the family along. A concession stand will probably be located on-site, so you can feed the gang.

You'll be given tickets or some other form of identification to show that you're registered for each event. Pay careful attention to any announcements that you hear. Soon after the scheduled starting time, ring numbers are assigned for each division.

While many divisions are performing simultaneously, usually only one event at a time is going on. Thus, all the judging of forms is done first, then the breaking competition is held, and finally, sparring is conducted. Grand champion competitions, in which the winners of each division compete against each other to determine the single-best competitor, are usually held at the end of the day.

Big tournaments may be held over a weekend. The preliminary rounds of each event are held on Saturday, and the semifinal and final rounds are held on Sunday.

Long division

Needless to say, grouping little 6-year-olds with the over-35 gang wouldn't be fair (to the over-35 gang). Therefore, each event has several divisions so that people of similar experience, size, and ability can compete with one another.

Gender and age

In general, tournaments have adult men's divisions, adult women's divisions, and children's divisions (which accommodate both sexes.) Sometimes, adult divisions are mixed, with men and women competing against each other. (This is most common in forms competition.) Adult divisions are generally 16 years (sometimes 18) and older, and the senior division is usually 35 years on up. An additional adult division is the instructors' division, so that instructors can compete against each other, not their students.

If many children participate, attempts are made to group them into as small of groups as possible for a couple of reasons:

✔ This makes it more likely that children of approximately the same size can compete against each other.

✔ It ensures that more children can win more medals. (My favorite children's division is *Sub-mini-pee-wee.* I think that's 5-year-olds.)

Rank

Within each general category, such as adult men's sparring, divisions are created for various belt ranks. At the largest tournaments, each belt level may be given its own division. At smaller tournaments, the categories are more general, such as "Beginner" and "Intermediate." Black belts always compete separately from nonblack belts. Black belt divisions may be grouped by degree *(dan).* See Chapter 5 for more on black belt degree and the *kyu/dan* system. So you may have an adult brown belt men's sparring competition, for example.

In general, women's divisions are fewer than men's because fewer women compete. Occasionally, the senior division is nonexistent, and the 45-year-olds have to compete with the 18-year-olds. All the nonblack belts may be grouped together. Attempts are made to ensure fairness. If a beginner is grouped with a more advanced student, the beginner is given several points to start, for example, and then the first person to reach five points wins. But especially if you're a woman, it pays to know ahead of time that all divisions are fluid.

Weight classes

Weight class also further divides fighters. Most sanctioning organizations have clear guidelines for weight classes. However, at smaller tournaments, a referee may just eyeball the competitors and split them into groups. Height may be the determining factor in these smaller competitions.

Again, because so few women compete, it pays to know how to work this ahead of time. If you're the only one in your weight class, you may be allowed to go outside your weight class, but this can put you at a disadvantage. Also, the competition may be cancelled if not enough competitors enter. Knowing which weight classes have the most competitors is to your advantage. Fight at that weight (if possible). For men, the opposite may be true: If a man can find a class with fewer competitors, he has a better chance of winning.

Style

This isn't your GQ rating. Many bigger tournaments are open to multiple styles, but this can cause difficulty during judging, so divisions may also include hard and soft style. Hard styles, such as Karate and Tae Kwon Do, compete against one another, while soft styles, such as Kung Fu, compete among themselves. Thus, you can have a senior adult fourth-degree black belt and above women's hard style weapons form division. Whew! Pay attention to those loudspeaker announcements, or you'll never find your ring.

Finding Tournaments

If you want to compete, you have to find a well-run tournament to enter. The best way to do this is through the recommendations of your fellow martial artists and your instructor.

You can also contact the sanctioning body for your martial art (see Appendix B for a list of organizations and associations) and get a list of upcoming sponsored events. If you're serious about competing, you need to understand how to accumulate enough wins at local and regional tournaments to be eligible for national and international competition. The sanctioning bodies can help; also, contact the Amateur Athletic Union for additional information.

Tournaments are also advertised in martial arts magazines, along with programs for learning *dim mak* (death touch; vulnerable pressure points on the human body that when touched can result in death) in ten easy steps. Check out *Black Belt* or *Martial Arts and Combat Sports* magazines for starters. (See Appendix B for contact information.)

Remember that just because you can't find any competitions in *Phoenix-Eye Fist Kung Fu* (Chapter 15) doesn't mean that you can't compete. You don't have to compete in tournaments specifically for your style. Many tournaments are open to multiple styles. And even in one-style tournaments, similar styles are usually welcome. (I used to win more Karate competitions than Tae Kwon Do competitions, and my black belt is in Tae Kwon Do!)

Choosing the right tournament

If you're enthusiastic about martial arts and march off to a tournament where you end up requiring 37 stitches in your head, you may find that your enthusiasm dims slightly.

This doesn't have to happen to you. Again, get the recommendations of people who have done it, including your instructor.

You also want to think about what kind of tournament you'd like to go to — a formal competition with many local as well as out-of-town competitors — or a more laid-back gathering of competitors who know each other. Check out the following list and the descriptions to help you get an idea of what's available:

- ✔ **Local and invitational:** Most importantly, work your way up. Start at local tournaments. For example, Dave's Karate Studio down the street from where you work out at Dragon Fire Martial Arts may decide to rent the local high school gym one Saturday afternoon and invite local martial artists for kicks. These types of *invitational* tournaments can be a good way to get your feet wet. Most of the competitors know each other, and although it may not be the most smooth-running event that you ever attended, it's unlikely that anyone will be taken out in an ambulance.

- ✔ **Regional:** In a similar vein, regional tournaments, drawing from several states, can be the next step. Again, these may be invitational, so that many of the martial artists know each other.

- ✔ **Open:** After you're ready to move out into the wider world, you can begin attending open tournaments — open to anyone in a clean uniform who is willing to pay the registration fee. These types of tournaments are usually sponsored by a martial arts organization, and wins may count toward competing in the national tournament.

- ✔ **National and international tournaments:** These are usually sponsored by a martial arts organization. To be eligible to participate, you have to have accumulated a certain number of wins at the local and regional level. But not all national and international competitions require this. Some allow you to participate as long as you pay the fee. This can be a great way to see the world, but don't attempt a national or international tournament until you have some experience.

Doing a dry run

There's no place like home, Toto. If you're not all that interested in traveling to other places (even Dave's Karate Studio down the street), or you can't afford the expense or the time away from other obligations, you can still take advantage of the benefits of competing by participating in informal competition.

Actually, every time you try to do better in class today than you did yesterday, you're competing (against yourself). All you have to do is take this one step further. For example, challenge yourself to score one clear, unblocked point on that black belt competitor who you can never seem to beat.

Enlist your fellow students. Have a friendly match where each acknowledges points scored during sparring; whoever accumulates the most points in two minutes wins. Get together after class and have a *round-robin* where various students match up and spar; only two spar at a time, and the rest judge. Then when that match is over, two different students spar, and the rest judge.

Ask a senior student or your instructor to watch you do your form and tell you what score she would assign it. During belt rank examinations, remember that you're trying to show your skill to the judge. That's a kind of competition.

Preparing to Strike Oil

You have the glossy brochure. You sent your registration fee. The car is gassed up and ready to take you to the tournament site. You have your uniform on, and your lucky mouthguard is in your pocket. What more do you need to get ready for competition?

Whoa. You need to prepare for competition long before the date of the competition rolls around. Serious athletes know that they have to train smart in order to peak at the right time. Thus, a marathoner sets her sights on the Boston Marathon, and plots, months in advance, what it takes to succeed. You should do the same.

Being aware of the peak season

Martial arts tournament season is generally late fall and winter. (Hey, it's an indoor activity.) Although tournaments can be held year-round, identifying the one or two (or three) competitions that really matter to you and organizing your training to peak during those times makes sense.

A few months ahead of time, you want to start conditioning your body, maybe losing a few pounds, and working out a little more. Have your coach critique the areas that need improvement and work at each of these areas. This is your spring training.

Your training should hit its highest velocity about three or four weeks before the actual date of the tournament. Then you can back off from this intensity and maintain a more everyday level of exertion. This helps prevent burnout and injuries.

Some martial artists have one big tournament they like to do each year, not having time for more. Others shoot for one big tournament but include a few others, so if they don't do well at the one, they have a back up.

Some martial artists hit tournaments every weekend for months. If this is you, be sure you get enough rest (and take a weekend off now and then) or you can overstress your body. Between tournaments, do only light martial arts workouts and save the more intense efforts for body conditioning, like aerobics and weight lifting.

Knowing the rules

Each competition has slightly different rules, and you must know these rules ahead of time in order to prepare appropriately. Certain techniques may be disallowed in sparring, for example. Or only certain forms are recognized. Your practice and preparation should take this into consideration.

My favorite sparring technique is a back fist to the head. I have scored more points than I can count with this technique. But it's not allowed in many tournament competitions, so I have to train myself *not* to use it. Otherwise, I would be disqualified for using an illegal technique.

Tournament competition takes place in *rings*. (I know. I know that it's called a ring, but it's square.) Depending on the competition, this is actually a square between eight and ten feet wide and eight and ten feet long. That may seem like plenty of room, but it isn't after you start doing your form or sparring. Practice with lines of tape or light chalk on the carpet to mark off the tournament space. If you keep stepping out of bounds during competition, the judges can penalize you. So be prepared ahead of time.

Keeping your head in the game

You can succeed in competition just by showing up. So don't let nerves overwhelm you or let your opponent's annoying arrogance get to you. You've already won, so relax.

Be confident going into the tournament. You prepared ahead of time, and you know what to do. Above all, don't allow yourself to get frustrated if you know that you can do better than you're doing. Just take a deep breath, look confident, and keep going.

Never let anyone know when you made a mistake. If you're supposed to do a front kick in your form and you do a side kick instead, that's okay. Just keep on going. Chances are, no one may even notice.

During one promotion test, along with a group of other brown belts, I did a form called *Hwarang* (an intermediate Tae Kwon Do form). I made a mistake with my footwork and ended up facing the wrong way. Serenely confident that I knew what I was dong, I didn't change direction even though everyone else finished in the opposite direction. Afterwards, the judge told me that he admired my focus and confidence. I did, however, earn the nickname, "Hwarang-way Lawler"!

Chapter 11

Working the Mind-Body-Spirit Connection

In This Chapter

▶ Becoming one with your martial art

▶ Developing patience and calm with simple exercises

▶ Organizing your life

▶ Experiencing harmony and healing

*I*n traditional martial arts training, the student's mental, ethical, and spiritual development is as important as physical training. Physical ability is useless without a strong character. A person can kick head high, but if he doesn't have persistence, then being able to kick head high isn't going to help him lead a richer, fuller life.

Although many aspects of the mind-body-spirit connection evolve naturally from training in the martial arts, you have to work at it. In the West, people are accustomed to living dichotomies: People are physical athletes, or they're brainy accountants. They don't realize that to reach their fullest human potential, they should be both . . . in fact, they should add a third factor: spirituality.

The Way of Martial Arts

Martial artists follow *the Way*. In Japanese and Korean martial arts, the word *do* means *way* or *path*. So a martial art like Aikido (Chapter 18) has the word *way* in its name. In Chinese martial arts, the word meaning *way* is *tao*. This ancient philosophy asserts that everything in the world is interrelated. If one can perform an action in harmony with the essence of the action, one is performing tao. This is best understood as being *at one* with something. Martial artists, after tireless practice, can reach the state where they become the training, and the training becomes them. It reminds me of that old question, "How do you separate the dancer from the dance?"

Traditionally, Taoism is credited to the Chinese philosopher Lao Tzu in the sixth century B.C. It is mainly concerned with the unknowable source, the Tao. As the Tao-Te-Ching says, "The Tao that can be described is not the true Tao."

The sign that symbolizes the *Way* (or Tao) is the yin-yang sign, which suggests that the Way is one of harmony and balance.

The mental aspects of the Way

Following the Way requires balance and moderation in all things. It requires simplicity and even passivity in the face of conflict and disorientation.

To follow the Way with honesty and integrity requires committing to living a highly ethical life. This can start on the smallest level. For example, in martial arts class, one way to perform *ethically* is to give your best effort all the time, even when no one else is looking, even when you're not being judged or competing with others. From that small step, you can seek to perform the "right" action in all aspects of your life. You may not win any awards, and sometimes, the price of integrity is high, but you know that you have followed the Way. And that's better than anything you can buy at Wal-Mart.

As you seek to understand and follow the Way, you begin to understand the interrelatedness of all things. You can reach a better understanding of your place in the world, even the universe, while at the same time neither overestimating nor underestimating your importance or the importance of others (including your dog and your boss). You learn that to become *at one* with the universe simply requires patience and the willingness to sit still for long periods of time.

To start your journey on the Way, simply make a commitment to learning how to choose the "right" action. All else will follow from that.

The physical aspects of the Way

You can follow the Way even if you aren't a martial artist. But being one helps. Your body isn't just a place to keep your brain warm; it's a vital living organism that needs care and attention. Just as you develop mental and creative talents to become a *whole* person, you also need to develop your physical talents.

You're more capable of physical action than you believe. The human body is an amazing machine, but people tend to limit what they do with them. This is especially true of adults who weren't particularly active or sports-oriented as children. But you can change your beliefs about what your body can do — even if you're older or have a disability.

Believing in what your body can do is empowering. If you can learn to do things with your body that you never believed possible, it convinces you that nothing is out of reach, and that you can do anything, even become President of the United States or at least CEO of a big corporation. How's that for a workout that only takes an hour a day a couple times a week?

By developing your body, learning how it works, you become more centered and comfortable with yourself.

Understanding what your body can do is empowering to everyone. But women, who are conditioned from birth to think of themselves as weaker than men, can truly achieve amazing physical results after they stop believing cultural fantasies masquerading as biological facts.

When you work hard in training, you open yourself to the Way. Because you concentrate all your mental and emotional energy on performing the techniques correctly and getting the most from class, you empty your mind of all other thoughts and distractions. That's right: When you're giving the most intense physical effort, you're actually meditating.

Most martial artists say one of their favorite parts of training is how it empties their minds of the worries and cares of the day. Not only can this lead to enlightenment, it can help relieve stress and anxiety.

When you practice a martial art (or any skill) to the point of mastery, you've achieved a state of Tao, or oneness with the art. You have become the art and the art has become you. This is one way to achieve enlightenment (if that's what you're after).

Touched by an angel — not

Some folks tend to think of *spiritual* and *religious* as the same thing. But they're not. In fact, the term *philosophical* might be a better one to use in this context. Martial arts aren't religious, but they do have a spiritual or philosophical component. You are expected to develop a good character and to behave in ethical and moral ways. But no specific doctrine is taught.

Instead, students are asked to cultivate certain qualities that can make them a better person, and indeed, a better martial artist.

For example, Tae Kwon Do students are asked to adhere to the Five Tenets: courtesy, integrity, perseverance, self-control, and indomitable spirit. These are qualities that anyone can admire, whatever one's religious background.

Meditation and Breathing Exercises

To become one with the universe requires a certain amount of patience, which, let it be said, not many of us possess. But you can acquire patience, which is a helpful trait to have even if you're not a Taoist.

Patience isn't quite the same as persistence. Patience is a bit quieter. It's calm, the opposite of action. Often, as I race through the days, I don't take the time that I should to calm down, de-stress, and spend a few minutes in search of the unknowable source.

By incorporating meditation and breathing exercises into your daily life, you can begin working the mind-body-spirit connection in some subtle and not-so-subtle ways.

Meditation basics

You have different kinds of meditation to choose from depending on what you're trying to accomplish. If you're trying to seek enlightenment and be one with the Buddha, you meditate one way. If you're trying not to yell at the kids, you meditate a slightly different way.

Zazen meditation or "empty mind" meditation is simply the act of emptying your mind and stopping all thoughts. This sounds easy enough to do in principle, but just try it. We have thousands of thoughts zinging in and out of our minds like city buses, and trying to get them to stop is quite a task, but a few simple maneuvers can help you to empty your mind.

Avoiding distractions

First, find a spot — a private and quiet place — where you're not going to be distracted by a teenager playing computer games. Some people use a white noise or special meditation CD or tape to cover up any ambient sounds; other people find these annoying and distracting. Turn off any bright lights and get comfortable. Unbutton your jeans if you have to. Sit in a relaxed position. Some people can recline, but this always makes me fall asleep.

Emptying your mind

Take several deep cleansing breaths and feel all the tension seep out of you. Then close your eyes and empty your mind of thoughts. Just keep it as blank as possible. If thoughts intrude, firmly dismiss them.

Some people find that spending a few minutes writing down what's on their mind before they try to meditate can help them clear their minds in order to meditate more effectively. Emptying your mind while simultaneously thinking, "I can't forget to call Mother tonight," is hard to do.

Using meditation aids

Because it can be difficult to simply empty your mind, many people use meditation aids to provide their minds with one thing to focus on while emptying it of all other thoughts and distractions. For example, some people choose a mantra, a sound that they repeat (not always out loud) over and over. Choosing a sound rather than a word is best, so that you don't end up thinking about the word, what it means, and how it's spelled, and so on.

Some people do meditate on a word or *koan* (philosophical puzzle), but the purpose of that kind of meditation is to explore the meaning of the word or the koan — not to empty one's mind. In fact, using the koan to achieve *satori* (enlightenment) is typical of Zen Buddhist sects. Even if you're not a Zen Buddhist, it can be a fun type of meditation to practice and can help to solve problems. Just feed the problem into your mind and focus on it and only it for as long as you can stand it. After a while, if nothing else, you'll be really tired of thinking about the problem and can go onto something else.

Some people use a simple visual image as a kind of mantra. This is what I do. I think of a plain candle flame, just a stationary yellow flame. Nothing spectacular about it. It doesn't move. It doesn't turn red or green. It's just something for my mind to think about while it isn't thinking of anything else.

Visualization

One type of meditation that's useful for martial artists is visualization. By visualizing success — whatever that is — you can achieve it. It might be visualizing yourself doing the perfect side kick. It might be visualizing yourself giving a flawless sales presentation. The purpose is to give yourself confidence that you can achieve the goal, walk you through achieving the goal, and identify the steps that you need to take to achieve the goal. It's like a visual, positive affirmation. Instead of saying, "I am the winner of the Boston Marathon," you visualize it, imagining it in all its details.

You can use this technique almost anywhere at anytime. To begin, find a comfortable position and close your eyes. Try to empty your mind as much as possible. Then imagine your athletic performance or whatever goal you want to achieve. Focus only on this visualization, ignoring all other distractions.

For example, visualize the perfect side kick. Imagine the steps taken to pull your leg to the chamber position, pivot on your supporting foot, and thrust your leg toward the target. Imagine how your body feels with each step. Visualize a successful strike through the target.

One of the best times to practice visualization is just before or just after martial arts class or competition. Just before class, imagine how well you'll do in class. Just after class, consider how well you did in class and visualize yourself doing even better next time.

Controlled breathing

By consciously and deliberately controlling your breathing, you can calm yourself down, build your endurance (by making sure that your body gets enough oxygen) and learn to focus.

You should always be aware of your breathing, especially as you work out. Some students forget to breathe when they're working out or breathe at the wrong time, which can make the workout much more difficult. Remember to breathe out during the exertion stage and breathe in during the resting stage of each technique.

Controlled or focused breathing is simple. Controlled breathing is best done standing to give your lungs enough room to expand properly, but you can do it while seated at your desk at work, too.

Expel most of the air from your lungs. Then, breathe in through your nose, counting slowly to three. Then breathe out through your mouth, again counting slowly to three. As you calm yourself, and as your heart rate slows, increase the amount of time each breath takes. For example, count to four for each inhalation and exhalation, and then count to five. After less than a minute, you'll feel calm, relaxed, and recovered from physical exertion.

Do controlled breathing whenever a short break presents itself during your workout. This gives you the energy that you need to exert the same intensity throughout your workout. Also, do a minute or two of controlled breathing after a workout and then do a few minutes of meditation or visualization in order to get the most from your training.

Rooted-tree breathing

I admit that I stole the idea of rooted-tree breathing from a friend who practices T'ai Chi and yoga. (Thank you, Debz!) Like controlled breathing, this exercise can calm you down and give you a little extra energy. Go through the following numbered steps to see how rooted-tree breathing works.

1. **Stand tall.**

   Think of a string attached to the top of your head pulling you upright. Pull your shoulders back to give your lungs room to breathe. Think of your spine as perfectly straight. Your feet should be planted about a shoulder's-width apart.

2. **Think of yourself as a tree.**

   Your feet are firmly rooted to the ground. As you inhale, think of pulling the energy up from the earth. Inhale deeply, making sure that your chest and abdomen expand. Lift your arms as you breathe to allow the most air into your body.

3. **Exhale, lowering your arms as you do so.**

   Think of expelling all the negative energy, anxiety, and tension that you have. Repeat the process, breathing slowly and smoothly in through the nose and out through the mouth.

Your *chi,* located in your abdomen, is your life force or inner energy. These breathing exercises can help you tap into and use your chi.

Developing Focus and Discipline

I have a weakness for potato chips and pistachio nut ice cream. Even worse, I would rather curl up on the sofa and read a good book than do curls at the gym. Fortunately, my martial arts training has taught me a little discipline.

You know that eating right and working out is good for you, and you feel good when you do it, but giving into the temptations that surround you is easy. And it's not just the potato chips that cause problems, either. Watching television when a person should be working or splurging on a new suit when the phone bill still isn't paid are both examples of a lack of discipline or self-control.

People need focus and discipline in all areas of our lives. Martial arts can help. In class, you're expected to listen without talking, to line up when told, to do the exercises as the instructor tells you to. This is the first step toward building discipline. Soon, you won't need the instructor to tell you; you'll be able to tell yourself, and this tendency toward discipline can affect your everyday life as well.

In the same way, you can develop focus by concentrating only on performing a certain technique in class and not allowing any other distractions to interfere. Again, the instructor and fellow students can help to reinforce this at first, but after a while, you'll automatically be able to focus on the task at hand.

The opposite is true as well. If you have focus and discipline outside the training hall, your efforts inside the training hall are easier: You show up for class regularly, on time, and prepared and ready to focus.

The science of euphoria: Endorphin rush hour

When you work hard physically, whether as a runner, a martial artist, or a triathlete, you can reach a state of detachment popularly called *runner's high* — the feeling that although what you're doing is difficult, you can just keep doing it forever, and you feel great. Some people call this getting in *the zone*.

At the end of a difficult training session, you can sit there, totally drenched with sweat, unable to move, with a goofy smile plastered on your face, because although it may require a crane and a hoist to get you on your feet, you never felt better. Any activity that requires much repetition, such as running or doing 300 front kicks in martial arts class, can give you this wonderful feeling. So, like rats in some mad experiment, you keep going back for more, even if it leaves you with sore hamstrings the next day.

Scientists have studied this effect and have determined that after a certain amount of physical exertion, your brain, essentially in self-defense, starts sending messages to your body. At first, these messages are along the lines of, "What do you think you're doing? At your age! That's too hard! We'll never do that!" But a few minutes later, the brain surrenders and starts producing *endorphins* — a chemical that has a narcotic-like effect only it's non-prescription. No wonder you feel good. Just use caution when operating heavy machinery.

Although your brain quits producing endorphins as soon as you stop this foolishness, the effect of the endorphins on your body can persist for some time after your workout. That's why you feel so great at first, and then why half an hour later, your legs feel so stiff. (A hot shower or tub bath after a workout can help your body relax, thus reducing muscle stress and can also help get rid of the build up of lactic acid that causes muscle soreness.)

Getting organized

One of the reasons that focusing on the task at hand is difficult is that we don't know what the task at hand should be. If you don't know whether you should be painting the kitchen or cooking dinner, focusing on either one is hard to do.

This is the wonderful thing about martial arts training. On the whole, you know what you should be doing. If it's time to do forms, then that's what you do. If it's time to practice techniques, then that's what you do. And if you *don't* know what you're doing, help is on the way! So if you're sparring and you're not quite certain which technique would be effective in this situation, your partner and the teacher can coach you.

This training can help you get a feel for how to stay focused and disciplined in your daily life.

Setting priorities

Part of being organized involves setting priorities. If you think of everything as equally important, then of course, what's really important doesn't get done. The tendency is to also let other people set priorities when they interrupt with urgent problems that aren't really our problems.

Before you can act with discipline and focus, you have to choose what you're going to be disciplined and focused about. If you want to earn a black belt in Aikido (Chapter 18), then understand the type of commitment that can take. Earning a black belt in Aikido while running a law office, attending medical school at night, and single-handedly raising your newborn triplets isn't likely. So choose those things that are important to you and don't bother with the rest.

That's it on a global scale. On a more mundane level, begin each day with a plan. What are the priorities for the day? What must get done? What needs to be done soon but isn't urgent? What can wait or be delegated to someone else? This process doesn't need to take more than a few minutes. If you have a spouse and/or family to consider, then determine your priorities together.

After you determine your priorities for the day, then make sure that you have all the *equipment* that you need to accomplish them. If you're going to go to class, then is your uniform clean? Is your equipment in a gym bag, ready for you to grab on your way out the door? How will you get to class, and who can take care of the kids while you're there? Having this organized ahead of time can help you maintain discipline and focus throughout the day. For more help with organizing, pick up *Organizing For Dummies* by Eileen Roth (Wiley).

Your enthusiasm for martial arts can actually distract you from being disciplined. This is what happens when you're so interested in all aspects of martial arts that you keep sampling different styles, teachers, and approaches instead of simply choosing one to start with and learning it well before trying anything else. A good guideline is to commit to training in your style for at least two years before trying anything else. Many people earn their black belts in one style before learning another. Trying to learn two (or more) simultaneously means that you won't learn either.

Martial Arts as Therapy

Now, I'm not saying that you're ready to fire your therapist, but martial arts can help you get a grip on emotional issues. Many people have discovered the healing power of martial arts.

Confronting your fears

Often, what holds people back in life is fear. People are afraid of failing, as well as succeeding — afraid of speaking up, and at the same time, remaining silent. No wonder folks feel stressed and anxious.

But learning martial arts is a powerful antidote to all that fear. The first time someone hits you or throws you to the mat, you're probably going to be afraid of getting hurt. The first time that you hit or throw someone else, you're probably going to be afraid of hurting him. But soon you realize that people aren't that fragile. You learn that you're strong, you can defend yourself, and even that you're worth defending. Watch out, boss!

Martial artists who have been abused often find themselves confronting the abuse during their training because all martial arts involve, essentially, violent physical action directed at you. This can be a tricky, emotional time. Learning to defend yourself can help you come to terms with the abuse, but you may need a little extra help. Talk to a trusted friend, join a support group, or talk to a counselor with experience in helping abused people.

Building blocks: Confidence and self-esteem

When you begin training in the martial arts, you feel pretty awkward and stupid. Be comforted: You also *look* pretty awkward and stupid. But that stage soon passes. In no time at all, you'll be performing the throws and locks as if you'd been doing it all your life. Physical mastery of skills like this makes you feel more self-confident and builds your self-esteem. It's our achievements that make us feel good about ourselves, whether that achievement is a perfect front kick or a good score on a math test.

At least one martial arts instructor tells her students to enjoy the beginner phase. "Revel in your awkwardness," she says. "Marvel at how you've had this body all your life and yet don't know what to do with it!"

As you learn the skills, you also develop the self-confidence to face your fears and to live your life the way you always wanted to. You begin to learn that you're a competent person and that you can take care of yourself (and others if you need to). Besides, if you can do a flying side kick, you can pretty much do anything: rebuild that Mustang's engine, start your own business, and earn a graduate degree.

Developing emotional muscle memory

I admit that I stole *this* idea from someone else, too. Carol Stambaugh, a social worker and martial arts instructor, first developed her theory of *emotional muscle memory* when she tried to describe why engaging in activities that are nerve-racking (such as entering a martial arts tournament) can be good for you.

Emotional muscle memory builds on the idea of *muscle memory* — simply the result of thousands of repetitions of a single technique. If you do a side kick 10,000 times, the 10,001th time that you do the kick, you don't really have to think about it. You just do it. If you've been practicing it perfectly, then you'll just do it perfectly.

The less you have to think about what you're doing, the more successful you'll be doing it. Imagine what it would be like if every time you stood up to walk to the refrigerator, you had to think: "Now, put one foot in front of the other . . . "

Riding the entrainment train

Music therapist Janalea Hoffman has written about the principle of *entrainment* or *synchronization of rhythm,* the idea that we all want to be in harmony (rhythm) with the universe. She points out that women who live together soon find their menstrual cycles are in sync. This is because their bodies know the universe wants everything to be in harmony.

Naturally, this principle can be applied to martial arts. One reason people find their training so beneficial mentally and emotionally as well as physically is because it helps them achieve this harmony. On a basic level, the repetitive movements reinforce the principle of rhythm. Sparring, which has its own type of rhythm, is satisfying for this reason, even if you don't win the match.

However, as Carol points out, emotions can take over. Practicing a side kick in class is one thing, but doing it when you're scared is another thing. You may panic, you may forget what to do, and you may miss.

That's where emotional muscle memory comes in. Just as you can practice your kick 1,000 times to build muscle memory, you can practice your techniques when you're scared in order to build muscle memory. In this way, you'll *rehearse* the emotions, so when they hit, your emotional muscle memory automatically takes over, and you just think, "Okay, I've felt this way before, but I did fine then, and I'll be fine now."

What this means is that you should put yourself in situations where you're nervous. You can build your emotional muscle memory by simply performing despite your nerves. Thus, competing in a tournament can help you build your reserves of emotional muscle memory. (It doesn't matter whether you win or lose, as long as you did something.) Think of rank promotion examinations as just another way to build your emotional muscle memory. Agree to do a martial arts demonstration for the local scouting organization. Performing in front of an audience might be scary, but it's good for you.

Chapter 12

Just Like in the Movies: The Lowdown on Weapons

In This Chapter

▶ Training with weapons at your own risk

▶ Learning about traditional martial arts weapons

▶ Understanding basic techniques for using traditional weapons

▶ Using environmental weapons

*O*ne of the most fascinating aspects of training in the martial arts is a weapon, especially because martial arts weapons are so odd and unusual. Heck, who wouldn't want a couple of ninja stars to toss around for fun? Who wouldn't want to learn how to use a sword just like a Samurai?

But when we talk about weapons training, we're actually talking about any one of the following:

✔ Actual training in how to use a weapon.

✔ Instruction in how to defend against a weapon by using a weapon or using empty hands.

✔ The use of traditional weapons only, or it can include modern weapons, as well as *environmental weapons,* which means anything within reach.

So to do justice to the concept of *weapons training,* this chapter briefly describes each of these aspects.

Weapons Disclaimer

In general, traditional weapons training serves one purpose: the preservation of ancient techniques. Weapons training that you receive, whether from an instructor or this book, is not guaranteed. You can hurt yourself if you try to use a weapon or if you try to defend against a weapon. Therefore, the information in this section is described for informational purposes only. Practice using weapons and defending yourself with weapons at your own risk.

What's a Weapon?

A weapon can be considered any means used against an adversary. Thus, your right foot can be a weapon, and so can a rock from your front yard. But in general, weapons are considered to be implements used in combat, such as a gun or a sword.

Some weapons are used to distract the opponent. The ninja stars of movie fame aren't actually thrown at people with the intent of injuring them. Instead, they're thrown at people to startle or cause them to back off.

Weapon categories: Would you like a blade with that?

Weapons are divided into categories, such as bladed, stick/staff, projectile, and composite. See the descriptions that follow:

- ✔ **Bladed weapons** include swords, knives, and halberds, all of which do damage through the use of the blade. Throwing weapons aren't included in this category even if they have blades.

- ✔ **Sticks and staffs** (or staves) are for blocking and striking. Spears and lances, which have long shafts, are considered part of this category even if they have a blade.

- ✔ **Projectile weapons** are thrown or shot at a target, such as arrows and *shuriken* (also known as *ninja stars*). (See Figure 12-1 and the "Shuriken" section, later in this chapter.)

- ✔ **Composite weapons** combine qualities of the preceding categories or achieve their means in an entirely different way. Weapons, such as *nunchuks* and *chainwhips,* fall under this category. (See more on nunchuks in the "Traditional Weapons" section, later in this chapter, and see more on chainwhips in the "Chainwhip" section, later in this chapter.)

Weapon ranges: Going my way?

Weapons are also divided into short-range and long-range weapons. In modern warfare, a long-range weapon can be "shot" from miles away, but *range* has a slightly different meaning when discussing traditional weapons.

Figure 12-1:
Shuriken,
also known
as ninja
stars, are
throwing
weapons.

Short- or close-range weapons include those less than two feet in length, as well as knives, clubs, and *tonfa*. (See Figure 12-2 and the "Tonfa" section, later in this chapter.) Medium-range weapons are those from two to four feet in length, such as the short staff and swords. Long-range weapons measure five feet or more and include spears and lances. Projectile weapons are also considered long-range weapons.

Weapons develop in a variety of ways. Terrain contributes. A lance can be deadly on the open plains but can't do much harm in a heavily wooded area. Local culture and politics also play a part: If weapons, such as the sword, are outlawed, odd-looking weapons, such as the nunchuk, develop.

Traditional Weapons

Traditional weapons have a long history in martial arts. Warrior weapons, such as the sword and the lance, were known throughout the world and were used by Asian martial artists. But unusual weapons, such as the nunchuk, the Escrima stick, and ninja stars developed out of specific needs in the cultures that gave rise to them.

- **Nunchuks** came about when Okinawans were banned from possessing weapons. The nunchuk is based on the *rice flail,* a farming implement; the Japanese overlords of Okinawa couldn't ban a simple farming tool.

- **Escrima sticks** first appeared in the Philippines after the Spanish conquest; the native people, banned from possessing swords, learned to use sticks to defend against the sword.

- **Ninja stars** were developed by the assassin clans in Japan as a way to harry and distract pursuers after the ninja had carried out their deadly deeds.

Figure 12-2:
The tonfa originated in Okinawa, Japan.

Using traditional weapons

Special training is required to use traditional weapons. The purpose of traditional weapons training is *not* fending off muggers with your handy broadsword; rather, traditional weapons capture and re-create some of the ancient ways.

Some martial arts, such as Escrima (see Chapter 19) and certain forms of Kung Fu (see Chapter 15), teach basic techniques that can be performed empty handed or with a weapon. The beginner is taught the empty-hand technique; then, after that's mastered, she is given advanced instruction using the same technique with a weapon.

Sword

In general, people think of the Japanese Samurai *katana* (see Figure 12-3) with its long, narrow, curving blade when they think of a martial arts sword. Depending on the culture and the time period, swords were used differently and even shaped differently. In Japan, the Samurai katana was revered as an awesome tool for nobles and considered a badge of honor. Japanese women carried the *kaiken,* a small sword or dagger, for self-defense or to commit *seppuku* (ritual suicide). In China, the preference was for broadswords with one cutting edge. Broadswords are still used in many Chinese martial arts forms.

Figure 12-3:
The Samurai katana was a badge of honor.

Narrow, long swords are generally used to thrust and slash. Lighter and shorter swords are used for hacking, jabbing, and deflecting. The broadsword, which is quite heavy, was used for horse-to-horse fighting.

Naginata

This Japanese weapon resembles a halberd. Consisting of a curved blade with a single cutting edge attached to a long handle, the *naginata* looks something like a sword attached to a pole. The blade can be from one to five feet long and the shaft from five to nine feet long. Originally, foot soldiers used the naginata for close fighting. But Japanese noblewomen and Buddhist monks were also trained in its use, and the martial art that features it, *Naginata-do,* is still extremely popular among women. For training purposes, a bamboo blade replaces the real McCoy.

The primary technique is a circular slash, which can be used against the sword. Modern contests between *Kendo* (sword art) practitioners and Naginata-do practitioners are popular.

Bo and jo

The *bo* staff (see Figure 12-4) is five or six feet long. The much shorter *jo* staff is really a stick. Staffs and sticks are used to thrust, strike, and sweep. In Escrima (a Filipino stick fighting martial art), practitioners sometimes use two sticks and can trap and lock the opponent's stick.

Figure 12-4:
The bo staff
is used to
thrust,
strike, and
sweep.

Tonfa

Like the jo staff, the *tonfa* (see Figure 12-2) is a stick that can be used to strike and thrust. The tonfa is essentially a two-foot baton with a handle attached at a right angle to it. An Okinawan weapon, it was originally the handle of a rice mill. It can be used against the sword or to defend against other sticks.

Shuriken

Originally, the ninja used these throwing weapons (also known as *ninja stars*), which are made of steel with sharpened edges (see Figure 12-1). They're thrown one at a time or several together. Their purpose is to distract the opponent, although being struck by one can be quite dangerous.

Chainwhip

This Chinese weapon is made of chain links, which can be coiled and easily hid. You can strike, wrap, or sweep with a chainwhip to block and disarm an opponent, much like a sword or staff does.

Nunchuk

This is a flail consisting of two short pieces of wood about eighteen inches long attached with a short length of rope or chain. Originally a farming tool (a rice flail), it can be used to crush, poke, or jab.

Defense against traditional weapons

To defend against traditional weapons, one can use traditional weapons. For example, a sword can be used to defend against a sword. Sticks can be used to defend against staffs and swords. The nunchuk and tonfa can be used against sticks and swords. Using traditional weapons against traditional weapons requires advanced training.

Most martial arts styles also teach empty-hand techniques against traditional weapons. For example, *the high block,* which is a basic block in Karate and Tae Kwon Do, uses the fleshy part of the forearm to defend the top of the head and the forehead. One main use for this block is to defend against someone trying to hit you over the head with an implement. Other techniques, like the spear block and the staff block, really have no modern use, unless someone's trying to jab you with a broom handle.

The high kicks in Tae Kwon Do came from an ancient Korean martial art and were intended to knock a warrior off his horse. Thus, if a fighter dismounted, he would still be able to defend himself against his opponents on horseback.

Modern Weapons

Moderns weapons are those weapons used commonly today to commit crimes and for self-defense. Thus, a knife, which has been around for a couple thousand years, can also be considered a modern weapon.

Using modern weapons

Using knives and guns requires special training. Very little modern weapon use is taught to martial artists. If you're interested in learning, you have to seek separate instruction.

Sadly, most homicides involve a weapon, frequently a gun; and even more distressing, the owner of the weapon involved is often a person who bought it for self-defense. Remember that if you're enraged and you have a gun at hand, what may otherwise be a slightly messy fistfight can become a homicide. Think long and carefully before keeping a weapon in your home. If you do, make certain that it's inaccessible to children. Keep it locked up and make sure the key is with you at all times.

Some schools and instructors teach students how to use a knife. This can be a reasonable skill to learn if you anticipate having to take a knife away from an attacker and use it against him. Using a knife for self-defense is a messy, bloody business. If you want to learn to use a weapon for self-defense, a gun is a more reliable alternative, although remember that it can be used against you, especially if you're not trained to use it yourself.

Defending against modern weapons

Naturally, if one of your reasons for training in martial arts is to protect yourself and your loved ones, you want to learn how to defend yourself against weapons. But defending against modern weapons is tricky and difficult. Not only does it require thorough knowledge of martial arts techniques, but it also requires a complete understanding of modern weapons, along with special weapons defense training, and even then, the results are by no means guaranteed.

Note: If an attacker confronts you with a weapon, using whatever force that's necessary to stop the attack is justifiable. Also, you must decide for yourself ahead of time how you want to handle such a situation. Merely turning and running may get you out of harm's way, especially if your attacker is not well trained in the use of weapons. However, this is by no means guaranteed. And how can you know whether the attacker is well trained?

Some martial arts instructors claim that the empty-hand techniques that they teach can be used against an armed attacker. Investigate these claims thoroughly and practice the technique repeatedly from all possible angles and positions before ever assuming the instructor is correct. Remember, it's your life that may be at risk.

Environmental Weapons

Although some people like to keep handguns around to protect themselves from attack, this presents certain drawbacks. A gun can be used in an argument with deadly results. An attacker may use a gun against its owner. Children can play with a gun, again with deadly results. So having a handgun in your possession is a serious responsibility and not one to take lightly.

At the same time, that handgun can only protect you if it's within reach and loaded when you're attacked. This makes it extremely dangerous.

You should never keep a loaded weapon in a house with children, where children visit, or with a household member who is mentally unstable or possibly suicidal.

Also, in some parts of the world, carrying concealed weapons is against the law; only law enforcement personnel are licensed to carry a weapon. This means that you can't keep your gun with you when you leave the house. So it won't be much good to have a .38 in your dresser drawer when you're jumped on your way home from the grocery store.

For this reason, using environmental weapons is worthwhile if your empty hands (and feet) are not enough. Environmental weapons are any implements in your surroundings that can be used against an attacker.

Look around

Take an inventory of your surroundings. Look around and see what's nearby that you can use as a weapon. Think of the various ways weapons are used: to strike, cut, thrust, block, and distract. What can be used in those different ways? Keys can be thrown to distract an attacker; a book can block a strike; a phone can be thrown; a letter opener can cut or thrust; a blow to the head with a heavy candlestick can KO an intruder. A brick wall can be used by shoving your attacker into it. Be creative.

Practice this awareness wherever you are. When you're in the kitchen, consider what you can use as a weapon if you were attacked there. How about the bathroom? What about while you're in bed? When you're in the office working late, what can be used to stop an attack?

What you know, the attacker can know

Whether you use an environmental weapon or some other implement to stop an attack, being aware of the weapons at your disposal is important because an attacker can use one against you. Thus, you need to be prepared for the fact that while you may not be able to pick up the kitchen knife and shove it into the attacker's chest, she may not have the same qualms. So just because an attacker starts out unarmed doesn't mean she'll end up unarmed. This is also a good reason to stop the attack as soon as you can, finish it, and get away.

By being aware of the items in your surroundings that can be used against you, you'll be in a better position to defend yourself. Awareness of your surroundings can also help you think of prevention in a different way. For example, maybe you're kind of laid-back about keeping the door to the garage locked. If an attacker broke into most suburban garages, he'd have enough tools at his disposal to demolish Fort Knox. So don't make it easier for a potential attacker. Be stringent about your safety precautions.

Defending yourself against environmental weapons also takes special training. But in general, environmental weapons are less deadly than weapons such as handguns, and are therefore easier to defend against empty-handed. For example, someone attacking you with a steak knife has to get close enough to do damage. You can keep him out of range with kicks.

Always get specialized instruction from an instructor with appropriate credentials before assuming that you can defend yourself against any kind of weapon.

Chapter 13

Using Martial Arts Outside of Class

*W*hen people ask you, "Have you ever had to use your martial arts training?" You may hope that the answer is, "No!" But the answer really should be, "Yes, I use my martial arts training every day."

Why? Because what you learn in martial arts training applies to your everyday life, even if you never have to lift a finger to defend yourself against a man with a bat. If you learn focus and discipline in training, then you can have more success in life. If you keep in shape, you'll live longer and have fewer health problems. Many aspects of training can contribute to a happy, rewarding daily life.

But training in martial arts also comes with responsibilities and obligations in daily life, too. Understanding these responsibilities and taking them seriously is important.

Representing Your Art in the World

Although you may never wear a T-shirt saying, "Martial artist in training," the fact is that you represent your art and your school even when you're outside the training hall. You wouldn't want to embarrass your art or school by behaving in any way that may be considered dishonorable, unethical, or lacking in integrity.

It should be your goal to set a good example of martial arts for non-martial artists to see. Not only can you show the world what a good martial artist really is, you can help dispel some of the misconceptions about the martial arts that still linger among non-martial artists, such as the stereotype that martial artists are violent or that practicing the martial arts is like joining a cult.

Think of your school and your art as being just like your mother. If you're contemplating any act that would embarrass Mama, it would embarrass your art and your instructor.

Keeping your cool

One of the most important ways to represent your school and your art well is to always keep your emotions under control. People who have tantrums while standing in line at the grocery store generally don't command a great deal of respect. Always being polite and courteous to people, even if they're nasty to you, is a good way to reflect well on your art.

Keeping your emotions in check also has a practical value: You're less likely to get into a situation where you have to use your self-defense techniques. Many, many violent confrontations start with two people exchanging heated words.

Keeping your cool in training and at competitions is important. Displaying a temper or cursing in frustration is disconcerting to fellow students and is considered unsportsman-like conduct at a tournament — this behavior can even get you disqualified from competition.

Wearing your uniform with caution

Some people dress in their traditional martial arts uniform, then hop in the car, and go to class. Maybe they don't have much time and don't want to mess with changing at the school. Maybe the locker facilities are nonexistent. In any case, be careful about wearing your uniform outside the training hall:

- ✔ First, the uniform really only has meaning inside the training hall, and strutting around in it at the mall on Saturday afternoon isn't exactly a good idea.

- ✔ Second, wearing your uniform can be like an invitation to have some tough guy challenge you to a fight. Preventing fights — not provoking them — is your responsibility. And that some people react this way is sad, but they do.

Bring your uniform in a gym bag and dress at the school. If this is impossible, wear a T-shirt underneath and put your uniform top on at the school. If you need to run errands afterward, take your uniform top and belt off and keep the T-shirt and uniform pants on. You won't win any fashion awards, but the bullies may leave you alone, and you can do your grocery shopping in peace.

Some instructors actually forbid their students from wearing their uniforms outside the training hall. Be sure to obey this rule if it's in place at your school.

No kicking your boss

You should never, under any circumstances, use your martial arts techniques to attack someone. You should only use your techniques to defend yourself and those who are under your protection. This doesn't mean that you have to wait until the mugger is hitting you over the head with a 2-x-4-inch board to defend yourself. But it does mean that you should never provoke an attack and that you should be certain a threat is imminent before you use physical self-defense. Always walk away when you can. See Chapter 9 for more information on self-defense.

When you sign on to train in martial arts, you may not actually take a solemn vow to use your martial arts knowledge only for the good, like superheroes do, but nonetheless, you have a serious obligation to never use your knowledge in a harmful way. By signing on as a martial artist, you essentially do make this pledge, even if you don't recite it out loud. So no kicking your boss, not even if you think it would provide a useful attitude adjustment. (Of course, if your boss comes out of the office swinging, you have every right to duck and counterattack as necessary.)

Every now and then, the newspaper reports how a boxer got into a fight with some poor civilian and has thrown him through the window. This shameful behavior gives all combat sports a bad reputation. A trained fighter can inflict serious damage, much more than an untrained fighter can. If you ever behave like this, not only are you looking at jail time, but you have also forfeited your right to wear your martial arts belt, the symbol of your rank. Keep your cool and never attack another person, no matter what he says to you.

Entering the no-boasting zone

When you were a kid, you may have been in a boasting contest with another kid. "I'm bigger than you are!" you may have said. It may even have been true. In the same way, martial artists sometimes boast about how good they are when they should keep their mouths shut — even if what they're saying is true.

You should never boast about your martial arts prowess. Most people won't care, anyway. Others may take you up on your challenge. And it's not exactly an expression of humility to tell your buddies at the bar: "Yeah, and I can whup your butt with *both* arms tied behind my back! Yeah, and blindfolded, too!" If your buddies have any sense, they'll dump the beer on your swollen head.

Martial artists develop confidence as a result of their training, but it should be a quiet confidence. A person who knows how tough she is doesn't need to advertise it.

Keeping the trade secrets secret

Your instructor has many years of training in the martial arts. She has a commitment to the art and to teaching it. She also provides a framework for the knowledge, offers a safe place to study it, and tries to prevent injuries from occurring.

So when you learn how to throw an opponent to the ground, the first action that you should take is to *not* rush home and teach your best friend the technique. This is an extremely dangerous practice for several reasons:

- First, teaching without context is not only irresponsible but also useless. Maybe that throw only works in certain situations. What if the person that you teach never learns that you aren't supposed to attack unprovoked?

- Second, you haven't mastered the technique yourself. How can you teach someone correctly if you don't know the correct method yourself? You may have done it a few times or even a few dozen times, but that doesn't mean that you've mastered the technique.

- Third, your best friend may injure herself or someone else by trying the technique at home.

Paradoxically, teaching is the best way to learn a martial art. Every martial artist should take the opportunity to teach others when possible. So what does this mean? It means that you should always get your instructor's permission to teach before you do so. It also means that you should take special care when you teach to make certain that you've mastered the techniques and are instructing correctly and that you're offering a safe place — an appropriate context for learning to take place.

If you want to teach, start with your fellow students. Take the time to get to know lower belts and help them learn about the martial art and the school.

Giving back to your school and your art

You owe your instructor more than just this month's tuition payment, and you owe your martial art more than just the bow you do before the start of class. You should always be looking for opportunities to repay your instructor (or your school) and your art for the privilege you've been given of learning at least a couple of life's little secrets.

You can do this a variety of ways. You can help out during class, especially as you become higher in rank. You can teach a class now and then when your instructor needs to take the evening off. You can help the training hall stay clean by picking up after yourself and others and by volunteering to vacuum or sweep. You can write a newsletter for your school. Whatever skills and aptitudes you have, you can find some way to contribute them to the school.

By giving back to your instructor and school, you are in essence giving back to the art. But you can also give to the art in more obvious ways. For example, you can do your best to promote your art — not just by being a good role model but also by encouraging friends and family members to try it. After you have the credentials, you can open your own school or become an instructor at someone else's school. You can find ways to bring the martial art to people who would otherwise not be able to share in it. You could teach an after-school program in a school, or you could offer a scholarship for a disadvantaged child to take lessons.

You can help organize competitions and/or obtain good publicity and PR for your art. The possibilities are limitless.

Incorporating Martial Arts Beliefs into Your Daily Life

When you begin martial arts training, you start on *the Way*. What this means is described more fully in Chapter 11, but essentially, it means that you're committing to living a balanced, moderate life.

Martial arts beliefs don't conflict with religious beliefs or other spiritual practices. They supplement them. So you have no reason to avoid learning all that you can about the martial arts beliefs specific to your martial art.

Finding balance

The symbol of Tao, and of martial arts, is the yin-yang symbol, which represents the conflicting, yet harmonious, elements that make up the universe. These elements can't exist without one another. You can't have night without day; you can't know happiness without sadness. So martial arts philosophy embraces the understanding that good and bad things happen and that everything in the universe is connected.

To be a great martial artist, you must learn to achieve balance in your daily life as well as in the training hall. In the training hall, a well-balanced martial artist may be one who is fit, trains, and performs forms, techniques, practice, and sparring equally well, and who conscientiously adheres to the rules of the training hall. But if this fantastically well-balanced martial artist goes home and never reads a book or wonders about the beauty of the unknowable, he isn't really a good martial artist after all.

A good martial artist balances the *body* (mastering the physical techniques of the martial arts) with the *mind* (stimulating the intellect, as well as disciplining the emotions) and the *spirit* (engaging one's curiosity about spiritual aspects — the nature of the universe, the soul, and the human condition).

Using the tenets

Most martial arts share basic beliefs about how to build character and strengthen individual personalities through martial arts training. The most common of these basic beliefs are called *the Five Tenets.* Although different schools and styles may use different names for these tenets, for the most part, all accept the general concepts of the Five Tenets as being important to martial arts training. For example, Karate emphasizes commitment to training no matter what the obstacles. This would be similar to the tenet of *perseverance,* which is committing to a goal and working to achieve it no matter how many obstacles get in the way.

These tenets are used in the training hall and in everyday life.

Be certain to ask your instructor about the guidelines of the school. Sometimes, these lessons are learned informally; in other schools, you're expected to memorize the tenets, describe how they're used in everyday life, and try to live by them.

Courtesy

In the training hall, courtesy means bowing to your senior students and the instructors, calling the instructors, "Ma'am" and "Sir" or "Sensei" (or some equivalent). Bowing to the *kamidana* (an altar to the spirits) that's placed at the front of some training halls is also courteous. In other schools, you may be expected to bow to a flag representing the country of origin of the martial art (and also the U.S. flag). These are simply salutations, sort of like shaking hands with someone.

Outside the training hall, courtesy means acting with a certain amount of humility. It means letting the person who has one item to purchase go ahead of you in line at your grocery store when you have 72 items in your cart.

Courtesy also means deferring to others, especially the elderly, the very young, and the disabled. Being courteous also means not losing your temper even if someone is discourteous to you.

Being courteous doesn't mean allowing other people to treat you like a doormat. It simply means remaining calm and gracious. You can insist that people treat you with respect even without raising your voice.

Integrity

Integrity is the art of behaving in an ethical, moral manner in all ways and in all matters. In the training hall, integrity is a commitment to learning the art and to teaching it responsibly. It shows integrity if you try to practice perfectly even when no one is looking and you won't win any gold medal for it. Integrity is also representing your school in an honorable way at competitions and demonstrations and simply during class.

Every day outside the training hall, you have challenges to your integrity. You can often see the big challenges coming: Someone offers you a lucrative campaign contribution if only you award the contract to their company. But other, small challenges can be a test to your integrity, too, and you may not realize it. And to have true integrity, you have to act in the right way even about these smaller challenges: A friend asks you to look the other way while she shoplifts lipstick. You walk away from the cashier with an extra five because he miscounted the change. You may use the phone and copy machine at work for personal reasons rather than strictly for business. Perhaps you stand around the water cooler and chat with fellow employees rather than do the work that you're paid to do.

By the number of people who fail to act with integrity over the big challenges (such as illegal campaign contributions), you may wonder what difference it makes whether you send your personal mail through the office mail meter. But it does make a difference. You'll know that you're not acting with integrity. No amount of doing well in competition can rebuild your self-esteem after you decide "everyone's doing it."

Perseverance

In martial arts, perseverance means trying the technique over and over again until you master it, even if it does take you ten years. It means continuing to attempt to break the board even if you missed the first six times. Perseverance means coming to class even when the last class didn't go so well. And it means trying some more even if the instructor criticized your form the last time you did it.

In everyday life, perseverance is crucial to success in any endeavor. When you're trying to break into a demanding, competitive field, such as acting, you have to keep going to auditions even though you may face considerable rejection. In relationships, you may feel like giving up, but if you persevere, you can often get through the tough times.

Before you commit yourself to a goal or a project, make certain that it's worthwhile, and that your goal is something that you truly want to achieve. Remaining dedicated is easier if you consciously choose the goal and aren't simply doing something that your parents think that you should do or that your spouse feels is a worthy pursuit, but you do not.

Perseverance despite rejection or lack of support can be difficult, but a true warrior does it. Many people have succeeded in areas where they initially met with resistance and even without the encouragement of friends and family members. You can do it too by hanging in there and never giving up hope.

Self-control

In martial arts, as in life, self-control is of two kinds. One is physical and one is emotional.

- ✔ **Physical self-control:** In martial arts, self-control often means physical control over one's body. In sparring, you may be expected to spar with no contact or light contact. This requires you to understand what your body can do and to have restraint over it. It means being able to use your techniques correctly and accurately. This type of physical control comes only through disciplined practice. Outside the training hall, physical self-control allows you to carry yourself with dignity and grace. This can do wonders for your self-confidence. If you feel comfortable in your own skin, others naturally respond to your confidence.

- ✔ **Emotional self-control:** In martial arts, emotional control is also important. You should be able to focus at will. You should never let your emotions get the best of you. In a competition, you may disagree with the referee's call, but by remaining in control of your emotions, you still come out a winner. Emotional and physical self-control in the training hall make one a good role model as well as a good martial artist.

  In daily life, emotional self-control helps you get through the inevitable frustrations while remaining on an even, balanced level. When you're able to respond to your 2-year-old's temper tantrums with calm and patience, not only do you feel better about yourself and your parenting skills, but also, your child feels calmer and more confident as well.

THE SENSEI SAYS

Controlling negative emotions

Often, people act out their negative emotions by yelling at others, punching the wall, and otherwise letting go. Losing control both emotionally and physically can be dangerous not just to you but also to others. Punching the wall when your wife disagrees with you is an implied threat to your wife. So don't do it. Instead, learn to control your emotions and express them calmly.

Unfortunately, some martial artists use negative emotions to focus their energy. Occasionally, when someone is having difficulty breaking a board or sparring an opponent, I'll hear a spectator (maybe a martial artist) yell, "Get mad at it!" or "Pretend the guy you're sparring is a boss you hate!" A good martial artist would never do this. You can be focused, determined, and even aggressive without getting mad. By forcing yourself to become angry in order to perform well, you're abusing yourself. You're also *practicing* your anger, which can lead to problems controlling your emotions. *Never* use negative emotions to generate energy and never encourage others to do so.

Indomitable spirit

Indomitable spirit is keeping an unconquerable, courageous attitude no matter what happens. In the training hall, refusing to allow defeat to get you down or to think of yourself as being defeated is an example of an indomitable spirit. You may have lost a match, but that's not the same as being defeated. It doesn't mean you're a bad martial artist or a failure.

THE SENSEI SAYS

One martial artist tells her students this definition: "Perseverance is the action; indomitable spirit is the attitude." Therefore, indomitable spirit and perseverance are closely connected. If you persevere, you're showing indomitable spirit; a person with an indomitable spirit perseveres.

Outside the training hall, keeping a courageous, optimistic attitude can help you get through emotionally difficult times. If you've lost your job, instead of feeling that you're a failure and no one would hire a loser like you, you can think of the job loss as an opportunity. You can pursue other jobs with optimism and vigor. (Employers are more likely to hire a confident, positive person). You can think about changing careers, starting your own business, or going back to school.

If you or someone you love is sick, remain upbeat and positive. This helps you or your loved one heal or at least feel more accepting of the changes that result from the sickness.

Using Martial Arts Training Every Day

In addition to using the philosophy of martial arts in your everyday life, you can use the training itself in your everyday life. Chapter 11 describes some ways to work the mind-body-spirit connection in your everyday life. A few of the more important ways that you can use your martial arts training follow.

Let's get physical

By training in the martial arts, you're committing to improving your level of fitness and your general health. Fitness not only contributes to your ability to throw your opponent to the mat, but it also contributes to your ability to get along in daily life.

General health

Health and wellness professionals agree that part of remaining vibrant and strong throughout your life is participating in physical activities all your life. Getting and staying fit can help you live longer and enjoy the life that you have. Being overweight and out of shape can contribute to problems, such as heart attack and stroke. By committing to regular training in martial arts, you can enjoy better general health in your daily life as well.

Cardiovascular health and endurance

Not all martial arts are aerobic in nature, but most can be. And martial artists can supplement their training with cardiovascular workouts that not only improve their martial arts performance but also improve their health.

Training in martial arts also improves your endurance, which means that you can get through long and trying days without as much fatigue. You can be sharper mentally if you're tougher physically.

Physical strength and agility

All martial arts increase your strength. Even if you don't supplement your martial arts training with weight lifting, you build muscle as you work out. This makes you stronger in your everyday life — more capable of doing the ordinary activities of daily life.

In the same way, martial arts stress the development of flexibility and agility. This is especially important as you grow older. The more flexible and agile a person is, the less likely she is to fall or to strain or sprain joints and muscles. Staying physically active also reduces problems associated with arthritis, which many people suffer with as they grow older.

Building muscle mass also builds bone mass. Because loss of bone mass, known as *osteoporosis,* can cause many problems including increased susceptibility to broken bones, pumping iron (or at least building strength during martial arts training) can prevent long-term health problems.

Playing reindeer games

Learning a martial art, even if you have never been physically active before, can make you more comfortable with your body and thus more open to learning other physical skills or playing other sports. This can open up a whole new world of skills-building and friendships with like-minded people. It also means you won't feel so stupid at the company picnic when everyone else heads to the playing fields to play softball. You can trot alongside them and catch a couple of fly balls, too.

Looking outside yourself

When you train in martial arts, you train in an individual sport, but you're not isolated. In order to learn all aspects of a martial art, you have to perform mock combat (such as sparring) or practice drills with other martial artists. When you do this, you learn to cooperate with people who have similar goals. You start to cheer them on, too. In fact, pretty soon, every time you talk about a friend or acquaintance, you'll say, "I met him in martial arts." And that's great because martial artists are some of the best people to hang around.

Selflessness

When you root for other people to succeed, whether you're cheering on a fellow student at a competition or holding your breath while one of your friends performs an especially difficult technique during a rank promotion exam, you stop focusing on *you* so much. (This is a good thing.) The same selflessness, the feeling of being invested in someone else's success, happens when you give back to your art or when you take time out of your training to teach someone else a new move.

You may find that this selflessness and awareness of others makes you more patient in your daily life and also more willing to help out those around you.

Camaraderie

Where else can you find a group of people who like getting kicked in the head? Although martial artists come in all shapes, sizes, and varieties, you'll find yourself drawn to other martial artists because you share one all-consuming passion. And that's great.

When I started training in martial arts, I was a suburban kid in graduate school. Everybody I knew was just like me, but after I started training, I met people from different races, from diverse social and economic backgrounds, and of all different ages and professions. It was a joy to learn that people of every conceivable background can still unite behind one common cause. And learning to value different characteristics about different people was good for me.

When you make friends only at work or in your neighborhood, you may tend to have only friends who are just like you. Having friends from all walks of life can be much more fun.

Achieving your goals

Training in the martial arts successfully is really just a matter of setting goals and persevering until you achieve them. By learning how to do this, you can gain the skills that you need to achieve whatever goals you dream of in your life outside the training hall. You'll understand how to:

- ✔ Choose and set goals
- ✔ Work toward your goals
- ✔ Handle the inevitable setbacks
- ✔ Enjoy your success after you reach your goal

Hopefully, after you reach a martial arts goal, you'll celebrate with your martial arts friends.

Martial arts training influences all areas of a practitioner's life. It makes you more confident, braver, and willing to take the risks that you always wanted to take. Whatever your goals are, your martial arts training will help you get there.

Part III
Styles, Techniques, and Tactics: An Up-Close Look

The 5th Wave   By Rich Tennant

BARRY STOPS HIS ATTACKERS IN THEIR TRACKS USING A CRANE TECHNIQUE, WHICH ALSO INADVERTENTLY ATTRACKS A FLOCK OF CRANES.

Careful. Those Cranes might be dangerous.

In this part . . .

I offer you a close look at each of the most popular martial arts. In addition to describing the philosophy, basic moves, and training methods, I also offer a little history.

Chapter 14

Karate

In This Chapter

▶ Discovering the history of Karate

▶ Understanding the origin of Karate weapons

▶ Learning basic Karate techniques

Karate is probably the best-known martial art in the West. Whenever most people think of martial arts, Karate is what springs to mind. However, Karate may be done in one of many styles. This chapter helps you to sort them out.

The word *Karate* originally meant *China hand* — the art was named after its Chinese origins. But the founder of modern Karate, Funakoshi Gichin, changed the pronunciation of the Japanese symbols so that they would mean *empty hand.* Although Karate does teach the use of weapons, most of the techniques are also taught empty hand — that is, without weapons.

Some of the most famous professional martial artists, such as Bill Wallace, fought Karate-style. (And Bill Wallace became world champion several times over even though, because of a chronic injury, he could only kick with one foot.)

Physical Considerations

Because Karate comprises so many styles, almost anyone in any physical condition with almost any physical attributes can succeed. But some points to keep in mind are

✔ **Stocky:** Solid stances mean that heavier, stockier people are less likely to be off-balanced.

✔ **Muscular:** An emphasis on power and correct use of techniques means that muscular types can succeed.

✔ **Not so flexible:** Most kicks are to the low or middle section, so awesome flexibility isn't necessary for success.

Avoid schools that have *Kenpo* or *Full contact* anywhere in the description of the style if you're not into heavy physical contact.

Okinawan versus Japanese Karate

Karate originally developed on the island of Okinawa. From this island, it was exported to mainland Japan, where new styles of Karate were created. Both Okinawan and Japanese styles of Karate are taught throughout the world.

Modern Karate spread to Japan in 1922 and to the United States shortly after World War II — less than 25 years later.

Okinawan characteristics

Okinawan Karate styles, such as *Shorin-Ryu, Goju-Ryu,* and *Kempo,* use circular techniques instead of direct, linear strikes. (This is owing to their Chinese origin.) All parts of the body are used as weapons, including elbows and knees, shins, and fingers. Stances are higher and more natural, allowing more mobility but less stability.

Shorin-Ryu

This style of Okinawan Karate is one of the original styles; its name literally means *Shaolin Way* after the famed Chinese Shaolin monastery, which according to legend was the birthplace of martial arts.

There are three main branches: *Shobayshi-Ryu, Kobayashi-Ryu,* and *Matsubayashi-Ryu.* A fourth branch, *Matsumara Orthodox,* is extremely rare.

Forms are emphasized over other aspects of training. *Forms* (often called *kata* or *hyung*) are precise patterns of specific movements incorporating martial arts techniques. For more on forms, see Chapter 5.

Goju-Ryu

This style of Karate was founded in the early 1930s. *Goju-Ryu* combines hard *(go)* techniques with soft *(ju)* techniques — that is, the direct and linear moves with the indirect and circular moves, respectively. These techniques work together. Emphasis is on correct breathing and kata. *Chinese Kempo* (which isn't quite the same as *Okinawan Kempo* — described in the next section) influenced the founder of Goju-Ryu, Miyagi Chojun.

Kempo

Sometimes called *Okinawan Kempo,* this style was greatly influenced by Chinese martial arts, which accounts for its circular movements and evasive techniques. It emphasizes self-defense and self-improvement as twin goals of training.

Japanese characteristics

Japanese Karate styles, such as *Shotokan* and *Wado-Ryu,* on the other hand, emphasize direct, linear strikes, the use of mostly hands and feet (rather than other body parts) and lower stances that allow the practitioner to maintain stability and generate more power. (See the "Shotokan" and "Wado-Ryu" sections coming up next in this chapter.)

Ryu means *school* and often refers to a specific style of Karate.

Shotokan

Funakoshi Gichin, the father of modern Karate, developed this style of Karate. *Shotokan* was Funakoshi's pen name and the name his students gave the style of Karate he taught. Essentially, the teaching philosophy is to learn a few techniques completely. Incomplete understanding of numerous techniques is not, according to Funakoshi, effective martial arts training. Being incompetent with 50 different techniques won't help you against an attacker, whereas if you know even one technique really well, you have a better chance. The techniques of Shotokan Karate are based on a stable stance with thrusting movements that increase power.

Wado-Ryu

A Karate school founded by one of Funakoshi Gichin's students, Otsuka Hidenori, the name means, "the School of the Way of Harmony." Wado-Ryu combines techniques of Jujutsu with the linear strikes of Japanese Karate. Evasion and body shifting are also emphasized. Unlike Shotokan, higher stances and shorter punches are used. Through physical training in the techniques, you're expected to develop mental awareness.

Traditional Training Methods

In the past, Karate students conditioned their bodies using various painful techniques. They struck *makiwara boards* (padded striking posts) with their hands to condition them. They thrust their hands or fingers into pails of sand, called *kan-shu,* to toughen their hands. They carried weighted jars, called *kame,* to increase their grip strength. They also used the *chikaraisha,* an

Okinawan device used to increase strength. This was a heavy stone with a handle attached. Lifting it strengthened the wrists and forearms. A chikaraisha was often carried while practitioners performed kata.

A *Karate-ka* is a person who practices Karate. A form (also called *kata*) is a pattern of techniques done according to a prearranged formula, like a traditional dance. Forms practice teaches Karate-ka (and other martial artists) how to do the techniques and how to move from one stance to another. Kata emphasizes the development of grace and agility.

Some people still enjoy performing these traditional strength-building exercises although others are happy to rely on modern methods. Many schools keep a makiwara board on hand just for old times' sake, and using it can be fun, as long as you use it correctly. (Otherwise, you'll be visiting your friendly orthopedic surgeon.) *Never* kick a makiwara board, not even if a 7-year-old challenges you to. Always make sure that your hands are in the correct striking position before using the post to condition your hands.

Basic Training

Karate training includes *kihon* (basic drills), *kata* (forms), *kumite* (sparring of various kinds), *bunkai* (application of techniques) and body conditioning exercises. When entering or leaving the training hall, you bow to the front of the room *(shomen)*. This is merely a sign of respect. When you greet instructors and senior belts or when you begin any training with partners, you bow to show respect, humility, and the correct attitude. (The correct attitude is *not,* "I am too important to bow to other people.")

The bow that Karate students make is called the *rei.*

The formal kneeling bow, known as *seiza,* is still sometimes used in traditional Karate schools to start and end class.

Traditional Karate practice emphasizes the connection between mind, body, and spirit:

- ✔ **Mind:** Learn concentration, focus, and self-discipline.
- ✔ **Body:** Become more fit and you learn to defend yourself.
- ✔ **Spirit:** Try to live in harmony and balance with the world around you.

The Karate training hall is called a *dojo.* If several schools are organized under one head instructor, the main training hall is called the *hombu dojo.* An instructor is *sensei.* A head instructor of a group of schools is *shihan.* The traditional practice uniform is *gi,* and the belt that keeps it closed is *obi.*

Techniques of Karate

Although Karate has many different styles, each emphasizing different approaches to fighting, most kinds of Karate share some similarities. For example, all styles teach stances, blocks, punches, and kicks — the various types are described later on in this section.

Stances

Stances in Karate provide the foundation for all techniques. If you don't have a good stance, you don't have a good technique. It's that simple. Techniques done from a poor stance are ineffective. Remember that the stance is your base, and your power comes from your base.

A *low stance* (one with the knees more bent) gives more stability, but a *high stance* (one with the knees less bent) gives more mobility. How high or low your stances are depends on your style, your instructor, and what you're trying to accomplish. (For example, in kata training, low stances allow you to generate power and show your good technique; in sparring, high stances allow you to move into and out of range more easily.)

How high or low your stances are also depends on your knees. Those of us with bad knees have a harder time with low stances because bending the knees puts more pressure on them. Doing joint-strengthening exercises, such as lifting weights, can help this.

Each stance — and indeed every technique — has its strengths and weaknesses. Figuring out what these are and taking advantage of them is your job as a martial artist.

Attention stance (Musubi dachi)

The *attention stance* is performed with heels together and arms at your sides. It's used while listening to the instructor or before bowing to senior students and partners. It puts you mentally and physically in the right *position* to begin training.

Front stance (Zenkutsu dachi)

The legs are kept about a shoulder's width apart in the *front stance*. Both feet face forward. The front leg is bent at a 90-degree angle, while the back leg is kept straight. The front leg bears slightly more weight than the back leg.

Back stance (Kokutsu dachi)

This stance is often used in sparring. A side-facing stance, it is performed by pointing one foot forward and the other at a 90-degree angle to it — pointing to the side. Most of the weight is on the back leg.

Hourglass stance (Sanchin dachi)

In this stance, toes and knees are turned inward to give extra stability to the fighter. Not a mobile stance, this stance is mostly used in kata.

Horse stance (Kiba dachi)

The *horse stance* is used in almost every style of martial arts, and in all cases, this stance is one of the first stances taught to beginners. The knees are bent and feet are positioned parallel to each other with toes pointing forward in this solid stance. Weight is distributed equally between both legs, as shown in Figure 14-1 in this chapter.

Guards, guards!

Guard positions are used to protect your body and head from attack. Essentially, you simply keep your hands up and ready to defend against your opponent's strikes.

- **Middle guard position:** You make your hands into fists and bend your elbows so that your arms protect your chest and rib cage.

- **Low-guard position:** One of your hands drops down to protect your forward leg.

- **High-guard position:** Both arms come up to protect the head, but this leaves the chest and ribs unprotected.

Figure 14-1: The horse stance (Kiba dachi).

Blocks

To block an attack, you simply use your arm (or less often, your leg) to push the attack away. This prevents a kick or punch from striking to a more vulnerable part of your anatomy. A block is usually a movement, not just a static position; it has a starting place and an ending place, and the movement in between is generally a sweeping motion designed to move an attacker's hand, foot, stick, or whatever out of the way.

Upper block (Jodan uke)

Sometimes called a *high block,* in this technique, the arm comes up to protect the head and deflect a strike to the high target area of the body.

Crescent block (Soto ude uke)

In this technique, the arm moves from the outside to the inside to protect the midsection and sweep away any technique. When this block is performed from the inside to the outside, it's called *Uchi Ude Uke.*

Downward block (Gedan barai uke)

In the *downward block,* the arm sweeps across the lower part of the body to defend against a kick or punch to the legs.

Blocks use a twist of the wrist at the end of the technique in order to add more power and to ensure that the correct part of the arm meets the attack.

Punches

In a Karate-style punch, you make your hand into a fist, chamber your arm at your waist with your elbow bent and your palm facing upward, and thrust toward the target straight from the waist, twisting your wrist as your punch lands so that your palm now faces down.

If you're aiming high, the punch travels up from the waist; if you're aiming low, it travels down from the waist; if you're punching to the middle, it travels straight from your waist to the target.

Boxers argue that punches should start from the shoulder — not the waist — but that's *boxing,* not Karate.

Some Karate styles have the middle knuckle protrude slightly from the fist to help prevent the wrist from rolling.

High punches are always performed at eye level, not over the top of someone's head (as beginners commonly do); middle punches are always performed to the *solar plexus* (between the rib cage and the navel); and low punches are always performed to the groin. Ouch!

Punching with your bare knuckles is different from punching with gloves or sparring gear on. In a self-defense situation, if you bop someone in the jaw with your bare knuckles, you're going to be sporting some pretty swollen knuckles. (You may also be rolling on the ground in pain, cradling your broken hand.) Instead, strike to the softer parts of your attacker's anatomy, such as nose, throat, groin, or solar plexus — *not* the sternum or rib cage. *Remember:* Bone against bone breaks bones.

Straight punch (Oi tsuki)

A *straight punch* is done on the same side as the forward leg in any stance. For example, if you're in a front stance with your left leg forward, then you would do a straight punch by striking with your left hand.

Reverse punch (Gyaku tsuki)

The *reverse punch* is done with the hand on the same side as the back leg in any stance. For example, if you're in a front stance with your left leg forward and your right leg back, a reverse punch would be done with your right hand.

Other hand techniques

You can hit someone with pretty much any part of your hand, and it's a legitimate Karate technique. The variations are practically endless. You can use the back of your hand, the back of your fist, and the palm of your hand, among other surfaces.

The quintessential Karate strike, the *knife-hand strike (Shuto uchi)* is done with an open hand. The palm and the fingers are kept straight, and the fingers are held tightly together. The thumb is bent, and the side of the hand is used as the striking surface, as shown in Figure 14-2.

Just for kicks

Karate has five basic kicks. They can be performed with either leg in almost any stance, although you'll find that performing some kicks in some stances and other kicks in other stances is easier.

In most styles of Karate, the more upright that you keep your body when kicking, then the better. You're harder to put off-balance this way.

Figure 14-2:
The knife-hand strike.

Kicks should be performed quickly. You should pull your leg back as fast as possible so that your opponent doesn't grab it and dump you on your head.

Front kick (Mae geri)

To perform a *front kick,* shown in Figure 14-3, chamber your leg (bending it at the knee) and thrust your leg directly forward. You strike with the ball of your foot.

Round or roundhouse kick (Mawashi geri)

The *round kick* sweeps from the side to a low, middle, or high target, using the instep or ball of your foot as the striking surface.

You can use your shin (instead of your foot) to strike if you're in close. This is a great self-defense technique because it can cause much damage to your attacker.

Side kick (Yoko geri)

The *side kick* (see Figure 14-4) is done by chambering your leg, pivoting on your supporting foot, and striking with the heel or edge of your kicking foot.

Figure 14-3:
The front
kick.

Figure 14-4:
The side
kick.

Back kick (Ushiro geri)

The *back kick* is also called the *reverse kick,* the *turn-back kick,* or the *reverse-side kick.* To do it, you pivot backward on your supporting foot, chambering your kicking leg as you turn, and then strike out with the heel of your kicking foot.

Crescent kick (Mikazuki geri)

This kick doesn't require a chamber. You simply swing your leg up and to the inside (or outside, depending on where your target is in relation to your leg), and then sweep your leg across and down. The heel or the ball of the foot can be used to strike the target.

Smash-mouth Karate

Although the emphasis in Karate is on using various parts of your hands and your feet to strike the opponent, you can also use your knees and elbows to strike. These techniques are often called *smashes* — knee smashes and elbow smashes. Essentially, you just smash your knee or elbow into a soft portion of the opponent's anatomy (such as the underside of the jaw, the groin, or the solar plexus), and voilà! You win the fight.

Elbow and knee smashes aren't often allowed in competition, but they do make excellent self-defense techniques.

Sweeps, throws, and takedowns

Karate styles also teach the use of

- **Sweeps:** You sweep the opponent's legs out from under.
- **Throws:** Pushing or pulling the opponent off his feet.
- **Takedowns:** Any other method of forcing the opponent to hit the deck.

You don't necessarily have to be bigger and badder than your opponent to knock him to the floor. You just have to apply the correct leverage at the right time. Figure 14-5 shows an example.

Sweeps, throws, and takedowns are sometimes allowed in Karate competition. Not only should you use them if they are, but you should look out for them. These techniques are also extremely effective in self-defense situations.

Figure 14-5:
A takedown.

Weapons, we've got weapons

After you master the basic empty-hand techniques, you may graduate to learning how to use traditional Karate weapons. You can do many of the same techniques with or without a weapon. For example, your guard position may be the same whether you have a *nunchuk* (see Figure 14-6) in your hand or not; and you can perform a crescent block empty hand or with a *tonfa* (see Figure 14-6). For more on weapons, including the nunchuk and the tonfa, see Chapter 12.

However, because the weapons of Karate are so unusual, using them all effectively requires special training. You have to learn which empty-hand techniques can also be done with a weapon (and with which weapon). Trying to use a nunchuk while performing a high block will probably result in you braining yourself. Special weapons kata are taught that show the correct use of the weapons.

You can take a page out of the book of the ancient Okinawans and look around you to discover all kinds of potential weapons that could be used in self-defense — a letter opener, a hammer, and even an umbrella.

Figure 14-6:
Blocking
techniques
with
weapons.

A little Okinawa history

Okinawa, an island in the East China Sea, is where the art of Karate first flourished. Okinawa was subject to Chinese, Japanese, and native influences, all of which contributed to the development of the techniques of Karate.

Chinese settlers arriving in the late fourteenth century brought Chinese self-defense techniques with them, and Chinese martial artists taught their fighting systems to Okinawans. Their techniques combined with an indigenous fighting system called *te.*

In the fifteenth century, ownership of weapons by anyone other than the ruling class was banned. So the members of the lower classes — merchants and peasants — used everyday implements for weapons, including flails *(nunchuks),* staffs *(bo),* and sickles *(kama).* The ruling classes probably wished they'd left well enough alone after they saw how effective a farming tool could be against a sword.

By the seventeenth century, a fighting system combining Japanese and Chinese techniques had developed on Okinawa. It was given the name *Kara-te,* which has stuck for a couple hundred years.

All classes of Okinawan society — including the military or warrior classes, the peasants, and the merchant class — quickly picked up the techniques and used them in self-defense. (All right, some of them may have used the techniques to attack other people, but that's not what the techniques were intended for.)

Chapter 15

Kung Fu

In This Chapter

▶ Discovering the many Kung Fu styles

▶ Thinking about your body type

▶ Breathing with Chi Kung exercises

▶ Using traditional training methods

Ah, yes, Grasshopper . . . the styles of Kung Fu are many, but they share some similarities. In this chapter, you learn the basics about the most popular styles, plus discover the related arts of *Chi Kung (Qi Gong)* and *Wushu.* For more on Chi Kung, see the "Chi Kung Exercises" section, later in this chapter.

The name *Kung Fu* means *human effort.* Chinese martial arts would be more appropriately called *Wushu,* which means *arts of war.* But the word *Wushu* is now applied to a performance-oriented Chinese combat sport that empha- sizes acrobatic techniques. Even the Chinese now use the term *Kung Fu* to refer to their martial arts.

Throughout Chinese history, Kung Fu styles were developed and passed along in secret. Kung Fu was a secret practice because the motivation behind it sprang out of political or religious groups that were in opposition to the existing government. Kung Fu was a way of protecting themselves in the event that they would be harassed or arrested by official decree. Little infor- mation was written down and public demonstrations were few and far between. Many styles may still remain secret or have been lost forever because they weren't passed down. Secret societies trained the *Chinese boxers* (martial artists). These secret societies advanced political, religious, and even criminal aims and taught martial arts to members. Some of these secret societies still exist.

The best-known Kung Fu expert is Bruce Lee, who popularized this style of martial arts first through teaching and then through acting. When Bruce Lee died in 1973, Kung Fu was at its height of popularity because of him. Even though he invented *Jeet Kune Do* (see Chapter 22), it was his expertise in Kung Fu that started the craze.

Categories of Kung Fu Styles

Hundreds of styles of Kung Fu exist. Some resemble gymnastics more than they do combat training; some include grappling techniques, others include Karate-type hand techniques, and still others teach unusual stances and esoteric movements otherwise seen only in the animal kingdom.

In order to get a grip, you need to have some understanding of how the styles relate to each other — how they're similar and how they're different.

Fortunately, Kung Fu styles are conveniently divided into different categories for just this purpose. The categories are: Northern styles, Southern styles, Internal styles, and External styles. (Keep in mind that these categories, like all categories, are highly artificial, and you can find Northern styles that look like Southern styles. Not to mention Internal styles that look like External styles.)

Kung Fu includes the arts of self-defense *(Koshu)*, combat sports *(Wushu)*, and exercises for health *(Chi Kung)*.

Northern versus Southern styles

Traditionally, the inhabitants of northern China were tall, slender people. The martial arts they developed took advantage of this physical type, and so Northern styles typically emphasize kicking techniques and footwork for which being tall and long-legged is a plus.

The shorter, stockier inhabitants of southern China, on the other hand, developed their martial artistry to take advantage of their anatomy: Southern style typically emphasizes punching techniques.

Internal versus External styles

Kung Fu styles can also be classified as Internal or External. External styles are based on physical techniques, power, and strength. Force and speed are developed. Focusing on developing inner energy *(chi)*, which improves concentration and focus, the Internal styles require more time to master than the External styles. (For more information on your chi, see Appendix A.) Internal styles tend to be more defensive in nature, using soft, circular techniques.

Don't Get Bent Out of Shape

Just as Northern and Southern styles of Kung Fu were adapted to meet the needs of people with certain body types, you may have more success in Kung Fu if you choose a style that suits your body type.

- ✔ **Tall and lean:** If you're tall and lean, then the Northern styles may work better for you.

- ✔ **Short and stocky:** If you're shorter and stockier, then a Southern style is probably for you.

- ✔ **Short and lean:** According to legend, a woman developed Wing Chun (described in the "Wing Chun" section, later in this chapter), which suits smaller people who lack heft and height.

- ✔ **Agile:** Flexibility isn't such an important factor in Kung Fu because kicks are generally low, but you need to develop agility to do the *sticky-hands* techniques and the body shifting and unusual postures that some styles require.

In general, you don't think of Kung Fu, with its traditionally soft, circular movements, as being especially hard on your body. But remember that some styles are full contact, which means that you or your partner will sustain a knockout. Make sure that you know how much contact to expect before you agree to be someone's sparring partner.

Popular Kung Fu Styles

Many Kung Fu styles are based on the movements of animals. The founders of these so-called animal styles watched animals in nature, analyzed how they fought, determined what techniques they used to win, and then tried to adapt what they saw into a fighting system that humans can use, even though human anatomy is slightly different.

Northern Praying Mantis

Northern Praying Mantis is a Kung Fu style based on an animal, or in this case, an insect. According to legend, the founder, Wong Long, watched the speed and strength of the praying mantis and tried to duplicate its powerful jaw movements.

Northern Praying Mantis style is based on successive, rapid-fire techniques intended to overwhelm the opponent. The mantis claw, a grabbing motion that requires a powerful wrist and forearm, distinguishes this style, which uses both linear and circular techniques.

Monkey style

Monkey style *(Tai Sing)* is known for its tumbling and rolling techniques, so artists must be flexible and agile. Kao Tze, who watched monkeys play and fight while he was imprisoned, is the founder of this style. He discovered that the monkeys used five basic fighting patterns, and he attempted to duplicate them in his style. Figure 15-1 shows the Monkey style in action.

- **Drunken Monkey:** Elusive and hard to catch, the Drunken Monkey isn't really drunk but is just pretending to be. The Drunken Monkey confuses and takes advantage of the enemy.

- **Stone Monkey:** Using sheer physical force to dominate opponents, the Stone Monkey is strong and powerful and overwhelms the competition.

- **Lost Monkey:** Looking confused and uncertain, the Lost Monkey is actually neither. She changes footwork frequently so that opponents can't detect her rhythm.

- **Standing Monkey:** The Standing Monkey uses traditional stances and relies less on rolling and falling.

- **Wooden Monkey:** Aggressive but quiet, the Wooden Monkey attacks ferociously when he spots an opening.

Choy-Li-Fut

This style, one of the most popular styles of Kung Fu in Asia, combines hard *(go)* techniques with soft *(ju)* techniques — that is, the direct and linear moves with the indirect and circular moves, respectively. These techniques work together. Choy-Li-Fut also combines Northern and Southern characteristics. Speed, balance, and power are all necessary to perform the techniques appropriately. Chan Heung founded this style in 1836, and it has its origins in Shaolin martial arts. Originally a secret society, the system trained martial artists to fight against the imperial Manchurian army.

The Choy-Li-Fut style includes numerous hand and weapons forms — more than 100 exist in the style. (*Forms,* also referred to as *kata* or *hyung,* are patterns of techniques that hone your fighting skills. See Chapter 5 for more on forms.) The forms include both Internal and External styles, making this one of the most comprehensive of Chinese fighting systems. The External style training is taught first; after the student masters these forms, he's ready to begin Internal style training, such as the development of *chi.* (See Appendix A for more on chi.) Most of the forms contain at least 100 movements, and some contain as many as 300. Doing such forms builds strength and endurance.

Figure 15-1:
The Monkey
style.

Many schools teach Choy-Li-Fut as a full-contact style, and some of the best full-contact martial arts competitors study this style. Beware if you get in the ring with any of them!

Main characteristics

The practitioner must be strong but flexible. A balanced stance is used, with the waist as the pivot point. Short-hand techniques balance the circular long-arm techniques.

Think of *long-arm techniques* this way: The martial artist can extend her arm completely, generating full power. For *short-hand techniques,* she can strike in close with equally powerful strikes. In the first case, the power is generated through relaxed movement, and in the latter case, the power comes from the pivot of the entire body into the strike.

The Choy-Li-Fut martial artist's arm is supposed to be like a rope — loose and flexible — and her hand is supposed to be like a rock — solid and strong.

The arsenal of techniques

Four basic punching techniques are taught: the straight punch, the back fist, the uppercut, and the roundhouse. Elbow strikes, knee strikes, sweeps, throws, and grappling techniques are also used. Pressure-point strikes are taught to advanced practitioners.

Weapons training

Weapons used include staff, spear, broadsword, double-edged sword, trident, and cane. Battle axes, butterfly knives, chainwhips, and double-hook swords are also used. (See Chapter 12 for more information on weapons.)

Wing Chun

According to legend, a woman was the founder of this style — one of the few styles of martial arts founded by a woman. The story goes that a young girl, Yim Wing Chun, wanted to learn Shaolin martial arts, and a nun, Ng Mui, taught her to use simple, direct techniques and quick counterattacks. The style emphasizes self-defense over flashy, difficult maneuvers.

Training methods include the wooden dummy and sticky hands *(chi sao)* technique. (Look in the "Traditional Training" section, later in this chapter, for more information on chi sao.)

Wing Chun has several different schools. Sifu Yip Man taught Bruce Lee who practiced the most popular and most famous school of Wing Chun. Wing Chun Kung Fu is the only martial art Bruce Lee ever studied formally. This so-called "slant body" school is a highly aggressive style of martial art, with no wasted energy.

A *sifu* is a martial arts teacher in Chinese.

Wing Chun teaches that you have five ways to defeat the enemy:

- Joint locks
- Kicks
- Strikes
- Throwing
- Weapons

Thus, the techniques taught are generally divided into those five categories.

A straight, linear approach is used because the shortest distance between two points is a straight line. Thus, this is the most efficient approach. Mostly hand techniques, which are faster than kicks, are used, and kicks are targeted only to the low area. Techniques allow a block and an attack to be performed in the same movement.

Two other Wing Chun schools include *side body* and *pao fa lein,* which emphasizes weapons use.

White Crane

Also called *Llama* or *Tibetan White Crane.* Although this is a Southern style, *White Crane* has footwork and kicks that seem more similar to Northern styles. Purely a defensive system, White Crane practitioners never attack. It uses the opponent's force and energy against him.

The most obvious characteristic of White Crane style is how the practitioner keeps his arms outstretched for balance (see Figure 15-2). One hand draws the opponent's attention while the other hand strikes.

The opponent never knows which hand is the distracting hand and which is the attacking hand because it can change in a moment. The White Crane practitioner allows little close physical contact and tries to keep out of range of the opponent as much as possible

Figure 15-2:
White Crane
style.

The White Crane practitioner strikes quickly and moves constantly, using low stances and circling techniques. The White Crane expert can kick high with great speed but only low kicks are used in combat; the side kick is especially popular.

Chi Kung Exercises

Chi Kung (Qi Gong) exercises are related to Kung Fu and are often taught along with Kung Fu or T'ai Chi (see Chapter 23). These exercises aren't martial arts techniques in and of themselves, but they supplement the martial arts techniques that you learn in Kung Fu and T'ai Chi. Chi Kung exercises help release the negative energy that interferes with your ability to relax. Your ability to relax is crucial in terms of maintaining mental health, and also in making calm, effective choices when under stress (such as when a maniac with a knife jumps out of the bushes while you're on your daily walk with the dog).

Active Chi Kung requires movement, and *passive Chi Kung* involves mental techniques, such as imagery, to produce similar results.

Chi means *inner energy,* and *kung* means *work,* so *Chi Kung* is *inner energy work.*

Because chi, your inner energy, can help you perform your techniques, it pays to be able to tap into it. Chi Kung breathing exercises are used for this purpose, especially by Internal Kung Fu styles.

Whether you actually practice Chi Kung, you should pay attention to your breathing especially during martial arts practice. Correct breathing helps keep your blood oxygenated and improves endurance. Most of the emphasis in Chi Kung is on breathing deeply, even yawning. Meditation may be involved, simply to rid the mind of negative energy.

Traditional Training

Because the art of Kung Fu is centuries old, practitioners have used many traditional training methods. Some are still popular today; others have been discarded to avoid raising your health insurance rates. See if you can tell which ones have been discarded and which methods are still in use in the following list:

- **Sticky Hands (Chi Sao):** This Wing Chun exercise involves two people who face each other (see Figure 15-3). They place their wrists and fore-arms together and then move their wrists in small circles, maintaining physical contact at all times. This exercise sensitizes the marital artist to his opponent and helps him learn to predict the opponent's next move. The partners work faster and faster, challenging each other to focus only on the experience at hand.

- **Wooden Training Dummy (Mook Jong):** The Wing Chun wooden training dummy consists of an approximately human-size, upright post with various projections extending from it. Two projections resemble arms, and one resembles a leg. Other projections may be placed at the midsection so that the different techniques can be attempted at various target areas.

The training dummy allows you to use your techniques full power (which in general you don't do against a partner), and helps you toughen your muscles and bones. Figure 15-4 shows a mook jong training dummy in use.

The *mon fat jong* training dummy is the luxury edition: Springs recoil when you strike it so that you can see if you applied your techniques correctly and so that you can determine how much power you're generating.

Figure 15-3:
Sticky
Hands.

✔ **Striking Posts (Chi Shing Chung):** To build leg strength and to condition the legs, posts are sunk into the ground. The martial artist kicks them, eventually building enough muscle and conditioning his legs so that the artist can break the post with a kick.

Mei-hwa-chuang are posts that are driven into the ground, atop which the martial artist performed his techniques. Staying on top of the posts while performing a form or executing various techniques requires balance and agility.

✔ **Weight Equipment:** The *chashi* is a heavy block with a handle that builds arm strength. Traditional Chinese martial artists use it like a free weight.

Figure 15-4:
Practicing
with a mook
jong training
dummy.

Kung Fu Weapons

Some Chinese weapons are obscure, and some are well-known, but Chinese weapons number in the hundreds. (See Chapter 12 for more information on martial arts weapons.)

Kung Fu history

Some historical records describe Chinese martial arts, which trace back to 5000 B.C. Throughout its history, China fought off invaders and struggled with internal divisions. It's not surprising that methods of self-defense and even of attack were developed throughout the centuries of conflict.

During the Warring States period (475–221 B.C.), violence erupted throughout the country. At this time, many thousands of ordinary peasants and merchants learned martial arts techniques to protect themselves. Martial arts were no longer a privilege of the warrior class.

A freelance martial artist, Liu Pang, unsatisfied with the state of the country, became the leader of an army of like-minded followers. He (with a little help from his army) overthrew the emperor and established himself as the first emperor of the Han Dynasty in 202 B.C.

During this era, a doctor, Hua-to, created a series of exercises based on the movements of animals. These exercises are thought to be the origin of many Kung Fu animal styles.

But according to legend, the Indian monk Bodhidharma (460–534 A.D.) brought martial arts to China when he taught the basic principles of physical fitness to the monastics at the Shaolin Temple. Bodhidharma was the founder of Zen Buddhism, and he traveled throughout Asia, promulgating his spiritual doctrine.

Even if Chinese martial arts had been well-established before the arrival of Bodhidharma, it's true that at the Shaolin Temple (first in the Hunan province in the north and then in the Fukien province in the south), monastics learned and taught the martial arts.

An irritated emperor eventually burned the Shaolin temple down, and many monastics were executed. Those not wishing to meet that fate fled, taking their martial arts with them. This is how Chinese martial arts spread throughout Asia.

Many styles of Kung Fu came with Chinese immigrants to America in the nineteenth and twentieth centuries. This was especially true after the suppression of the Boxer Rebellion (1900), and thousands of Chinese martial artists were forced to flee their country.

At first, Chinese teachers continued to keep their arts secrets, teaching their methods to only a select few students who had proven to be ethical and trustworthy individuals. They refused to teach non-Chinese students for the good reason that the Chinese were already seriously oppressed, and giving the outsiders yet another tool of oppression would be foolish. But over time, this changed, and many non-Chinese began to learn and teach Kung Fu. Bruce Lee was one of the first to teach non-Chinese students in the 1960s.

Historically, the Chinese martial artist would carry at least three weapons: One was primary, another was hidden, and the third was a dart. All were useful for different self-defense needs. The Chinese martial artist would be most skilled in the use of the primary weapon, such as a sword; he would keep a hidden weapon (such as a dagger tucked in the belt) to respond to surprise attacks; and he would carry a dart weapon (such as a sleeve arrow) for in-close fighting or for long-distance attacks.

Chinese weapons are still used in Kung Fu styles, mostly during the performance of kune. Pairs of Chinese broadswords are most often seen.

A *kune* is Chinese for *form*.

Kung Fu Techniques

Because so many styles exist, showing basic techniques common to all of them is impossible. In general, Kung Fu styles teach postures (stances), guards, blocks (which are often called *deflections* because they merely redirect the opponent's energy and are not full-power blocking techniques), fist attacks, and foot attacks. Some styles teach grappling techniques, throws, joint locks, and vital point striking.

Chapter 16

Tae Kwon Do

In This Chapter

▶ Learning what physical attributes may help

▶ Finding out what those flashy jumping kicks are for

▶ Building endurance with Tae Kwon Do

▶ Discovering how to do basic techniques

Drop those Tae-Bo tapes. If your only exposure to Tae Kwon Do has been through Billy Blanks videos, look out! In Tae Kwon Do, you can learn flashy jumping kicks, high kicks, and spinning kicks that would make an aerobics teacher dizzy. (You may also fall down plenty while attempting to master these techniques, but that's just a basic part of training.)

The high kicks, although not necessarily practical for street defense, are useful in competition; the jumping kicks are a nod toward tradition: Ancient Korean martial arts taught them so that a foot soldier could knock a mounted warrior off his horse. Spinning techniques generate much power and can be performed quickly.

Korean Karate, as Tae Kwon Do used to be called, is the modern version of ancient Korean fighting systems. Tae Kwon Do resembles Karate because of its emphasis on linear strikes, but vast differences exist between them (and not just because Tae Kwon Do originated in Korea and Karate originated in Okinawa). This chapter helps you understand more about Tae Kwon Do, now the most popular martial art in the United States and growing in popularity around the world.

General Hong-Hi Choi is credited as the founder of modern Tae Kwon Do, which was given its name in 1955.

Hard Bodies, Hard Heads

Contact is usually controlled, so you probably won't break too many ribs in this style, but expect some bruises (mostly from falling down while you try to learn the kicks). Also, board-breaking is practiced in many Tae Kwon Do schools, so if you're not interested in stacking firewood for the winter, make sure you know what you're getting into.

- ✔ **Fast:** Tae Kwon Do emphasizes kicks: high kicks, jumping kicks, spinning kicks, and even humble kicks to the shin, so you need to be fast on your feet.

- ✔ **Flexible:** Natural or acquired flexibility is a must to perform the techniques most effectively.

- ✔ **Strong and lean:** Lean but muscular people often have the advantage because Tae Kwon Do relies on speed and power

- ✔ **Tall:** Tall people can reach farther with the kicks; kicks to the head score more points than kicks to the body.

The emphasis of training is on empty hand (without weapons) techniques. Weapons are not traditionally taught in Tae Kwon Do even though you may come across a Korean sword and the Korean martial art of archery. Many techniques were developed to defend against weapons. (Some techniques, such as the staff block, aren't necessarily applicable to modern threats but are fun to perform.) The Tae Kwon Do practitioner learns literally dozens of techniques, any of which may be suitable for a particular self-defense situation — all without having to pick up a weapon.

The Five Tenets

Tae Kwon Do practitioners are expected to develop mind, body, and spirit. To this end, they build character by following the Five Tenets of Tae Kwon Do: courtesy, integrity, perseverance, self-control, and indomitable spirit. See Chapter 13 for more information on the Five Tenets.

The Five Tenets aren't spiritual or religious in nature. They're just qualities a good person should strive to have. You're expected to follow the Five Tenets in the *dojang* and outside it.

A *dojang* is a Korean training hall.

Tae Kwon Do versus Tae Kwon Do

Tae Kwon Do has several styles, which are governed by different sanctioning organizations. Although the techniques that the different organizations teach are the same, they do differ in the *forms* (see Chapter 5) that they teach and in how sparring is taught and scored.

The words *hyung* and *poomse* mean *form*.

Traditional Tae Kwon Do

Traditional Tae Kwon Do schools follow the guidelines of General Hong-Hi Choi, the founder of modern Tae Kwon Do. They tend to be affiliated with his organization, the International Tae Kwon Do Federation (ITF).

Traditional schools teach all aspects of Tae Kwon Do equally. That is, sparring isn't considered more important than forms, and repeated practice of techniques is as important as board-breaking. Competition isn't the main purpose of training. In traditional Tae Kwon Do schools, you learn all the techniques eventually, not just those that are most effective for sparring or a street fight.

Traditional Tae Kwon Do training includes the following:

- Board-breaking
- Body-conditioning exercises and drills
- Forms
- Repetition of techniques
- Sparring (both step-sparring and free-sparring)

Step sparring is a method of practicing fighting techniques under carefully controlled circumstances. The attacking partner performs a technique — a kick or a punch — and the defending partner uses a pre-arranged series of blocks and counter-attacks to respond to the strike. Both partners know what to expect and since little or no contact is allowed, students can learn the building blocks of sparring without feeling intimidated or scared and without worrying about getting hurt.

Free sparring, also called free fighting or free-style sparring, is a type of mock combat in which partners attack, defend and counter-attack continuously without using any pre-arranged pattern of techniques. Contact may be heavier; neither partner knows what the other partner is going to do, so it more accurately mimics what an actual fight is like. Free sparring improves timing, blocking, evading and footwork skills, but is slightly riskier since fighters can miscalculate and land a stronger blow than intended.

Traditional Tae Kwon Do sparring is scored on a point system. Any technique that lands unblocked on a legal target area earns a point. Thus, speed and finesse are more important than power. These matches tend to be no contact or light contact.

Sport or Olympic style Tae Kwon Do

But many Tae Kwon Do schools have a more sport- or competition-oriented approach. The World Taekwondo Federation (WTF) sanctions Olympic and international tournaments, so you must choose an affiliated school if you're going to go for the gold.

In the United States, only certified United States Taekwondo Union (USTU) schools are recognized by the WTF. Thus, you need to enroll in a USTU school to compete in WTF competition. In other countries, the WTF recognizes other schools and organizations. Check to see if a particular school is WTF-affiliated if that's important to you.

WTF-style schools emphasize learning the most effective techniques, rather than building an arsenal of rarely used jumping reverse inside-outside crescent kicks.

In WTF sparring, a trembling shock or blow must occur for a point to be awarded. That is, the opponent's body must visibly move through space as a result of the blow. Simply landing an unblocked technique isn't enough. Thus, power is more important than speed and finesse. These matches tend to have heavier contact.

Other Tae Kwon Do approaches

Other organizations accredit Tae Kwon Do schools. These include the American Taekwondo Association (ATA) and the United States Taekwondo Federation (USTF). Outside the United States, you'll find the British United Tae Kwon Do Federation, the International Tae Kwon Do Association and the International Tae Kwon Do Council, among others.

Kwan means *school* in Korean. Early schools of Tae Kwon Do were *moo duk kwan, chung do kwan,* and *ji do kwan.*

Because Tae Kwon Do schools offer different approaches to training, you should have an idea of what your goals are before you sign on with a school. There's nothing wrong with going to a traditional Tae Kwon Do school to learn that jump reverse inside-outside crescent kick, but if your heart is set on going to the Olympics, you have to choose a WTF-style school.

Because of their different approaches, be aware that even in local and regional competitions or in open competitions (where you can do any style as long as you show up in a clean uniform), the rules are different depending on which organization is sanctioning or organizing the event. Know what the rules are before you spar. See Chapter 10 for more information about competition.

Training Methods

Because conditioning and flexibility are so important to the Tae Kwon Do practitioner, training focuses on repeatedly performing the techniques and on doing stretches to improve and maintain flexibility and agility. Try fighting a three-minute round with no endurance training to get an idea of why the conditioning is important.

The exercises described in the next section, "Strength and endurance training," may be part of a class or training session, but you can also do them on your own to improve your ability to do Tae Kwon Do.

Strength and endurance training

Cross training, including aerobic activity and weight lifting, can help you become a better martial artist, but it isn't required. See Chapter 8 for more information on training.

Instead of hopping on the treadmill or pumping iron, doing the techniques of Tae Kwon Do over and over can build strength and endurance. Sparring the heavy bag for three-minute rounds helps you build the endurance that you need to spar against a live opponent.

Performing techniques in slow motion — for example, taking 30 seconds to complete a side kick — builds strength, balance, and concentration.

Stretching techniques

Doing full-body stretching every day helps you maintain excellent flexibility. Although you can choose from one of several different methods of stretching, such as flexing a muscle before you stretch it, you don't need a complicated approach to stretching. Just keep the basics in mind: Move slowly and smoothly into the stretch position, hold the position for at least ten seconds (and as many as 30 seconds), and then relax.

When doing stretches, don't bounce! And never stretch a muscle until it hurts. If you feel pain when stretching, stop immediately and relax. If the pain persists, see your doctor.

Proprioceptive neuromuscular facilitation (PNF) (phew!) is a technique where you flex a muscle before you stretch it. *Active-isolated* (AI) stretching is a technique where you flex the opposing muscle group before the stretch — for example, you flex your hamstrings just before stretching your quadriceps. Both of these approaches improve the quality of your stretching.

Doing a whole body-stretching routine is sensible, moving from your neck to your ankles, every day. However, you can pay special attention to the stretches that give you the flexibility that you need to do the kicks:

✔ **Side leg/knee bend stretch:** In this technique, you extend one leg to the side and bend the other knee, keeping that foot flat on the floor. Be careful using this technique if you have knee trouble.

✔ **Open stretch:** For this technique, sit on the floor and spread your legs apart as far as possible. Then roll your hips slightly forward so that your body weight is over your legs, helping them to stretch. A variation of this stretch requires you to try to touch your chest to the floor.

✔ **Front-split stretch:** This stretch is done by extending one leg fully in front of you and extending the other behind you. Then touch your chest toward your knee.

✔ **Kick-stretches:** Partner stretches can be done using kicking techniques. For example, you perform a front or side kick, and your partner raises your kicking leg as high as possible, that is, without causing you pain. After holding the stretch for ten or more seconds, the partner releases your leg, and you slowly lower it to the ground. To build strength, attempt to hold your leg in place after your partner releases it.

Basic Techniques

Tae Kwon Do teaches stances, blocks, and fist and foot attacks. Some schools teach intermediate and advanced students *throwing* and *takedown techniques,* in which you essentially force your partner/opponent to the ground, and may also do wrestling-type techniques; *joint locking,* which is the manipulation of joints and immobilization of limbs for the purpose of stopping an attack without permanently injuring the attacker and *vital point striking,* which are strikes to the vulnerable areas of the body, such as the eyes and groin, where a solid hit can do the most damage.

Stances

All techniques are taught in stances. The stance aids the correct performance of the technique. Lower stances (knees more bent) give stability to the martial artist, and higher stances (knees less bent) give more mobility.

Front stance (Chongul ja sae)

In this stance (also called the *forward stance*), the forward leg is bent at the knee and the back leg is extended straight (both feet flat on the ground). The weight is evenly distributed between both legs, although the forward leg may have slightly more weight on it (see Figure 16-1).

Figure 16-1:
Front
stance.

Back stance or fighting stance (Hugul ja sae or Ja yu dae ryun sae)

This is a side-facing stance that makes you a narrower target (see Figure 16-2). The forward foot points straight ahead while the chest and hips face to the side. The back foot is at a 90-degree angle to the front foot. The back leg is bent, and most of the weight rests on the back leg.

In the fighting stance, which is just a modified version of the back stance, the weight is more evenly distributed, and the chest and hips face slightly more forward. This allows the martial artist more mobility, and she can use either leg to kick without shifting weight.

Figure 16-2:
Back
stance.

Horse stance (Kim jae sae)

This technique strengthens the legs and is used in some forms. In it, both feet face forward, and both knees are bent. Weight is distributed evenly on both legs.

Blocks

Blocks are usually full power techniques that move the opponent's attacking limb out of the way. Because the techniques take power to perform but aren't strikes that can score a point or disable an attacker, Tae Kwon Do practitioners also practice footwork, evasion, and body-shifting to move out of the line of an attack.

Low block (Hadan maki)

In this technique, the arm sweeps down from the shoulder across the leg, to push aside an attack to the lower body. The martial artist never reaches down to complete the block. Refer to Figure 16-1, which shows a low block from the front stance.

High block (Sangdan maki)

The arm sweeps up, bent at the elbow, to protect the face and top of the head from an attack.

Crescent blocks (Jungdan maki)

The arm, bent at the elbow, sweeps from inside to outside or from outside to inside to move an attack away from the midsection.

Knife-hand blocks (Sudo maki)

In most blocks, the hand is made into a fist. But in *knife-hand blocks,* the hand shapes itself into a knife, and the knife edge of the hand and the side of the forearm actually perform the block.

A single knife-hand block is performed by keeping the palm and fingers straight. The fingers are held tightly together. The arm, with elbow bent, sweeps across the midsection from inside to outside.

A double knife-hand block is performed with both hands together. Both arms extend back and then sweep across the body, ending with elbows bent, one arm covering the midsection and the other protecting the front or side of the body, depending on what stance you're in when you do it.

In all blocks, the wrist is twisted at the end of the technique to add power and to ensure that the correct blocking surface of the arm (the fleshy part of the forearm) actually makes the block.

Kicks

Tae Kwon Do is well-known for its flashy kicking techniques. The basic kicks, however, aren't difficult to learn. They become more complicated when you do them to the high section, as jumping techniques, and as *double kicks* (one kick after the other in quick succession). Figure 16-3 shows a cool flying side kick.

Front kick (Ap chaki)

For this technique, you simply chamber your kicking leg by bending your knee and then striking with your foot straight to the target, as shown in Figure 16-4. The ball of your foot is the kicking surface. However, if you're trying to smack someone in the groin, you can use your instep.

Figure 16-3:
Flying side kick.

Figure 16-4:
Front kick.

Roundhouse kick (Doll rye chaki)

This kick comes sweeping from the side of the body to the target (see Figure 16-5). The instep of the foot is used. (Sometimes, the ball of the foot is used, especially when breaking a board with this technique.)

Figure 16-5:
Roundhouse
kick.

Side kick (Yup chaki)

For the *side kick,* chamber your kicking leg and pivot on your supporting foot until your heel faces your target. Strike out with the heel or knife edge of your kicking foot, as shown in Figure 16-6.

Crescent kicks (Chiki chaki)

Crescent kicks are done by swinging your leg up and to the inside or the outside (depending on where the target is) and then across and down. As your foot reaches the height of its arc and starts to come across, that's when the strike (with the side of your foot) occurs.

A variation, the *axe kick,* is done when the strike occurs after the foot reaches the height of its arc. In this case, the foot slashes directly downward and the heel of the foot is the striking surface.

Reverse kick (Dwet chaki)

The *reverse kick,* also called the *turn-back kick* and the *reverse-side kick,* is accomplished by spinning to the rear, chambering your kicking leg as you revolve, and striking the target with the heel or knife edge of your foot.

Figure 16-6:
Side kick.

Hand strikes

Tae Kwon Do is known for its kicking techniques, but it has quite an arsenal of hand techniques as well. The basic punch and its variations are used, but so are knife-hand strikes, back-fist strikes, and numerous others.

Punch (Chung kwon chigi)

Chamber your arm at your waist to perform the punch. Your elbow is bent, and your hand is a fist. You thrust your fist out, twisting your hips into the technique to give it power, and pulling your opposite arm back as a balance.

The *straight punch* is performed on the same side as your forward leg. So if you're in a front stance with your left leg forward, a straight punch would be done with your left hand.

The *reverse punch* is performed on the opposite side as your forward leg. (It generally has more power than a straight punch.) So if you're in a front stance with your right leg forward, a reverse punch would be done with your left hand, as shown in Figure 16-7.

Figure 16-7:
Reverse
punch.

Palm strike (Chang kwon chigi)

The *palm strike* is done with the heel of the palm. It is performed like a punch, but your hand is in a different position. Your fingers should be held tightly together and your heel positioned slightly in front of your fingers. Some people bend their fingers to strengthen the hand.

Knife-hand strike (Sudo chigi)

This technique uses the edge of the hand as the striking surface. You open your hand, keeping your fingers tight together, and your thumb bent. You strike with the side of your hand opposite your thumb.

Back-fist strike (Choo muk dung chigi)

For this technique, you make your hand into a fist, but you strike with the back of your fist. This protects your knuckles, especially if you're striking to a hard area of the body (such as the head) with unprotected hands.

Tae Kwon Do history

In the early history of Korea, indigenous Korean fighting techniques were combined with Chinese and Mongolian fighting techniques to create *Subak,* a martial art learned by the warrior class. A related martial art, called *Tae Kyun,* also emerged in this early period. It combined native techniques with the influences of other cultures. Its founder, Won Kang Bopsa, taught the techniques to a group of noble youths called the *Hwarang* (flowering youth). These young men grew up to be important military leaders. They were taught a curriculum consisting of martial strategy, including Tae Kyun, Buddhism, etiquette, and the arts and sciences. This curriculum was called *Hwarang-do* (the way of the flowering youth).

This type of training was mandatory for high-ranking youths until the tenth century when Confucianism replaced Buddhism as the dominant philosophical belief. Confucianism emphasized cultural and intellectual achievements rather than martial successes.

Korea was subject to Japanese and Chinese influences for many centuries. In 1592, Japan invaded but the army was ousted by the Koreans, with the help of the Chinese, who were then permitted exclusive access to Korea.

In the ensuing centuries, Korea suffered a series of invasions — first from Mongolia and then from Japan — that drove its martial arts underground. After World War II, Korea gained independence from Japan, and Koreans began to look for ways to encourage their native culture to flourish again. Korean martial artists began to systematize the various Korean martial arts techniques.

In the early twentieth century, Japan conquered Korea and occupied the country until the end of World War II.

Thus, Chinese and Japanese warrior techniques influenced Korean martial arts. Although other cultures, such as Okinawan, developed ways to use weapons even when they were banned, for the most part, Korean martial artists didn't use weapons in their fighting systems. (However, fighting techniques for using the Korean sword do exist, alongside a system of Korean archery.)

Chapter 17

Judo

In This Chapter

▶ Accommodating all body types — tall, short, big, and small

▶ Beginning at the beginning and then learning more

▶ Discovering Judo principles and its evolution

▶ Finding out about basic Judo techniques

*L*ooking for that competitive edge? Hoping to hone your skills on the tournament circuit? Judo is one martial art that can be (and is) played like a sport. Unlike other traditional martial arts, competition has become one of the most important (if not *the* most important) elements in Judo, with people throwing and pinning each other to the mat in sanctioned competition every week of the year. Although some people take up Judo just for recreation, most eventually become involved in competition.

Judo relies on grappling, sweeping, and throwing techniques rather than the kicks and punches of Karate and Tae Kwon Do. So it looks less like a traditional martial art and more like classical wrestling. (No, not World Wrestling Entertainment-style! No bashing people over the head with chairs.)

In this chapter, you learn about where Judo came from, what it looks like now, and where it's going.

Because of the emphasis on competition, you often hear Judo teachers called *coaches* rather than *instructors*.

The word *shiai* is Japanese for *competition*. It is through competition, as well as regular training sessions, that Judo practitioners improve their skills.

Complex Simplicity

Judo is "the Way of Gentleness," even though the point is to throw people to the ground and keep them there. (Ouch!) Jigoro Kano created Judo in 1882 based on the techniques of Jujutsu, a deadly combat art.

He developed the principles and techniques of Judo according to the concept of maximum efficiency with minimum effort. That is, it made better sense to use body position, footwork, and leverage to defeat an opponent rather than relying on sheer size and strength. Not everyone has sheer size and strength on tap. As a method of self-defense, Judo can be used by anyone — adult or child, man or woman — regardless of size. A small opponent who knows Judo can defeat a large opponent who does not.

Jigoro Kano believed that through the study of Judo, an individual could improve (perhaps even perfect) her mind *and* body.

Physical Fitness Requirements

In Judo competition, fighters are paired with people of the same gender and age group and in the same weight class. So being heavier or lighter isn't necessarily an advantage (or disadvantage) in competition.

- ✔ **Hefty:** If you intend to use Judo as a means of self-defense, having some heft doesn't hurt, but in competition this advantage is nullified by weight class pairings.

- ✔ **Agile:** Agility is important for defense and to perform the throwing and grappling techniques.

- ✔ **Strong upper body:** Although technique is most important, a strong upper body can help you defeat your opponent through more effective throws and holds.

- ✔ **Strong grip:** Grip strength helps you do the throws and holds. This can be developed over time.

In early training, time is spent learning how to fall and how to perform grips. So even if you're not in spectacular shape to start, you can get the endurance you need by the time you need it.

Less is more

In 1964, when the Olympics were held in Tokyo, Judo became an Olympic sport. From this point on, emphasis was placed more on the sport aspect of Judo and less on the art aspect.

The more sport Judo evolved, the more pared-down the techniques became, so that instead of learning dozens of throws, most Judo practitioners now learn only the most effective ones. The older, less effective techniques are now found only in the *kata* (forms), which are rarely performed. Remember: *Kata* (forms) are pre-arranged patterns of techniques. See Chapter 5 for more on forms.

Categories of Techniques

A Judo curriculum was established by the early twentieth century that included the following categories of techniques, which all students learn and which all teachers must master:

- **Kuzushi:** Off-balancing the opponent
- **Tsukuri to kake:** Planning and performing an attack
- **Ukemi:** Breakfalls
- **Nage no kata:** Throwing the opponent
- **Katame no kata:** Grappling and locking techniques
- **Goshin jutsu:** Self-defense combat techniques
- **Kime no kata:** Submission techniques

In Judo practice, *tori* is the partner who throws, and *uke* is the partner who is thrown.

Class Is Now in Session

Judo is taught through the repetitive practice of techniques. A whole class session may be devoted to practicing just one throw. *Kata,* which were originally used to practice Judo techniques, are disappearing from Judo practice. *Randori,* which is sparring, may also be taught in repetition.

Although Judo has forms *(kata)* that students can learn, forms tend to be neglected and are not taught very often. Most Judo techniques can be found in the now-neglected kata. However, some of the techniques taught in these forms would be dangerous to do during *randori.*

Doing the basics

All *Judoka* (practitioners of Judo) are taught in a similar way. First, beginners are taught breakfalls — how to fall without breaking anything. After you're no longer afraid of falling, you learn basic clothing grips, correct stances, and footwork.

After you have even a basic understanding of these, the study of Judo proper begins. You learn throws, holds, and other grappling techniques that become progressively more difficult to do but progressively more effective.

As with all martial arts techniques, some of the techniques you learn are more suited to your skills and abilities and natural inclinations than others; these are the techniques that can form the core of your personal arsenal. Each technique has its strengths and weaknesses; you have to learn what they are and how to exploit the strengths and defend against the weaknesses. This is why the mastery of any martial art takes so long, and at the same time, why it's so much fun.

Just because a technique is difficult to do doesn't mean that you should give up. Devote some time each week to the practice of techniques that aren't your favorites, and you'll have them when you need them.

Typical training

A typical class includes a warm-up period, including mobility and conditioning exercises, then breakfall practice, throwing drills with and without partners, arm and neck locks, and then grappling (groundwork), where you learn to pin your opponent.

When your partner *taps out* — that is, taps the mat with his hand — it means that you win, and it's time to let your partner up. Always heed the tap out, also known as *the submission signal*. Otherwise, you can cause an injury. Besides, you want your partner to listen when *you* tap out. Passing out in class is no way to become an accomplished Judoka.

Unlike other martial arts, Judo has no style or school variation, such as Karate (see Chapter 14). If you practice Judo, you practice Judo. Because all the techniques and commands are taught using Japanese, people from countries all around the world can participate in competition without any misunderstandings. Hmm . . . maybe not without *any* misunderstandings.

The International Judo Federation (IJF) sanctions Judo competitions and spreads the acceptance and teaching of Judo throughout the world.

Mobility and Stretching Exercises

Exercises to help the Judoka gain flexibility, balance, and strength have long been part of Judo training. In general, the instructor starts the training session with some of these exercises after a bit of a warm up to get those cold muscles ready to stretch. You should also do these exercises on your own at other times to get the greatest benefit from your training. You may not have to kick head high in Judo, but you do have to be as slippery as an eel, and to become eel-like, you have to be flexible and agile.

These mobility and stretching exercises include

- ✔ **Toe touches:** Try to touch your forehead to the floor without bending your knees.

- ✔ **One-knee squats:** Extend one leg and squat over the other, trying to maintain balance. (This is harder than it seems.)

- ✔ **Partial rolls:** You start on your back with arms and legs extended, then swing your legs up and try to touch the mat behind your head with your toes, and then return to the original flat-on-your-back position but continue moving your upper body forward until your hands touch your toes.

- ✔ **Crunches:** Along with similar body-conditioning exercises.

- ✔ **Groundwork-simulating exercises:** You practice various groundwork techniques to improve your flexibility.

Breakfalls (Ukemi)

Breakfalls — falling correctly without injury — are among the first techniques that you'll be taught. You may be taught to land in a certain way and then to roll across the mat, springing into a standing position. Rolling helps absorb some of the impact of the fall and improves your flexibility and agility. Quickly moving to a standing position prevents an opponent from throwing and then pinning you.

You learn how to do breakfalls to the back and to the front. So no matter how your opponent throws you, you can land without breaking your nose or your tailbone.

Avoiding injury

In general, your main goal is to keep your head from striking the ground and causing a regrettable loss of consciousness. In a forward fall, this means keeping your head lifted up — unless you tuck your head and roll forward in a somersault. In a backward fall, it means keeping your head tucked to your chest.

Your secondary goal is to prevent other parts of your body from sustaining damage. So landing on a padded portion of your anatomy — shoulders, buttocks, or hips — is best. Never extend your arm and attempt to absorb the impact through your hand. Although this is instinctual, it's a good way to break your wrist or arm. Instead, keep your joints loose and roll or slide to absorb the impact of the fall.

Frustrating your opponent

You want to break your fall in such a way as to prevent your partner/opponent from taking advantage of the fall and pinning you to the ground. This may mean rolling to a standing position or falling and immediately assuming a guarded position or falling and pulling your partner with you so that you can throw him as you go. Actually, special throwing techniques, such as *tomoe-nage* (stomach throw) and *sumi-gaeshi* (corner throw), allow you to do this. (These techniques, as you might imagine, take a bit of practice.) See Figure 17-1 for an example of a commonly used breakfall.

Figure 17-1:
Breakfall
from a
standing
position.

Throwing Techniques

Each throwing technique consists of two parts:

> ✔ **Entry:** Starting the throw and getting into the correct position.
>
> ✔ **Breaking:** Disturbing the opponent's balance so that you can throw her.

These two components are often practiced separately hundreds of times each, then combined together, and practiced with a partner.

Gripping the Gi

Most of the throws require special grips on the opponent's *judogi* (Judo uniform). These handgrips are an important part of the throwing technique and may be practiced separately from the throw itself.

Because many of the throwing and grappling techniques of Judo rely on gripping the judogi, be aware that they may not be as effective in self-defense as they are on the mat. An attacker may not have a convenient lapel to grab, his shirt might tear, or he may even be shirtless. Understand that applying martial arts techniques to street fighting may require some modification of the techniques.

The judogi is especially designed to stand up to the rigors of grappling and throwing in the training hall. Substituting other workout clothing or a different type of martial arts uniform isn't recommended.

In the throes of throwing

Dozens of throws can be done using a variety of body positions for the entry and using many different body parts for leverage, such as shoulders, hips, thighs, and ankles. Most Judoka have four or five favorite throws that they use most frequently.

Each throw has its strengths and weaknesses. When a throw becomes popular, people learn how to exploit its weaknesses. So throws go in and out of style. Even the most advanced practitioners use several basic throws, described in the following sections.

Body drop (Tai-otoshi)

In this technique, the Judoka moves in front of the opponent, keeping both feet wide apart. Grabbing the opponent's sleeve and lapel, the Judoka pulls the opponent over her hip and foot to drop the opponent in front, as shown in Figure 17-2.)

Figure 17-2:
Body drop
throw.

a.

b.

Two-handed shoulder drop (Morote-seoi-nage)

This technique is similar to the body drop, except the opponent is thrown over the shoulder, as shown in Figure 17-3. Executed correctly, this is a difficult technique to defend against. Done quickly, all the opponent sees is the floor

Leg sweep (Harai-goshi)

For this technique, the Judoka steps in front of the opponent. Then using one leg, she sweeps the opponent off his feet, striking the opponent's near leg above the knee to do so, as shown in Figure 17-4.

Inner thigh sweep (Uchi-mata)

This technique is similar to the leg sweep, only the Judoka places her sweeping leg *between* the opponent's legs, and then lifts and throws the opponent over her leg.

Figure 17-3:
Two-handed
shoulder
drop.

Figure 17-4:
Leg sweep.

a.

b.

Defending against throws

To defend against throws, you can use footwork to keep your body out of the correct throwing position. Much of your training focuses on how to prevent people from doing to you what you want to do to them. If your partner does manage to throw you, you learn how to move your body slightly during or after the throw to prevent perfect execution of the throw (which prevents your opponent from scoring a full point and winning the match).

Sometimes, you may have to sacrifice your position in order to gain an advantage. This is often done by dropping to the mat and taking your opponent with you, but positioning yourself in such a way that you can then pin your opponent to the mat.

Groundwork (Grappling) Techniques

According to Judo rules, a throw must be attempted first before grappling can be done. You can't just bow to your opponent, fall to the mat, grab your opponent, and get to work, even though that sounds like fun.

Although the must-throw-first rule seems to emphasize throwing techniques, groundwork is an essential part of Judo. Pinning your opponent and holding the pin — preferably for 30 seconds — scores points in competition. Judo has many different holding techniques, but unlike throws, the effective Judoka learns, masters, and uses all the holds.

Because many street fights *go to the ground* — that is, an attacker grabs you and throws you down — the grappling techniques of Judo can be used in self-defense situations.

- **Basic scarf hold** (Hon-kesa-gatame): Think like you're a scarf, and you'll get this technique down. After your opponent has been thrown, you can easily slide into this position. Well, *easily* is a relative term. If you're big, you just land on your opponent and cover his chest with your body, trap the opponent's right arm between your chest and arm, and lock your hands behind the opponent's neck. If you're small, you sit alongside your opponent rather than on top of him, keeping your legs spread wide for a good foundation. It's harder for your opponent to throw you when you're in this position. Then perform the hold as I described it for a big person.

- **Broken scarf hold** (Kuzure-kesa-gatame): This hold is a variation of the basic scarf hold. Instead of locking your hands behind the opponent's neck, you keep the opponent's right arm tucked between your arm and chest and hold it there; your left arm grabs the opponent's jacket at the shoulder.

✔ **Shoulder hold** (Kata-gatame): In this technique, you wedge one leg against the opponent's body, keeping your other leg extended to provide support. You lock your arms around the opponent's neck, keeping your head close to the opponent's. One of the opponent's arms (usually the left arm) should be trapped between your shoulder and head. This may sound like a difficult hold to get into, but it's even more difficult to get out of.

✔ **Basic upper four quarters hold** (Hon-kami-shiho-gatame): In this technique, you and your opponent are in such a position that your bodies are extending in opposite directions. You pin the opponent's upper body with your upper body. You slide your arms under the opponent's shoulders and grab the opponent's belt. You can also perform this pin from a crouching position. The hold can also be done from the side in which case it goes by a different name: basic side four quarters hold (hon-yoko-shiho-gatame).

✔ **Neck and arm locks:** These techniques can be dangerous to use, so the Judoka must have some experience in groundwork and should know how to respond to a *tap out* or submission signal before attempting them. These techniques often require using the judogi (uniform) to make the lock effective. For example, in the Normal-cross strangle *(nami-juji-jime)*, the Judoka grabs the opponent's lapels in a cross grab so that the Judoka's wrists cross and then pulls the opponent toward her.

The only type of arm lock a Judoka can use in competition is one in which pressure is applied to the elbow. Shoulder and wristlocks, which Judoka may learn from forms or at higher ranks, are harder to control in competition and can result in serious damage to the opponent. Use 'em all you want against muggers, but remember that they'll disqualify you in competition.

Combining Techniques

Past the beginning stages, the Judoka learns how to combine techniques in order to create the opportunity to throw the opponent. A single, well-executed technique can easily throw a beginner, but the more advanced practitioner is not so easy to handle. For this reason, an effective Judoka learns how to use more than one technique in succession *(ren-zoku-waza)* to find a weakness in the opponent's defense. The Judoka may attempt a throw from one angle, and if unsuccessful, may try a throw from the opposite angle or at least from a different angle.

Continuing with the attack even if initially unsuccessful is what separates the good Judoka from the merely competent. This requires a competitive and aggressive instinct to keep going; assuming that at some moment the opponent may relax his guard, that moment of relaxation can be exploited.

Judo history

Jigoro Kano (1860–1938) studied the principles of *Jujutsu,* a combat art practiced in Japan for hundreds of years to train the Samurai. He felt that the study of Jujutsu had several drawbacks. For example, he saw that doing the techniques had the potential to cause physical harm — sometimes permanent harm and even lethal harm — to the practitioner and his partner or opponent. You can't have a friendly sparring match to improve your skills if someone's likely to end up with a broken skull.

Because the practice of Jujutsu was so dangerous, few people undertook its study, and becoming technically accomplished was difficult. Jigoro Kano envisioned a martial art that took the cream of Jujutsu techniques, but that many ordinary people would be able to learn both as a sport and as a means of self-defense.

Jigoro Kano also believed that the Jujutsu techniques could only be done using brute force, and he felt that a good system of self-defense would work even for people who weren't big and muscular. To counteract these problems, Kano refined the techniques of Jujutsu so that the practitioner's use of leverage, mental effort, and physical skill counted for more than mere muscle mass. Thus, Kano created Judo. And for the next 50 years, until his death in 1938, Kano spread the word about his art throughout the world.

Chapter 18

Aikido

In This Chapter

▶ Understanding Aikido as a strictly defensive art
▶ Redirecting and deflecting the energy of any attack
▶ Breathing and breakfalling through the basics
▶ Rock 'n' rollin' and pivoting around your opponent

*A*ikido means the Way of Harmony with the Ki. (*Ki* or *chi* means your inner energy.) So even though Steven Seagal breaks heads, arms, and legs using Aikido techniques in his action flicks, the true purpose of Aikido is finding and maintaining a balance between mind, body, and spirit. An advanced Aikido practitioner can use the most complex throws and locks to defend against an attacker while never permanently injuring the attacker.

The techniques of Aikido were developed to help practitioners overcome physical and mental barriers and to learn how to be more in tune with the surrounding world.

The circular movements in Aikido symbolize wholeness and unity, which can counteract disharmony, disunity, and violence.

The founder of Aikido, Ueshiba Morihei, wanted to create a martial art that was purely defensive in nature. The techniques are designed to use the attacker's force against him.

The Aikido practitioner doesn't kick or punch the opponent. Joint locks and throws are used, and the Aikido practitioner may touch the opponent's body in order to redirect the opponent's energy.

Aikido has no attack. Aikido emphasizes physical fitness, strength, agility, and a nonviolent attitude.

Your Physical Resources

Aikido doesn't rely on an exhaustive (and exhausting) arsenal of kicks and punches. You don't necessarily expend every ounce of energy controlling or throwing your opponent. Your opponent is the one who expends plenty of energy. But Aikido, done right, can be hard work.

- **Durable:** People of all shapes and sizes can perform the techniques of Aikido, but you do have to have some stamina.

- **Flexible:** Aikido requires agility and flexibility in order to do all the circular movements effectively and to perform the body shifting and evasion necessary to avoid injury in a self-defense situation.

  Rolling, falling, and kneeling for extended periods of time can be hard on the joints. If getting up from the floor is a major task for you, Aikido may prove frustrating.

- **Strong:** Although your strength comes from your *hara* (center), having a solid, muscular body helps you perform the techniques.

Hard and Soft Aikido

Like Karate, Aikido comes in a variety of styles, but Aikido has far fewer styles than Karate. Some Aikido schools use more direct (hard) techniques to defend against an attack, and others rely on the traditional indirect (soft) techniques. (Think straight line versus circle.)

Because the founder of Aikido thought of it as a way to develop individuals, not as a sport with winners and losers, Aikido is noncompetitive, at least in traditional schools. But people do work with partners to improve their skills.

Showing Rank

Most traditional Aikido schools recognize essentially two ranks: *white belt* (beginner) and *black belt* (advanced). Some schools are so laid-back that they don't even go this far, figuring that you know where you are in the scheme of things and don't need to announce it by tying a bit of colored cloth around your waist.

Some Aikido schools award more belt ranks, such as a white belt for beginners, a colored belt (perhaps blue or brown) for intermediate students, and a black belt for advanced students. Sometimes, these belts are divided into various levels, depending on one's experience and expertise. See Chapter 5 for more information on ranks and ranking systems.

Aikido practitioners wear the *dogi,* which is similar to Karate and Judo uniforms. When students achieve the rank of black belt, they're allowed to wear the *hakama* — a pair of wide-legged trousers that looks like a skirt but was worn by the Samurai, beginning in the eighth century A.D. In some schools, all students wear the hakama.

Ready, Set, Relax!

At the beginning levels of Aikido training, students learn basic techniques, including stances and footwork, and they learn *breakfall* skills. A *breakfall* is a way to fall without hurting anyone.

As students progress in their training, greater emphasis is placed on self-examination. (This may not be a pretty sight.) The purpose of self-examination is to arrive at self-understanding — to know why you do what you do — in the hope that self-improvement follows.

Meditation helps students learn to tap into their *chi.* (For more on chi, see Appendix A.) Aikido practitioners learn to train their minds to remain calm and open and to respond appropriately to an attack. They also use breathing techniques to find and use their chi. They concentrate on feeling their breath travel from nose to abdomen. During this period of focused breathing and concentration, the Aikido student may use visualization to *see* himself doing the techniques exactly right.

Hara is a central concept in Aikido (and some other martial arts). It is the location of the chi, usually thought to exist in the abdomen. All the strength of Aikido comes from this center.

See Chapter 11 for more information on working the mind-body-spirit connection.

Aikido Curriculum

Aikido has over 700 techniques to master, so learning them all takes a long time. They're divided into two categories:

- **Nage waza:** Throwing techniques
- **Katame waza:** Controlling techniques

Aikido also has five basic defensive techniques, with practically countless variations of each:

- **Atemi:** Vital point-striking
- **Tai sabaki:** Body-shifting and evasion
- **Irimi:** Entering into a throw
- **Rofuse:** Throwing
- **Kansetu:** Immobilizing the attacker using joint locks

At the advanced stages of training, Aikido practitioners may learn to use weapons. Aikido weapons include the *bokken, jo,* and *tanto* (wooden versions of the sword, staff, and knife, respectively). See Chapter 12 for more information on weapons.

The Best Defense Is a Good Defense

Aikido teaches self-defense techniques against many kinds of attack. Many joint locks and throws can be used against unarmed attackers, who may grab your wrist or shoulder. Self-defense techniques against basic blows, such as punches to the head and abdomen, are taught, as are techniques that defend against some combination of grabs and blows.

Aikido also teaches defense against traditional weapons, such as sticks and staffs, as well as against modern weapons, such as knives and firearms. Because defense against armed attackers is extremely complex, you have to be an advanced student to learn the tricks of the trade.

Defensive strategies consist of training in the three stages of defense:

- Decision
- Perception
- Reaction

If any element is missing or poorly handled, the results can be disastrous. For example, an attack that isn't perceived quickly enough can result in a disaster.

The *Aikidoka* (Aikido practitioner) tries to reduce the amount of time between perception and reaction. Heightened awareness, quick decision-making, and fast, effective reaction are practiced.

Flexibility Training

Because Aikido relies on agility and flexibility to perform the techniques most effectively, you should work on increasing your flexibility through drills and exercises.

Some of these exercises may be done in a training session or class. You should also do them on your own.

Seated toe touches

In this stretching/flexibility exercise, you sit on the floor and extend your legs straight out in front of you. Keeping your knees relaxed but not bent, reach forward and touch your toes.

Check out the following variations:

✔ Spread your legs as far apart as possible. Bend at the waist, trying to touch your chest to the floor between your legs. Extend your arms and fingers out as far as possible in front of your to give an added stretch.

✔ Pivot your upper body and stretch over your left leg, trying to touch your hands to your foot. Do the same over your right leg.

✔ Bring your feet together, knees bent and soles touching. Bend your upper body over your ankles, trying to touch your forehead to the floor.

Kneeling stretches

In the *seiza* (kneeling) position, have someone hold your knees to the ground while you lie back, trying to put your back on the floor. If you're not that agile or if you have knee problems, extend one leg while keeping the other bent under you, and perform the exercise that way, and then switch legs.

Side bends

Stand with your feet slightly apart. Reach over your head with your left arm while bending at the waist to the right. Repeat on the opposite side.

Upper-body twist

Stand with your feet slightly apart. Put your hands low on your hips and twist your upper body to the right and then to the left.

Eight-direction exercise

To build your center and practice the circular techniques used in Aikido, try the following drill:

1. Stand with your arms at your side and your feet slightly apart. Slide your left foot forward, moving your hips forward and feeling your center. As you step, swing your arms forward and up until they're at eye level. Then bring your hips back to the starting position and allow your arms to fall down to your sides.

2. Pivot 180 degrees to the right (pivot on both feet). Repeat the process: Step forward with your left foot, swing your arms up, and so on.

3: Pivot 90 degrees to the left and step forward with your left foot. Repeat the arm swinging process here and in each of the following steps.

4: Pivot 180 degrees to the right and step forward with your right foot.

5: Pivot 45 degrees to your left and step forward with your left foot.

6: Pivot 180 degrees to your right and step forward with your right foot.

7: Pivot 270 degrees to your left and step forward with your left foot.

8: Pivot 180 degrees to your right and step forward with your right foot.

   You can repeat it by stepping out with your right foot and pivoting to the left.

Rolls (But No Donuts)

In Aikido, you learn to use rolling techniques to evade attack and to prevent injury during a fall.

By rolling, you can quickly get to your feet after being thrown. You can do the rolls from a sitting position or a standing position. (If you're kneeling, you can easily move to a sitting position to perform a roll.) Rolls are to the front or to the back.

Backward rolls

Starting from the sitting position is slightly easier than from a standing position. To do a backward roll from a sitting position: Keep one leg bent under the other and then rock backward and land in the same sitting position, as shown in Figure 18-1.

Figure 18-1:
Backward
roll.

For a backward roll from a standing position, you would simply begin in a natural standing position. Then drop to the sitting position and perform the roll as you would from a sitting position.

Forward rolls

To roll forward from the standing position:

1. Step forward, bending your upper body and the knee of your forward leg. Keep your back leg straight.

2. Place your back arm next to your back foot. Keep your forward arm curved over your head.

3. Tuck your head between your forward foot and your backhand, rolling along your forward arm and shoulder. Keep your body curved and your legs drawn up, as shown in Figure 18-2.

You can do several continuous rolls, or you can return to the standing position.

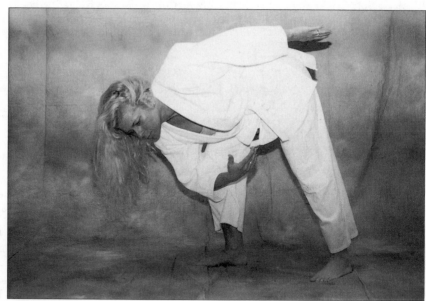

Figure 18-2:
Forward
roll.

Basic Techniques

Striking techniques are limited to a few blows to the vital areas (vulnerable areas such as the groin) that are mainly used for distraction. All techniques can be (and are) performed from standing or kneeling positions, against standing or kneeling attackers.

The techniques of Aikido are learned through the performance of *kata* (forms), the repeated practice of techniques, and in a type of freestyle sparring between partners. (For more on forms, see Chapter 5.)

Students learn to free themselves from holds and to prevent throws as well as to throw the opponent and immobilize her using controlling techniques. When sparring, you may be presented with a challenge: Multiple opponents may restrain you or attack you with a variety of techniques all at the same time and then expect you to free yourself.

Stances

When attacked, you assume a specific stance. Stances are sometimes called *postures,* not to be confused with posturing. The stance helps you perform the defensive techniques correctly.

Unlike other martial arts, Aikido doesn't have a myriad of stances. The basic stance in Aikido is the natural stance, which is shown in Figure 18-3. The head, spine, and abdomen all maintain a vertical line — just like Mama tried to teach you. Your feet may be side by side (natural stance), or your right foot may be ahead (right natural stance) or your left foot may be ahead (left natural stance).

In any of the natural stances, hands are used to guard the body. They may be held low, natural (middle), or high, depending on the attack.

Figure 18-3:
Natural
stance.

Footwork

In Aikido, you can step in eight linear directions to avoid an attack: forward, backward, each side, and four diagonals.

But circular movement is essential in Aikido footwork. So when you're under attack, you can pivot out of the way, thus avoiding the linear path of the strike. You can also spin to avoid an attack.

You're taught to combine the circular footwork with the linear footwork. For example, pivot out of the way of an attack and then step directly forward to perform a throw or hold.

Basic immobilizations

You have dozens of ways to immobilize an attacker, depending on how she attacks, where you are, and what you're doing when attacked. But in all immobilizations, circular movements are used to avoid the attack, to redirect the energy of the attack, and to control the attacker. Pressure can be brought against the attacker's wrists, shoulders, elbow, and other vulnerable body parts.

Basic arm lock

Assume the attacker thrusts or punches toward your abdomen.

1. Pivot away from the attack by stepping away with your back leg.

2. As the attacker's arm slides past you, grab the attacker's wrist in one of your hands and her upper arm (just above the elbow) in your other hand.

3. Position the attacker's arm so that her palm faces upward. Pull up on the wrist while pressing down on the upper arm or elbow (see Figure 18-4).

4. As you grab the attacker's arm, you can continue the circular movement, pulling the attacker of her feet.

The attacker loses her balance and falls face first to the ground.

Figure 18-4:
Basic arm
lock.

Shoulder immobilization

You can use parts of your body to aid in the immobilization. Assume the attacker is pushing or punching toward your shoulder with his right hand.

1. Firmly grasp the attacker's hand with your right hand, keeping the attacker's fist tightly closed and pressed against your shoulder.

2. Twist the attacker's hand so that the palm faces upward.

3. With your left hand, grasp the opponent's arm above the wrist.

4. Press your forearm against the attacker's forearm. The entire weight of your body presses against the attacker (see Figure 18-5).

Generally, the attacker drops to his knees or falls to the floor as a result of the pressure.

Figure 18-5:
Shoulder immobiliz-
ation.

Throwing techniques

Many throwing techniques (also known as *projections* — your opponent becomes a projectile) build on the controlling techniques. Sometimes, simply taking a controlling or immobilizing technique a step or two further results in a throw.

A basic throw, commonly taught to all beginners, is called the *kokyu nage* (the 20-year technique). This technique can be used against many basic attacks, which is why it is often the first throw taught to Aikido beginners.

Assume that an attacker is about to grab your left wrist.

1. Insert your right hand between the attacker's hand and yours, grab the attacker's wrist, and pivot on your left foot.

2. As you pivot, you pull the attacker forward in front of your body.

3. With your left hand (your free hand), you pull the attacker's head against your body, reaching over the attacker's left shoulder (see Figure 18-6a).

4. You continue to pivot while performing this maneuver. Then you switch direction, bringing your right arm up in a circle. Your arm forces the attacker upward.

5. Then you bring your right arm across and down, forcing the attacker down on his back (see Figure 18-6b).

Figure 18-6: Kokyu nage (20-year throw).

a.

b.

Aikido history

Ueshiba Morihei, the founder of Aikido, investigated more than 200 martial arts styles to develop the techniques of Aikido. He was determined to rid his art of any dangerous or harmful martial philosophy.

To this end, he discouraged competition among martial artists, feeling that the purpose of Aikido was to help practitioners develop into the best people possible, not to award medals for performance.

Chapter 19

Escrima

In This Chapter

▶ Attacking the body or the weapon in self-defense

▶ Being fast, flexible, stocky, and strong helps

▶ Blocking with a stick and without one

▶ Understanding the fundamentals

*Y*ou can't beat it with a stick. But in this case, you *can* beat it with a stick — an Escrima stick, that is. Escrima is sometimes called "the art of traditional fencing," although practitioners use sticks rather than foils to do their deeds. The *Escrima stick* is a wood stick that's about 24 to 30 inches long (depending on style) and about an inch in diameter. Sometimes, one stick is used; sometimes, two sticks are used. An Escrima practitioner with one stick or two is like watching a drummer: It's fascinating, but you don't want to be the drum.

Escrima (from *skirmish* in Spanish) is a Filipino martial art, closely related to the martial arts of *Kali* and *Arnis,* which also developed in the Philippines — just in different regions. Kali and Arnis teachers teach similar techniques to Escrima teachers, although they probably all claim that their system is the best.

In Escrima, you use wooden fighting sticks in addition to your knuckles to defeat your opponent. Some empty-hand techniques — including kicking, punching, trapping, and grappling moves — are taught as a supplement to the stick fighting. Other weapons may also be taught, such as the sword and dagger. (In Spanish, that's *espada y daga*.) Some traditional schools also teach students how to use the shield and the spear. (See Chapter 12 for more information on weapons.) However, it's the stick that gets the most attention.

Body-shifting and footwork techniques help the Escrima practitioner avoid the opponent's attack. Conditioning exercises toughen hands and feet for striking blows.

Escrima techniques are used against armed and unarmed attackers. Usually, the techniques are practiced against other Escrima practitioners who use their sticks and other weapons, such as the sword and dagger, which you have to defend against using a measly little wood stick.

Escrimadors (male) and *Escrimadoras* (female) are martial artists who practice Escrima.

Different Strokes for Different Folks

Stick fighting has many schools and styles, and traditionally, every Escrima teacher thinks her method is best. Although each Escrima teacher has a different approach to teaching Escrima, essentially, you can take one of two main approaches to stick fighting:

- **Attack the opponent's body:** Effective but causes injuries
- **Attack the opponent's stick:** Less effective but causes fewer injuries.

Some schools combine approaches, so that you learn to attack the weapon of an armed attacker and the body of an unarmed attacker.

Getting Started

Escrima doesn't require much equipment, especially at first. You just put on some comfortable clothes, grab an Escrima stick, and get started.

Some schools have students wear an Escrima uniform, which consists of loose-fitting trousers and a short jacket over a T-shirt. You may or may not wear shoes during training; traditional martial arts are done barefoot, but dropping those sticks on your toes hurts.

If you plan to compete, you may have to invest in body armor. Some schools may ask you to wear padded safety equipment and headgear during training, much like the equipment that fencers wear. (You'd think this would be especially important if the school takes the approach of attacking the body rather than the stick, but these schools that tend to be more traditional *don't* have students wear protective equipment. Go figure.)

Most Escrima schools don't award belt ranks, although some are beginning to follow the Japanese style of kyu/dan rankings. Essentially, you know that you're making progress in Escrima if the number of bruises that you sustain in each training session continues to go down.

A *guro* is an Escrima instructor.

Escrima Fitness

Although kicks and grappling moves are not commonly used in Escrima, practitioners need to have a strong core and to be light on their feet. (If someone is coming after you with a sword in one hand and a dagger in the other, getting out of the way is the best action that you can take.)

- ✔ **Fast:** Upper body speed and power help you execute the techniques.

- ✔ **Agile:** Flexibility in the lower body is less important in Escrima than in other martial arts, but agile arms and upper body are needed for the most effective stick-fighting.

- ✔ **Stocky and strong:** A stocky, muscular physique can handle this style well.

Also, hopefully, you don't bruise easily. You're playing with sticks. Someone's going to get whacked.

Mental Attributes

The Escrimadora learns to develop several important mental attributes. Without these, she can't succeed in the art:

- ✔ **Awareness:** After an attack is initiated, *awareness* turns into focus.

- ✔ **Motivation:** The discipline to achieve your goals.

- ✔ **Visualization:** The ability to imagine or *see* yourself performing the techniques correctly.

- ✔ **Emotional self-control:** Mastery over fear and panic; learning to relax is fundamental.

See Chapter 11 for more information on the mind-body-spirit connection.

Traditional Training

During the Spanish conquest of the Philippines, the native martial arts were driven underground and only performed in public as dances and plays. Escrima's traditional training methods, the main way that these techniques are taught today, evidence Escrima history.

Pandalag

This traditional training method is the performance of offensive and defensive swings and strokes in repetitive drills. This is often the most dancelike of the traditional learning methods.

Sombra Tabak

These are traditional, prearranged patterns of practicing strikes, thrusts, and parries. They may be thought of as similar to *kata* (forms) — patterns of techniques used to improve the artist's footwork.

This is *free-sparring* (a form of mock combat in which partners attack, defend, and counterattack continuously). Two students try to defeat one another using all their techniques and skills. Although practitioners may wear padded safety equipment and only strike one another's sticks, this can still be a dangerous way to spend your Saturday afternoon. But it's fun.

Many Escrimadors also study Traditional Filipino healing arts, such as Hilot, probably because of the bruises they get during free-sparring.

Twelve: Your Lucky Number

In Escrima, good things (or at least important concepts) come in twelves. Escrima has twelve categories of study, twelve angles of attack, twelve vital areas, and twelve basic strikes. (See the "Traditional Training" section, earlier in this chapter.) The twelve angles of attack are actually attacks to the twelve vital areas of the body. Instead of learning to defend against a countless number of techniques, the Escrimador learns to defend against attacks to any of the vital areas. Whether the attacker is kicking, punching, or wielding an axe that's coming at your head doesn't matter; what matters is that you know how to defend against objects coming at your head. The twelve angles to defend against (and the vital areas to attack when it's your turn) are as follows:

- Left temple
- Right temple
- Left shoulder
- Right shoulder
- Stomach or groin
- Left side of the chest
- Right side of the chest
- Left knee
- Right knee
- Left eye
- Right eye
- Top of the head

Some schools may have a slightly different interpretation of the angles or may number them in a different order, but the concept remains the same.

The twelve basic strikes are any attacks to these twelve vital areas. Some of the strikes are sweeping blows, and others are thrusts. For example, you use the stick in a sweeping motion to attack the opponent's temple, but you use the stick to thrust in order to attack his chest.

Basic Techniques

In Escrima, the techniques are all done in the same way whether you're armed or unarmed. It doesn't matter which weapon you're using (stick, dagger, or empty hand), the techniques are done in the same way. This makes Escrima an efficient system of fighting. You don't have to learn a whole method of attack and defense for each weapon.

All techniques should be practiced with both the left hand and the right hand in order to maintain crucial balance in the martial artist's skills.

Empty-hand techniques

Although Escrima emphasizes the use of weapons, *anatomical* weapons — parts of your body — can be used to fight Escrima-style. Basic techniques include

- ✔ **Dagger hand:** Similar to the knife-hand used in Karate (see Chapter 14) and Tae Kwon Do (see Chapter 16) and is used for chopping strikes.

- ✔ **C-hand** or **Clamp hand:** A variation of the dagger hand — the fingers are bent instead of straight.

- ✔ **Fist:** The fingers are folded tightly together.

The knee is also used to strike, especially when the attacker is in close. The foot is used to kick, usually fast and low, in order to distract the opponent.

Using the Escrima stick

First, you need an *Escrima stick*. Depending on the style, the stick may be 24 to 30 inches long. Some teachers feel that longer sticks are more effective, and others feel that shorter sticks are more effective in close. Either way, the stick measures about an inch in diameter and is made of a hardwood or rattan. (Teachers also disagree on which is better: Hardwood can splinter and pieces can break off during training, which can be dangerous; rattan disintegrates much more rapidly and has to be replaced frequently.)

To hold the stick, you grip it near the end with your fingers and thumb wrapped around it, as shown in Figure 19-1. In some cases, such as for certain blocks, your thumb may be placed on the side of the stick while your fingers curl around the base of it. Your grip shouldn't be so tight that you can't maneuver the stick, nor should it be so loose that you drop the stick. (Dropping a hardwood Escrima stick on your toes can sting.)

The hand not holding the stick is the *alive hand* or just the *empty hand.* This hand is responsible for checking the opponent's hand or even the opponent's weapon.

Stances

Only a few stances (often called *positions*) are used in Escrima. An *attention stance* shows that you're paying attention and may be used at the beginning or end of class; a *salutation stance* shows courtesy to your partner or opponent. Essentially, you salute your opponent with the stick and then try to brain her with the stick.

Natural stance

The natural position is used while watching others in class or while talking to a fellow student or the instructor. Your feet should be comfortably apart, toes forward, with your stick under your left bicep, and your left hand on your right forearm. This shows that you're not about to attack anyone but can quickly assume the ready position.

Figure 19-1: Gripping an Escrima stick.

Ready stance

This position is taken when you're preparing to fight. You stand with your right side and foot forward, and your upper body is turned slightly away — this gives your opponent less target area to attack. The left arm, hand in a fist, guards your midsection. This hand, the *alive hand* (the hand holding the stick), should be in front of your navel. Your right hand holds the stick, which is placed across your body.

Salutation stance

The salutation is a courtesy you give to your instructor, fellow students and sparring partners. Start in the ready stance. Then shift your weight to your left foot and step back with your right foot. Bring your weapon up, with the end at the center of your forehead. Your other hand rests on your navel.

Footwork and body-shifting

Footwork and body-shifting are used to evade an attack. These are thought to be more effective than simply blocking an attack because a blocked attack can still cause injury to you. Remember, your opponent is swinging a stick at you.

In general, body-shifting is merely turning your upper body out of the way of a strike (especially thrusts), as shown in Figure 19-2.

Figure 19-2:
Body-
shifting.

Footwork moves your whole body out of the way. In Escrima, practitioners are often taught to move on diagonals toward and away from the opponent in order to avoid linear strikes.

Stick strikes

You may strike with the Escrima stick in one of several ways, such as those that follow:

- **Full-power sweeping strike:** Strike all the way through your target.

- **Fast strike:** Pull the stick back *(retraction)* immediately after the strike instead of sweeping all the way through the target.

- **Whipping or fanning strike:** Striking horizontally, vertically, or on the diagonal.

- **Twirling strike:** Striking in an upward or downward movement. (Don't let go of the stick!)

Blocking with the stick

Each block and counter is designed to protect against one of the angles of attack. It doesn't matter if the attacker is using a stick, a punch, or a knife to attack, the defense is the same.

All techniques in Escrima flow from block to counter. You don't just block your opponent's strike and then wait for her to have at you again. Instead, you block the strike (sometimes called *parrying*) and then you counter with a technique that could disarm or stop the attacker.

In the following descriptions, it's assumed that you'll be carrying the stick in your right hand. Lefties can use their left hand to swing the stick, but the procedures must then be reversed. (For a good Escrima teacher, this isn't a big deal to teach.)

Cross block against a strike

This is a basic technique done when the attacker is striking toward your left temple. As the attacker swings her stick, you step forward with your right leg and block her stick with yours; hold your stick at a slight angle. Bring your left hand up under the attackers stick to check it. Now the attacker's stick is trapped between your stick and your hand (see Figure 19-3).

Figure 19-3:
Strike
and parry.

To counter the strike, grab the opponent's attacking hand and step back with your left leg, bringing the opponent toward you. Swing your stick into her forearm, then retract your stick, and strike to the underside of the opponent's attacking wrist. You can continue with this countering technique until the attacker has dropped her weapon or promises to go home and live a good life. For example, you can thrust the stick into the attacker's solar plexus (just below the rib cage and sternum); you can hit the forearm again, and so on.

Cross block against a thrust

To use this technique, assume the attacker is thrusting his stick toward your solar plexus. As the attacker strikes, raise your stick arm waist high, keeping the stick at a slight downward angle to protect your solar plexus and groin. Place your left hand under your stick. Step back with your left leg. Intercept the attacker's stick with your own, as shown in Figure 19-4. Check the attacker's hand with your (unarmed) left hand. Keep your left hand on your attacker's hand.

Figure 19-4:
Jab and
parry.

For the counter, turn to face the attacker, striking his forearm. Retract your stick and strike to the attacker's wrist, or thrust your stick to his solar plexus. Continue striking, keeping your left hand in position to check the opponent's stick, until your opponent gives up.

Without a stick: Unarmed techniques

Usually, Escrima students are taught how to do all the techniques with a stick, and then they're taught how to do them unarmed. The techniques remain essentially the same no matter what, but doing them without the stick is slightly more difficult than with the stick.

Cross block unarmed

Assume that your attacker is punching toward your face. You simply cross your hands and move them toward the attacker, intercepting the attack (see Figure 19-5). Immediately redirect the energy of the attack by moving your hands to the side of your body, away from your center.

Figure 19-5:
Unarmed
parry.

Now you can counter the attack with an unarmed technique of your own, such as a punch.

C-Hand interception

Assume the attacker is punching toward your head. Move your right leg back and grab the attacker's wrist with your left hand. Keep your right hand up and guarding your body. Move the attacker's hand away from you to redirect the energy of the attack.

This type of attack requires speed and timing to intercept. That's why stepping out of the way of the attack *first* is important. Then if you miss the interception, you won't get nailed. To counter such an attack, follow up with a punch using your free hand.

Unarmed disarm

If you're unarmed and someone is attacking you with a stick or some other weapon, you need to be able to immobilize the weapon so that it can't be used to smack you in the head. You can use any of the controlling blocks you learned with the stick even if you don't have the stick. You can also use these controlling blocks to control the attacker's weapon and then take it away, even if you don't have a weapon yourself.

These techniques are difficult to perform effectively and should never be attempted in a real self-defense situation without considerable practice and training.

Basic trapping hands with disarm

In this case, assume the attacker is attacking with the Escrima stick to your head. Raise your hands to shoulder level with the right hand crossed over the left hand. Step forward with your right leg. At that moment, the stick should hit your left hand.

To perform the disarm:

1. Immediately turn your upper body to the left, redirecting the energy of the attack.

2. Grab the stick with your left hand.

3. Pull it upward and away from the attacker while striking the attacker's wrist with your right hand (see Figure 19-6).

Figure 19-6: Trapping hands.

Escrima history

Escrima came to the Philippines from Indonesia and Malaysia. A form of stick-fighting using the *tabak* (a short, sharpened stick) may have been the forerunner of Escrima.

When the Spanish conquered the Philippines late in the sixteenth century, Filipino systems of martial arts were driven underground, only to emerge in dances and plays, which, ironically, were performed for the entertainment of the Spaniards.

Over the next three centuries of Spanish rule, the techniques of Escrima changed because of the Spanish influence. Spanish styles of sword-fighting, especially the Spanish system of sword and dagger fighting (*espada y daga*), found a special expression in Escrima. Many Escrima masters teach Escrima in Spanish or English (the language of many of their students) rather than Tagalog, which is the official language of the Philippines.

Chapter 20

Hapkido

In This Chapter

▶ Being physically fit and centered is important

▶ Discovering the variety of Hapkido techniques

▶ Learning the importance of the counterattack

▶ Understanding how to attack your opponent's chi

*H*apkido (the Way of Coordinated Power) is a modern martial art from Korea that may someday rival the popularity of Tae Kwon Do if the people who teach it have their way. But don't mistake Hapkido for just another Karate-knockoff. Hapkido techniques have as much in common with Aikido techniques as they have with Hapkido's sister Korean martial art, Tae Kwon Do. So in addition to kicks and punches, Hapkido practitioners learn joint locks and throws.

Hapkido is a highly developed system of self-defense. Practitioners don't attack. They wait for the opponent to launch an attack, which they counter with devastating power techniques. Advanced students defend themselves with effortless locks and throws.

Those who learn Hapkido must understand the importance of expanding their physical and mental abilities and consciousness. The Hapkido practitioner uses *chi* to create inner balance and peace and tries to disrupt the attacker's chi to end the attack. *Chi* is your inner energy or life force. For more on your chi, see Appendix A. Cultivating your chi requires as much patience and work as cultivating your garden.

The name for Hapkido underwent many changes, including *Yu Kwon Sool, Ho Shin Mu Do,* and *Yu Sool,* until the name *Hapkido* was finally settled upon in 1963. After the founder's death in 1986, his upper-level students, some of whom had attained ranks of eighth- and ninth-degree black belt, went in different directions. As a result, Hapkido spans several different styles according to the inclinations of these high-ranking instructors. However, all the styles and schools stress the importance of learning striking and grappling techniques and developing the internal aspects of Hapkido.

Well-Rounded Fitness

The Hapkido practitioner has to kick, punch, throw, and grapple. The techniques of Hapkido are well rounded, so the practitioner of Hapkido must be well rounded, at least in terms of fitness. She relies on timing and speed to perform the techniques as counterattacks, so agility and flexibility are as important as power and strength.

- ✔ **All shapes and sizes:** Because of the variety of techniques available to the practitioner, height, body type, and gender don't matter.

- ✔ **Confident:** Self-confidence is a must. Being tentative with the techniques is downright dangerous.

- ✔ **Open-minded:** The Hapkido practitioner must be willing to learn about Eastern concepts that aren't readily embraced in the West.

- ✔ **Physically fit:** Overall good fitness is important for the Hapkido practitioner.

- ✔ **Strong and Flexible:** Strength and flexibility are equally important; you need to work on both to succeed.

Chi for Me

Using your chi in Hapkido means more than just summoning it when you *kiai* (also *kihop*) — the martial arts shout that helps you focus your energy, as discussed later in the section "You make me wanna shout (kihop)." Using your chi in Hapkido also means maintaining a healthy balance between mind, body, and spirit.

When your chi is blocked, it leads to sickness. At the minimum, blocked chi makes it difficult to practice the martial arts techniques.

In Hapkido, you may learn how to release your chi yourself through various breathing exercises. Hapkido practitioners often use meditation to help them relax and to help them understand how to use their chi.

Vital points (Kup so)

The location of the vital points is essential to the study of Hapkido. Vital points are vulnerable areas of a person's body, such as the groin and the throat. If you strike a vital point, you disrupt the opponent's chi, causing more damage and devastation than a typical punch to the jaw would cause.

Danjon rules

In order to maintain your balance and equilibrium, in all senses — physical, mental, and emotional — you must understand your body's *central point* (*danjon*).

The *danjon* is your natural center of gravity, located in your abdomen. It is also where your chi resides when you're not directing it against an attacker. Knowing where your center (*danjon*) is helps you become a more powerful martial artist. This is so, because, essentially, all your techniques start from that point of energy.

Chi breathing

To consciously discover your center and your chi, try this breathing technique commonly used in Hapkido:

1. Begin in a natural standing position. Bend your elbows slightly. Bend your wrists, so your palms are flat and parallel to the floor.

2. Place both hands in front of your abdomen (where your danjon is), keeping your hands slightly apart.

3. Breathe in slowly and deeply. Think of positive chi energy coming into your body. As you breathe, raise your hands to chest level, filling your lungs — your whole body — with invigorating chi energy and air, as shown in Figure 20-1a.

4. Wait a moment. Turn your palms down. Expel your breath, moving your palms down to their original position, as shown in Figure 20-1b.

This technique reminds you where to find your chi, relaxes you and prepares you for training. Although it's usually done before and during Hapkido training sessions, it can also be done at other times when you feel stressed and frazzled and need to become centered.

You make me wanna shout (Kihop)

Like other martial artists, the Hapkido practitioner draws on her chi while performing techniques to add power to the techniques. To do this, the martial artist inhales deeply and then shouts from the abdomen (where the chi is located) as the technique is performed.

Figure 20-1:
Chi
breathing
technique.

a.   b.

In Hapkido, the kihop is done not just when striking with kicks and punches, but when throwing as well.

The martial arts shout is called a *kiai* in Japanese arts and a *kihop* or *kihap* in Korean arts.

Defensive Strategy

Hapkido, like Aikido, is based on the concept of achieving maximum effectiveness with minimum effort. That is, Hapkido practice doesn't waste energy. All techniques are direct and effective, including all-defensive techniques.

- ✔ Your defense should be simple, effective, and in direct response to the attack.

- ✔ You should never move unnecessarily to counterattack.

Basic Techniques

Hapkido involves hundreds of techniques. Defensive techniques, counterattacking techniques, punches, kicks, blocks, and interceptions . . . you can run out of breath just naming them all. In fact, you learn over 500 hand techniques before you even become a black belt. That's not including the variety of kicking and punching techniques that you also learn.

When you begin training, you're taught the techniques necessary to find and use your chi, such as breathing exercises and meditation. At the same time, you learn the basic punching and kicking techniques. Next, you learn the techniques of disengagement. After you understand these, you move onto joint locks and defenses against kicks and punches. Advanced students eventually master the throwing techniques of Hapkido.

Every conceivable attack has a technique. The founder did his best to imagine every conceivable attack; that's why Hapkido has so many techniques.

Although you'll be exposed to all the techniques, you may choose those that work best for you, given your skills, abilities, and physical attributes, so don't let sheer numbers intimidate you. By the time it becomes your turn to teach the more than 500 techniques, you'll have spent years with them, and it won't seem so overwhelming.

The techniques build on each other so that a technique used to disengage becomes a technique used to control an attacker, which then becomes a technique to throw an attacker. Thus, you don't learn dozens of unrelated techniques. You learn dozens of techniques in context (and over time).

Breakfalls (Nakbeop)

Because throws are used in Hapkido and in street fights, you have to learn to fall correctly so that nothing breaks. Hapkido breakfalls include the forward roll, the backward fall, and the side fall.

Forward roll

When you're thrown (or fall, you klutz you) to the front, the best way to protect yourself is to roll. Step forward, lean over, and extend your forward arm towards the ground. Use this arm to guide your body but don't *land* on this arm. Tuck your chin in and roll forward. The back of your shoulder should touch the ground first. Continue moving forward to a standing position.

Backward fall

Keep your head tucked in towards your chest. Slap your hands and forearms onto the ground as you fall. Do not place your hands directly behind you and don't land directly on your palms.

Side fall

This technique is similar to the back fall. Again, keep your head tucked. Slap your hand and forearm to the ground, landing on your hip and shoulder.

The natural stance

Unlike other martial arts, such as Tae Kwon Do (Chapter 16) and Karate (Chapter 14), Hapkido has only one stance, and even this one stance isn't formal. The natural stance is the fighting stance in Hapkido.

Your legs should be about a shoulder's width apart for stability, with one leg slightly behind the other. The forward foot faces directly ahead; the back foot is at an angle to it. Your knees should remain slightly bent for mobility. Arms are raised shoulder high, and hands are made into fists.

From this natural stance, the Hapkido practitioner can move into whatever position is necessary to defend herself against an attack. Because the Hapkido practitioner gets her power from the *danjon* (the location of the *chi;* the center of the body), getting power from the stance is less important. In Hapkido, being flexible and able to react to the attacker is essential.

Hand techniques

The defensive methods that are used to disengage from an attack, execute a joint lock, and perform a throw are called *hand techniques.* More than 500 hand techniques are found in Hapkido and can be used to counter any type of attack.

Defensive techniques are done immediately upon an attack being launched. The longer that it takes you to react, then your chances of being able to effectively defend yourself decrease.

The thumb is the weakest part of the attacker's grip. In Hapkido, the thumb is usually attacked in order to disengage from a grab.

Hapkido practitioners, along with other martial artists, practice according to the *continual motion theory.* This is the theory that no one particular technique can necessarily end a physical confrontation, so you must follow up with a counterattacking technique — sometimes more than one counterattacking technique — until the threat is eliminated.

Disengaging techniques

Hapkido provides many techniques to defend against common grabs. Essentially, the purpose of a disengaging technique is to free yourself from an attacker's grab.

In Hapkido, all disengaging techniques are followed up with counterattacks, such as elbow strikes, punches, locks, or throws. A basic disengaging technique is the *wrist grab*.

1. Assume the attacker is facing you and grabs your right wrist with her left hand.
2. Step toward the attacker with your right foot.
3. Open your hand and keep your fingers tight together to flatten your hand into a knife hand. Bend your elbow and pull your right arm back.
4. Then thrust your right arm downward at an angle and across your body, disengaging the attacker's grip.
5. Then perform an elbow strike with that arm, and follow up with other counterattacks as necessary.

Joint-locking techniques

Joint locks are performed (and taught) after disengaging techniques. With a joint lock, you control the attacker's attacking limb. These are an effective replacement for counterattacks in those instances when you may not want to seriously injure your attacker, just stop him from continuing the attack.

Joint locks don't and shouldn't take much effort. If the lock is difficult to do, it's probably ineffective. The numbered steps that follow demonstrate a joint lock:

1. Assume the attacker is facing you and grabs your right wrist with his left hand.
2. The attacker, facing you, grabs your left wrist with his right hand (see Figure 20-2a).
3. Form a knife hand with your right hand.
4. Swing your arm up and twist your wrist, so your palm faces the floor.
5. With your left hand, grab the attacker's hand, digging your fingers under the bottom of his hand and place your thumb against the back of his hand.

6. Pull your right hand away while twisting the attacker's hand with your left hand.

7. Place your now-freed right hand next to your left on the attacker's hand, pressing his wrist down (see Figure 20-2b).

8. To increase pressure and pain, push down harder on the wrist.

Figure 20-2: Joint lock technique.

Practicing joint locks can be risky business. Make sure that you use extra care when doing these with a partner. You can cause serious damage to someone's joint if you're not careful.

Throwing techniques

Throws are generally taught to advanced students who have already mastered disengagements and joint locks. Like Aikido throws, Hapkido throws are based on redirecting the opponent's energy. Using leverage rather than brute force makes Hapkido throws nearly effortless.

The following numbered steps provide an example of a throw:

1. Assume that you're facing the attacker, and he grabs your right wrist with his left hand.

2. Make a knife hand with your right hand. Twist your wrist so your palm faces upward.

3. Step directly forward with your left leg to your attacker's right side.

4. Grab his right shoulder with your left (free) hand.

5. Swing the attacker's arm above his shoulder, while directing the shoulder toward the ground with your right hand.

6. Pivot to the right as you guide the attacker to the ground (see Figure 20-3). If the attacker is also a Hapkido practitioner, he can gently perform a forward roll to a standing position; otherwise, splat!

Figure 20-3:
Forward
throw.

Defense against strikes

An attacker may not reach out and grab you. She may kick or punch you. The founder of Hapkido was aware of that, so he designed techniques for just such a situation.

Hapkido defense against strikes is based on the principles that all hand and foot strikes come in one of two ways:

- **Linear attack:** Directly to the target
- **Roundhouse or circular attack:** Sweeping toward the target from or to the side

Thus, a hand or foot attack has two possible responses, depending on whether it's a direct or circular attack:

- To defend against linear attacks, you sidestep the attack and then counterattack.
- To defend against a roundhouse attack, you intercept the attack before impact.

In either case, timing is a crucial element to effectively defending yourself. If you side step too late, it doesn't matter how elegant your side step was; if your interception doesn't intercept the technique, it doesn't matter how macho you look doing it. Using these defense techniques requires continual and repeated practice.

Elbow controls

To defend against punches, you control the attacker's elbow. When the attacker strikes with a direct punch, sidestep the attack and place your knife hand against the attacker's elbow to block or deflect the punch and guide it away from you. This also serves to check the attacker's attacking arm; with your knife-hand against her elbow, the attacker can't launch another attack with that arm (see Figure 20-4). This technique can be used to defend against many common hand strikes.

For roundhouse punches, the knife hand is applied to the inner elbow; in essence, you intercept the technique with your knife hand before it has a chance to land on your skull.

Kick controls

A similar principle applies to defending against kicks.

- You can step out of the way and parry the kick with your knife hand.
- You can use a cross block, especially if the kick comes too fast for you to step out of the way or if several kicks come in succession and you can't keep sidestepping them. For the cross block, you simply cross your knife hands at the wrist and force them against the kicking leg, directing it downward. A variation of this technique allows you to throw the attacker.

✔ You can capture the leg after you've moved out of the way. For example, as the side kick goes by, you grab the leg at the thigh and ankle and control or throw the attacker.

✔ For roundhouse techniques, including roundhouse kicks and spinning-heel kicks, you move inside the kick to intercept the kick and grab the kicking leg or throw the kicker.

Figure 20-4:
Elbow
control.

Hapkido history

Choi Yong Shul developed and systemized Hapkido techniques, based on the traditional martial arts of Korea, in the 1930s. He added Aikido elements to the Korean techniques and combined strikes and kicks with grappling techniques and throws. Its current system was finalized in 1963.

Choi studied Aikijutsu under Takeda Sokaku, when Japanese forces occupying Korea forced Choi to work in Japan as a laborer. The founder of Aikido, Ueshiba Morihei, also studied Aikijutsu during Choi's time in Japan, spending seven years with Takeda Sokaku. Thus, both Hapkido and Aikido share a similar parentage.

Chapter 21

Muay Thai

In This Chapter

▶ Being fast and durable can help

▶ Learning about the different kinds of kickboxing

▶ Understanding Muay Thai strategy

▶ Discovering basic kickboxing techniques

*M*uay Thai kickboxing, sometimes called *Thai Boxing,* is a tough form of kickboxing that dates back several centuries, at least to the mid-sixteenth century. In Thailand, Muay Thai kickboxing is a hugely popular spectator sport.

Muay Thai, nicknamed *the science of eight limbs,* uses both hands, both feet, both knees, and both elbows as weapons. Pure Muay Thai is a brutal, difficult sport, but people who practice the less deadly styles of it appreciate the physical conditioning, strength, and endurance that they achieve.

Muay Thai and its other kickboxing incarnations are more sport than martial art, and Muay Thai practitioners bypass many of the rituals of traditional martial arts. But like training in any of the martial arts, training in Muay Thai builds self-confidence and physical fitness and reduces stress.

Be aware that aerobic kickboxing programs, such as *Cardio-Kickboxing, Tae Bo,* and *Aerobox,* are *not* self-defense programs. Fitness instructors, not martial artists, usually teach these classes, so they may not even be doing the techniques correctly. Aerobic kickboxing is an excellent way to get in shape, but if you want to learn to defend yourself, you'll need to take a self-defense class.

Fighting Fit

Muay Thai requires you to be in excellent shape. Beginners (who don't expect to be fighting anytime soon) can build their fitness through training in Muay

Thai. The body conditioning, endurance exercises, and drills can help them get in top shape.

✔ **Fast:** Techniques require speed and power.

✔ **Not so flexible:** Most kicks are low, so lower body flexibility is not as important as in other martial arts.

✔ **Durable:** Like boxing, endurance is needed to fight a complete match.

✔ **All shapes and sizes:** Technique rules, so smaller and shorter people can still whup up on bigger and taller but less skilled opponents.

More women than men are now training in kickboxing in the United States, and women are gaining on men in Canada and the United Kingdom.

Conditioning Versus Competition: Kickboxing Styles

Although kickboxing comes in many different styles with slightly different approaches to the techniques, essentially, schools are broken into two categories:

✔ **Schools that emphasize conditioning.** Such schools include those that teach aerobic kickboxing and that teach contact kickboxing but don't push competition as the main purpose of training.

✔ **Schools that emphasize competition.** These kickboxing gyms train people to fight in amateur and pro competitions, and they clearly state that as their purpose.

Some Muay Thai techniques, such as elbow strikes, aren't allowed in other types of kickboxing competition. However, these techniques can be practiced for self-defense. It makes more sense to hit someone with your elbow than with your fist. You're less likely to hurt yourself.

Training Methods

Kickboxers rely on cross-training to become excellent fighters. So not only do they train in their sport, but they also do weight training, aerobic training, flexibility exercises, and other drills to help them maintain their edge.

Weight training

Some kickboxers refuse to go near weights, believing they get all the workout that they need hitting the heavy bag. Others swear by weight training, but say it must be done right.

If you bulk up too much, you can interfere with your agility and speed, which are important to a kickboxer. That muscle-bound bully who used to kick sand in your face probably couldn't perform kickboxing techniques.

Kickboxers often do a full-body weight-training workout per session, or they alternate upper body workouts with lower body workouts. They don't necessarily need complicated weight training regimens. A weight-lifting workout for 40 minutes twice a week is generally more than enough weight training for a kickboxer.

Weight training shouldn't be done the day after a heavy contact kickboxing workout, although you can do it after an aerobic kickboxing session. Heavy workouts should be followed by light workouts. This gives your muscles time to recuperate and gain strength. A full-body workout should include arms, shoulders, legs, and abdomen.

Body conditioning

Weight training builds muscle mass, which helps in terms of sheer power. You can shove your competitor around the ring if your biceps are like small trees, and he has biceps like limp spaghetti.

But muscle endurance is what counts in kickboxing — not sheer strength. You have to keep lifting your hands to punch and your legs to kick. That's muscle endurance.

This type of muscle endurance is achieved through body-conditioning exercises, which are essentially those exercises that use your own body weight as resistance. Professional kickboxers do hundreds of crunches, pushups, and pull-ups every week. (Some of them do hundreds of crunches, pushups, and pull-ups every *day.*) You'll have to start doing the same if you hope to become that lean, mean fighting machine that you've always dreamed of being.

Cardio training

In addition to weight training, most kickboxers improve their endurance and cardiovascular fitness through cardio training. This can be running, swimming, biking, or an aerobics class, even an aerobic kickboxing class.

Flexibility training

In order to do the techniques with blazing speed, you have to have flexibility in your joints. If you feel stiff, you're not going to be able to launch that lightning-quick attack against your opponent to win the match.

By improving your flexibility, you're actually improving the range-of-motion in a joint. This increases your agility and makes you as slippery as an eel. (Try landing a punch on an eel, and you'll see that this is a good thing.)

Static stretches (no bouncing) can help you improve your flexibility, and hundreds of these exercises exist. Toe touches, open stretches, and the like can all help you improve your flexibility. You may also take a yoga class once a week to help improve your flexibility. (Practice the techniques at home, too, to get full benefit.)

Balance

You can always tell beginning kickboxers by how often they fall over trying to do a front kick. Maintaining your balance is essential in kickboxing, and it's something that you can even train to do. If you have no sense of balance at all, start moving through the following steps slowly:

1. Stand near a wall, and place one palm on the wall.

2. Bend your knee so that one leg is off the floor.

3. Stand in this position for thirty seconds. Relax and repeat with the other leg.

4. If this is a piece of cake (or after it becomes a piece of cake), let go of the wall.

5. Stand in the middle of the room and bend your knee, so one leg is off the floor.

6. Hold the position for thirty seconds and then relax and repeat with the other leg.

7. Close your eyes when you stand on one foot. Your vision helps you keep your balance, but it's good to be able to keep your balance even if your eyes are closed. (If sweat or even blood gets into your eyes when you're fighting, you still want to be able to fight without falling over.)

8. After you can do that, try kicking with one leg. Now try kicking with one leg with your eyes closed. When you can manage all that, you'll have a solid sense of balance.

Fitting it all in

"Great!" you say. "I can become a truly competitive kickboxer, but unfortunately, with all that training, I won't actually be able to keep my job."

Relax. It just sounds more complicated than it is. First, you don't have to do all the training immediately. Start out with an aerobic kickboxing class and build from there. Or do some one-on-one training with a kickboxing coach and learn what areas you need to work on most and start with those.

Stretching, body conditioning, and balance exercises can be done throughout the day whenever you get a chance. They may also be part of your kickboxing workout.

Weight training doesn't need to be done more than twice a week. On really busy weeks, one full-body workout can be enough. These sessions don't have to take more than forty minutes, either.

Cardio training should be done three times per week. These sessions don't have to take more than half an hour, but an hour is ideal.

Don't forget to have one day of rest each week to give your body a chance to recuperate from all that training.

A Kickboxing Workout Routine

What should a kickboxing routine look like for a beginner? It looks hard. That's what it looks like, and it's only going to get harder. But that's how you develop awesome kicks and punches, rock hard abs, and enough stamina to catch the bus even when you're running late.

Although training sessions vary in length and intensity, usually an hour or so is sufficient time to get a good workout in. You may go to a class, you may work with a trainer one-on-one, or you may do the workout in the privacy of your own living room. Or you may do some combination of all three approaches.

A sample beginner's kickboxing workout may look like this. (You may take a breather every now and then between activities.)

1. Jump rope or similar cardio (five minutes)
2. Stair climb machine or similar cardio (five minutes)

3. Stretches (five minutes)

4. Crunches (20+ repetitions)

5. Punch the focus mitt or heavy bag (two two-minute rounds)

6. Kick the kicking target bag or heavy bag (two two-minute rounds)

7. Kick and punch the heavy bag with combinations (two two-minute rounds)

8. Pushups (20+ repetitions)

9. Crunches (20+ repetitions)

10. Stretches (five minutes)

Sparring for Fun and Profit

When you do aerobic kickboxing, you never actually kick and punch other people, and they never actually kick and punch you. If you're totally sane, this seems like a reasonable approach to you. But you're missing out on much of life's lessons if you never spar another kickboxer in the ring.

If you just practice your techniques on the heavy bag, you won't learn the importance of timing, and although you may practice *combos* — combinations of kicks and punches that flow together without stopping — you won't learn what techniques actually work best for you until you spar with another fighter.

Sparring with partners in the gym can be plenty of fun. You learn how to defend against another person's kicks and punches, which is good training for self-defense, and you learn how to kick and punch another person who knows what you're trying to do and is on the lookout for it. You have to develop timing, confidence, and sheer grit.

You may never want to go beyond this type of sparring, and that's fine. You'll still get great benefits from your training.

Safety considerations

Incompetent training can cause injuries, especially when you get to the stage of sparring in the ring. Make sure your instructor has appropriate credentials. For kickboxing, someone who has kickboxed professionally is a better bet than someone who just has a black belt in a martial art.

In kickboxing, you wear safety equipment when you spar to prevent injuries. This includes a mouthguard, headgear, gloves, and shin guards. Also, most kickboxing gyms let you set the amount of contact you're comfortable with. A good rule of thumb is to kick other people only as hard as you want to be kicked back. (In professional kickboxing, you're going to try to knock out the opponent, and so the contact is going to be much harder.)

Along with incompetent instruction, you could get hurt if you or your sparring partner is wearing defective or worn safety equipment or no equipment at all. Make sure that your equipment is in good shape and replace it as soon as it shows signs of wear. Torn equipment shouldn't be used and must be replaced immediately.

Competitive sparring

If you really enjoy the friendly sparring sessions in the gym, you may also want to fight in sanctioned competition as an amateur and perhaps some day as a professional. Both men and women can fight as amateurs and professionals, but neither makes much money at it.

If you do so, you need to make sure that you have a good trainer who knows how to prepare fighters for matches. Professionals need a manager to help promote their career and arrange their matches.

In addition to your regular training sessions, if you plan to compete in amateur tournaments or professional bouts, you need some special training. This is no time to try to go it alone. Seek the advice of experienced kickboxers and your teacher. See Chapter 10 for more information on competition.

In 1974, the Professional Kickboxers Association (PKA) was founded to promote kickboxing throughout the world. The first official sanctioning organization, the PKA set the rules for amateur and professional competition.

Basic Techniques

In Muay Thai, about 30 techniques are used. In other forms of kickboxing, slightly fewer techniques make up the arsenal.

In some forms of kickboxing, you're not allowed to use elbow strikes.

If you compare this to the hundreds of martial arts techniques, such as in Hapkido (Chapter 20) and Aikido (Chapter 18), you'll see that kickboxing has pared the techniques down to the minimum necessary to win a fight.

All techniques are taught through repetition and through sparring. No forms are taught in kickboxing.

Fighting stance

Kickboxing has one stance, the *fighting stance,* which is shown in Figure 21-1. This is also called the *neutral stance.* You stand with your body slightly turned away from the target or opponent. One leg is slightly behind the other, and your legs are about a shoulder's width apart for stability. Knees are only slightly bent for mobility. Your weight is evenly distributed to both legs.

Your hands should be fists, and they should be up, guarding your face and body, with your elbows tucked to your ribs. Your chin should be tucked toward your chest. Although you should work both sides equally in training, usually you start with your dominant leg as your back leg — your power leg.

Punches

The punches used in kickboxing are similar to the punches used in boxing. You start with your hands up near your shoulders, and you pivot on your feet, turning your body weight into the punch to add power. This is different from traditional martial arts punches, where your hands start at your waist.

Jab

The *jab* is done with your forward (nondominant) hand. You simply punch forward from the shoulder, bringing your hand back to guard your head as quickly as possible. The jab is used to feel out the opponent — to see how she responds and not actually inflict damage or score points.

Cross

The *cross* is a power punch. You use your backhand (dominant hand) to perform it. You bring your fist forward, extending your arm from the shoulder and turning your body into the punch (see Figure 21-2).

Hook

The *hook* can be performed with either hand. Your arm starts in the *hook* position, with your elbow bent and your arm parallel to the floor. You turn your body into the hook instead of extending your arm. The bend (hook) in your elbow stays constant even on impact.

Figure 21-1:
Fighting
stance
(also
called
neutral
stance).

Overhand

The *overhand* punch is a circular punch that comes up from the shoulder and down on top of the opponent's head. This technique isn't commonly used and is most effective for taller fighters. It helps you get past an opponent's guard.

Uppercut

The *uppercut* can be done with either hand. It impacts the opponent's ribs or the underside of his jaw. For this technique, you drop your hand slightly past shoulder level and then bring your fist up and under the target.

Spinning back fist

This technique was borrowed from martial arts and can be done with either hand. For this technique, you hit with the back of your fist rather than your knuckles (hence its name). You extend your arm so that your elbow is only slightly bent, then rotate to the back (this builds speed) and smack your opponent's temple.

Figure 21-2:
A cross punch in action.

Elbows and knees

Elbow strikes may not be allowed in competition, but they're excellent self-defense tools. The point of the elbow can be used to strike, as can the front of the elbow. You can drive the point of the elbow into an attacker from behind or to the side. You can swing the front of your elbow in a sweeping motion to a vulnerable part of an attacker's anatomy, such as a nose.

Knee strikes may be used in kickboxing competition, and they're either straight or roundhouse. As shown in Figure 21-3, you can simply drive your knee into your opponent's solar plexus (just below his rib cage and sternum) or an attacker's groin, or you can swing your knee from the side to attack the ribs.

Kicks

Kicks are divided into two categories: defensive and offensive. *Defensive kicks* are fast and can be used to block an attack. They're done with the front leg. Using the back leg, *offensive kicks* are a bit slower but more powerful.

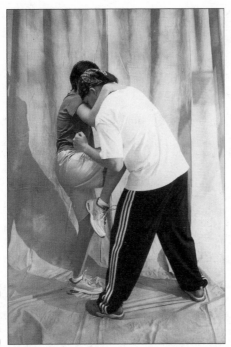

Figure 21-3:
Knee strike.

Roundhouse

This is the staple kick of your arsenal. The kick sweeps from the side to your target. You use your shin or your instep as the striking surface, as shown in Figure 21-4. You can use this type of kick often to target your opponent's shin, as shown in Figure 21-5. Traditionally, you would condition your legs for these devastating shin strikes by kicking small trees.

Front kick

For this kick, you strike directly in front of you. You fold your leg (chamber your leg by bending your knee) and then snap your leg forward, striking with the ball of your foot (see Figure 21-6).

Side kick

For this kick, you fold your kicking leg, then pivot on your supporting foot, and thrust your kicking leg forward, striking with the heel of your foot.

Turn back kick

This kick (also called the *reverse kick* or the *reverse side kick*) requires you to spin to the back as you fold your leg and then kick with the heel of your foot.

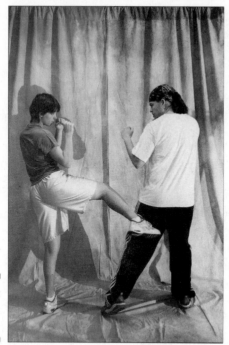

Figure 21-4:
Round-
house kick.

Figure 21-5:
Roundhouse
kick to shin.

Figure 21-6:
Front kick.

Leg sweeps and throws

Other techniques may be allowed in kickboxing competition or may be taught in training as aids to self-defense. Most leg sweeps and throws in kickboxing are straightforward and don't require difficult maneuvers. For example, one popular sweep just requires you to put your foot behind your opponent's foot and hook his foot out from under while you push.

Muay Thai history

Muay Thai kickboxing began in Thailand several centuries ago. No one is quite sure how kickboxing started, but it's possible that a martial arts influence came to Thailand from China. Empty-hand combat skills may have been taught as part of military training in Siam, the country that was the forerunner of modern Thailand.

Muay Thai kickboxing influenced the development of all other styles of kickboxing, and so did classical boxing. (Most modern kickboxers use boxing punches rather than traditional martial arts punches.) Another influence was *Savate,* a French form of fighting that used kicks. Sailors brought kicking techniques from China and used them in self-defense. Savate later became a popular sport.

Eventually, the techniques of these different fighting styles melded to create modern kickboxing.

Chapter 22

Jeet Kune Do and Eclectic Martial Arts

In This Chapter

▶ Finding out about underlying concepts

▶ Learning about the Way of No Way

▶ Understanding typical eclectic techniques

▶ Creating your own eclectic style

Most people have heard of Judo, Karate, Tae Kwon Do, and Kung Fu. (See Chapters 17, 14, 16, and 15, respectively.) If you tell your next-door neighbor that you're on your way to kickboxing class, he understands what you mean and will probably treat you more politely from now on.

But *Krav Maga, Pankration,* and *Jeet Kune Do*? What are those? Appetizers on the menu of a French restaurant?

Actually, they're all styles of martial arts, sometimes called *eclectic* martial arts. Why eclectic? Because they're unusual, and they take a buffet approach to martial arts training. Founders of these styles have spent years picking and choosing among many different techniques to come up with a system that includes only the best, most effective movements. That's what *eclectic* means. (You can look it up in the dictionary if you don't believe me.)

The most well known of the eclectic styles is Jeet Kune Do. The famous martial artist, teacher, and actor, Bruce Lee, developed this martial art according to his philosophy of martial arts training.

Defense by Interception

Jeet Kune Do is, literally, *the Way of the Intercepting Fist,* and it's a comprehensive martial art that uses only the best techniques, strategies, and tactics of martial arts. Just as intercepting a pass in football destroys the opponent's attack, intercepting a strike in a fight destroys the opponent's attack and puts you in the driver's seat. Now your offense can get out on the field and win one for the Gipper. As an advanced Jeet Kune Do practitioner, you would modify the techniques to suit your own skills, abilities, physical type, and personal style.

After Bruce Lee died, his senior students began teaching Jeet Kune Do from a variety of approaches. Although it's still not a style that you can find on every street corner, Jeet Kune Do is more accessible than it was 30 years ago.

Known as the first eclectic martial art, Jeet Kune Do (JKD) incorporates elements of Karate, Judo, and Jujutsu, along with classical wrestling and boxing. Like other eclectic martial arts, JKD structure isn't formal. You wear comfortable clothes, and JKD has no ranks. You won't learn forms. (Bruce Lee *hated* forms.) And you won't do prearranged drills — or not often, anyway. You just practice the techniques and spar.

Let Me Count the Eclectic Ways

Eclectic styles combine different elements of various martial arts to create a new martial art. People who have trained in traditional martial arts often think that the training is artificially rigid and that certain techniques are missing, so they begin to look for ways to supplement their training. The result is often an eclectic martial art.

Creating your own style of martial art, whether it's an eclectic style or not, has a long and honorable history. From the beginning of organized martial arts training, students have tried to refine techniques and to develop systems that are better than the ones currently in existence.

Drawbacks to the traditional approach

Supporters of eclectic styles feel that traditional approaches to martial arts training have drawbacks. For example, if you train in Karate, you may not learn much about throwing and grappling, so if you encountered someone in a street fight or in a tough-man competition who knew these techniques, you may be at a disadvantage. By the same token, if you learn Judo, and depend on throws and locks to defeat your competition, you may not know exactly what to do when that insane Karate-ka comes after you with fists (and feet) of fury.

Eclectic styles try to combine several methods to eliminate this problem. Most eclectic styles teach both striking and grappling skills.

Traditional martial artists say that if they use their techniques effectively, problems are nonexistent — nothing is missing. A grappler can throw a kicker to the ground; a kicker can keep a grappler at a distance, so the grappler can't throw him to the ground.

Eclectic styles

Martial arts has more eclectic styles than you can shake a stick at. Some of the better-known ones include the following:

- **Capoeira:** This African-Brazilian system of unarmed combat is based on self-defense techniques that slaves used in South America.

- **Hand-to-Hand Combat:** Military trainers use martial arts techniques to teach armed and unarmed combat strategies to recruits. You may see ads for programs used by the U.S. Navy SEALS or the like.

- **Krav Maga:** This is an Israeli form of self-defense that uses kicks, punches, and throws.

- **Mu Tau:** This is a martial art based on classical boxing and wrestling.

- **Pankration:** This is a style of Greek wrestling and boxing in which kicks, throws, and locks are used.

- **Self-Defense Programs:** Self-defense programs, which meet for short periods of time and attempt to teach basic self-defense techniques, may be considered eclectic martial arts. After all, the techniques are selected for ease of use and maximum effectiveness.

  In *padded attacker* courses, you try out your techniques against someone in heavily padded gear so that you can go full power and learn if you really can stop an attacker. These courses are generally geared toward women.

  The most serious martial artists feel that these courses may give students a false sense of security, especially if the techniques aren't practiced repeatedly over a long period of time. Learning the arts of combat can't be done in a weekend.

- **Shootboxing:** This martial art, which combines kickboxing and Judo, is popular in Japan.

- **Shootfighting:** This martial art combines shootboxing and wrestling.

- **Trapfighting:** This is an Americanized version of shootfighting.

- **Vale Tudo:** This is a Brazilian form of wrestling with roots in street fighting.

Physical Facts

Eclectic styles run the gamut from high-kicking, acrobatic *Capoeira* to the straightforward and deadly effective *Krav Maga*. You can even create your own eclectic style to suit your needs and abilities.

You'll need over-all fitness, including agility and strength, but the diversity of styles is so great that you can find one that's perfect for you, no matter what shape you're in. (Sumo, anyone?)

Because eclectic styles can be so accommodating — you use what you can use — they make a good choice for someone who has physical limitations, yet still wants to gain the benefits of training in the martial arts. Techniques can be modified to suit your abilities, and you can be challenged to perform more than you may think possible.

Jeet Kune Do Concepts

Jeet Kune Do isn't just a system of martial arts techniques. In fact, it isn't really a system of techniques at all. No wonder people call it the Way of No Way. The idea is that telling you what to do limits you too much. Instead of you trying to fit into a rigid system, the system adapts to you.

Like other martial arts, practicing Jeet Kune Do is a process of self-discovery. You won't get far if you expect the teacher to *fill you up* with knowledge. You have to *uncover* the knowledge yourself. Bruce Lee used to liken this to a sculptor who takes away clay to reveal the figure or design beneath.

Jeet Kune Do is a live, fluid, and constantly changing and adapting approach to fighting. According to Bruce Lee, the martial artist should "absorb what is useful; reject what is useless; add what is specifically your own."

This doesn't mean that Jeet Kune Do has no teachings. Certain basic principles capture the essence of Jeet Kune Do, but even these basic principles that follow can be abandoned if needed in order to defeat the opponent:

✔ You must always preserve the centerline.

✔ Your techniques must flow rhythmically.

✔ You must react to and fit your techniques to the opponent's attack.

Jeet Kune Do Curriculum

Bruce Lee developed a curriculum that you can learn as you discover more about the art. The areas of study include

- ✔ Basic kicks and punches (Only the most direct, efficient strikes are used.)
- ✔ Body shifting
- ✔ Evading, blocking, destroying, intercepting, and redirecting the attack
- ✔ Feinting
- ✔ Holds
- ✔ Nontelegraphic techniques (Your opponent can't tell what you're going to do before you do it.)
- ✔ Strategies of attacking and defending
- ✔ Theory of independent movement (Each limb moves separately.)
- ✔ Trapping and immobilizing techniques

Typical Training

Although every teacher of an eclectic style takes a different approach to teaching the concepts and techniques of that style, in general, eclectic martial arts are taught in an unstructured setting. You wear comfortable workout clothing, such as T-shirt and sweat pants. JKD doesn't have a traditional uniform or a traditional belt ranking system. You'll probably wear shoes, but in some styles, you may be able to work out barefoot. When you spar, you use some form of safety equipment to reduce the risk of injury. Your coach can help you decide what to wear and what type of equipment to invest in.

Your own interests and abilities dictate much of your training. If you're not self-disciplined and highly motivated, your teacher isn't going to do it for you.

Eclectic styles usually don't have forms, but you learn a few drills and follow prearranged routines. Mostly, you practice the techniques and spar using the techniques. You may also do plenty of body conditioning exercises, such as crunches, pushups, and pull-ups, and you may also do cardio work, such as running in a nearby park or up and down the stairs.

In some schools of Capoeira, students form a circle with a large space in the center; an assistant beats a drum to provide a rhythm. Students may clap to keep the beat, jump into the circle, and perform the techniques when they feel the need to do so.

Creating Your Own Martial Art

You don't have to follow the rules set down by others. You can create your own martial art. The history of martial artists striking out on their own and developing their own effective systems of combat and then teaching these new systems to other martial artists is long.

Developing a solid background

In general, you need to have a background in at least one martial art to create your own style. You can even call it *Joe-Do,* meaning *the Way of Joe,* or whatever you want. Spending time training seriously in a martial art, such as Karate, before creating your own system is essential to creating an effective system.

After you have a background in martial arts, you can then analyze what's missing, consider your own skills and abilities, and then add in techniques that you can use and discard the rest. You can keep your personal martial art to yourself, or you can teach it to the world like Bruce Lee did. It helps if you're as awesome as Bruce Lee.

Finding other techniques

After you have a grounding in a martial art, you need to explore other martial arts to see what they have to offer. From this research, you can develop a system that incorporates the best of all martial arts techniques.

You can attend classes in various martial arts for short periods of time or even long periods of time. No one sets a time limit on how long you may take to create your own marital art.

You can also attend seminars and workshops offered by experts in various martial arts. You can spend an intense few hours or maybe a few days with a master and learn several techniques that can complement your system. Depending on the length of the workshop or seminar and who is offering it, you may spend anywhere from $20 to $1,000 learning the "secrets of the Navy SEALS" or "Dim Mak Death Touch in ten easy steps."

Seminars and workshops are advertised in martial arts magazines, on the Internet, and through various listservs that cater to martial artists.

Even if you're devoted to a traditional martial art, such as Judo, you can benefit from attending workshops and seminars in different styles. These can improve your skills and expand your abilities.

Other ways to learn about techniques include the Internet, which has more martial arts sites than you can count, as well as videos, books, and magazines.

Basic Techniques of Jeet Kune Do

Although Jeet Kune Do is a philosophical approach to martial arts training rather than an arsenal of techniques that you're expected to learn before you're considered proficient, certain techniques and strategies are taught to students. The basic concepts of Jeet Kune Do, described in the "Jeet Kune Do Concepts" section, earlier in this chapter, are illustrated in the way the following techniques are practiced and applied in training.

The way of no stances

Jeet Kune Do doesn't have static stances for you to learn. JKD simply has transitions from one technique to another. The ideal is *balance in motion* — not balance in stasis.

The Jeet Kune Do practitioner strives to stay light on her feet while at the same time remaining balanced and difficult to knock over. She tries to keep her hands in such a position to guard the centerline and to intercept attacks, but no hard-and-fast rules govern this. Sometimes, you have to drop your guard to defeat the opponent. Only experience and training teaches you when to do what.

Evasion

Maneuvering your body to evade an attack is a fundamental principle of Jeet Kune Do. The *perfect* evasion is one where you avoid a strike and launch a counterattack at the same time.

For the most part, shifting your body can accomplish the necessary evasion, such as twisting your upper body out of the way. Footwork is sometimes used, but remember that an essential principle of Jeet Kune Do is to use as little energy and movement as is necessary to defeat the opponent. The direct, linear approach is the most effective.

For example, suppose an attacker is punching toward your nose, as shown in Figure 22-1. Twist your upper body to the side instead of sidestepping the punch to evade the strike and at the same time launch a counterattack (such as a punch) to the inside of the attacker's strike.

Figure 22-1:
Evasion
and strike.

Trapping

You can easily prevent the opponent from landing a strike by redirecting his attack. This requires confidence and agility, which come with time and training.

For example, suppose the attacker is punching your nose. As the strike comes, you launch your own counterattack inside of it, effectively redirecting the attacker's strike away from your body. Then you trap the attacker's arm between your counterattacking arm and your free hand as demonstrated in Figure 22-2.

Attacking by combination

You can combine several attacks — maybe punches, kicks, and leg sweeps — in an aggressive, nonstop sequence in order to disable or stop an attacker.

Your goal is to make your combination of techniques flow, like a boxer does, with the intention of disabling the attacker.

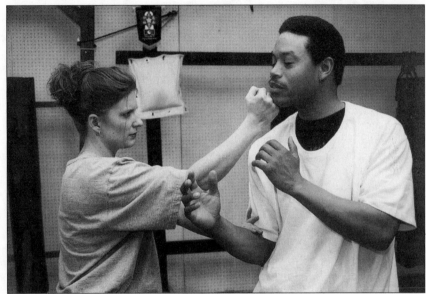

Figure 22-2:
Trapping
hands.

Attacking by drawing

This may also be called *attack by feinting*. You feint (fake) a technique without actually striking the opponent. This causes the opponent to launch a counter-attack. You trap the attacker's striking hand (see the "Trapping" section, earlier in this chapter) and then deliver your own disabling strike, as shown in Figure 22-3.

Kicks

In Jeet Kune Do, kicks are mostly used to set up punches, which are considered the more effective techniques. A kick is more effective against a fighter who isn't expecting it than against a fighter trained in martial arts.

Jeet Kune Do kicks are strong and quick, taking the most direct route. They're usually directed to a low-target area, as shown in Figure 22-4.

Figure 22-3:
Feint
and trap.

Figure 22-4:
Jeet Kune
Do kick.

Punches

Punches come at all angles and from whatever position your body is in (see Figure 22-5). However, all punches start from the center of your body — not from the side of your waist as in traditional martial arts, and not from the shoulder as in boxing. The fist can be vertical, horizontal, or diagonal on impact.

Figure 22-5:
Jeet Kune
Do punch.

Bruce Lee and Jeet Kune Do

Bruce Lee, known for bringing Kung Fu to the attention of Americans, developed Jeet Kune Do as a way to help people *liberate* themselves from classical or traditional martial arts, which he called "a mess." Lee, who studied Wing Chun Kung Fu under the respected Sifu Yip Man, also studied other martial arts in order to select the most effective techniques of the different styles and to meld them into one totally effective system of fighting. Remember Bruce Lee's words: "Know the principle, follow the principle, dissolve the principle."

Chapter 23

T'ai Chi Chuan

In This Chapter

▶ Comparing T'ai Chi Chuan to other martial arts

▶ Learning T'ai Chi is good for your health

▶ Discovering the differences among styles

▶ Finding out how to do exercises that flow

T'ai Chi Chuan (Grand Ultimate Fist) is one of the oldest martial arts in the world — so old that its origins are lost. Although great stories abound about how the techniques were developed and taught, most of these stories have to do with boastful martial artists defeating whole villages full of Kung Fu devotees, thereby converting them to the practice of T'ai Chi Chuan. Even if the stories aren't true, they're plenty of fun to learn about.

As many as half a billion people start each day with T'ai Chi Chuan exercises, and that many people can't be wrong. If you visited China, you'd see people doing the techniques in the park, in the town square, and in their living rooms. Office workers and factory workers gather before their shifts to do the exercises and prepare themselves to face the day.

Normally called simply *T'ai Chi,* this martial art/fitness exercise consists of slow, connected movements that reduce your level of tension, relax your breathing, and clear your mind.

The movements of T'ai Chi are based on the theory that moving correctly allows your *chi* to circulate freely. Blocked chi causes mental and physical illness. (For more on your chi, see Appendix A.) So by doing the exercises, you open up your *meridians* — the channels in your body that chi energy moves through. T'ai Chi practitioners believe that your chi or life energy flows through channels in your body and these channels can be blocked, which causes illness and discomfort.

T'ai Chi teaches students to yield, so that the attacker defeats herself. This concept is demonstrated through the *push hands* exercise, which is discussed later in the chapter in the section of the same name.

The movements of T'ai Chi have a self-defense application, and proficient T'ai Chi practitioners can exert great power with their techniques.

Martial Art or Not?

Although some would argue that T'ai Chi Chuan isn't really a martial art at all but simply a form of exercise, advanced practitioners would beg to disagree.

The partner exercises teach you how to redirect an attacker's energy while yielding to absorb the blow without injury; the movements in both armed and unarmed *forms* (often called *kata,* prearranged patterns of techniques — see Chapter 5) can be used to stop an attacker. Like Aikido, the aim isn't to destroy the opponent but simply to avoid the attack.

T'ai Chi practitioners say that just because you don't have to jump three feet in the air, scream a blood-curdling scream, and break concrete blocks with the side of your hand doesn't mean that T'ai Chi is for sissies or that you can't use the techniques to defeat the bad guys.

Weapons Use

T'ai Chi teaches the use of weapons, especially after the practitioner has mastered the unarmed forms and the partner exercises. Weapons include traditional Chinese weapons (T'ai Chi is, after all, a Chinese martial art), such as the double-edged straight sword, the curved sword, the spear, and the staff. Some styles of T'ai Chi teach more weapons forms than other styles. See Chapter 12 for more information on weapons use.

Benefits of T'ai Chi

Researchers have actually studied T'ai Chi to see if it really does provide the benefits that practitioners claim. (Apparently, it was a boring day at the lab.) The results of these studies point to the fact that T'ai Chi can do great things for your body and your mind.

T'ai Chi teaches you that your mind, body, and spirit must be unified for mental and physical health. To ignore one puts all the others in jeopardy.

By practicing T'ai Chi, you'll achieve the following:

- ✔ Cardiovascular fitness
- ✔ Improved muscle tone
- ✔ Increased joint flexibility
- ✔ Lower blood pressure
- ✔ Reduced stress
- ✔ Serenity of mind
- ✔ Unblocked chi

Physical Factors

T'ai Chi is a gentle way of practicing the martial arts. It's like the difference between high-impact aerobics and low-impact aerobics. You get cardiovascular benefits no matter which approach you take, and doing low-impact aerobics means that you don't have to replace your hips every five years.

If your joints aren't up to performing flying side kicks, then maybe T'ai Chi is for you. T'ai Chi practitioners aim to develop a so-called T'ai Chi body, but it isn't necessary to have this *before* you start T'ai Chi. (By the way, a T'ai Chi body is one that's agile, supple, and energetic.)

- ✔ **All ability levels:** T'ai Chi can accommodate individuals with varying degrees of ability. The techniques can be modified to suit your abilities. All the techniques of T'ai Chi are performed in the way that's most comfortable to you. If you can do head-high kicks, fantastic; if not, ankle-high kicking is no shame.
- ✔ **Older:** Many older individuals practice T'ai Chi as a way to become flexible and then to maintain that flexibility.
- ✔ **With physical drawbacks:** T'ai Chi can improve the health of individuals with medical problems. If strenuous exercise induces asthma, for example, you may find that the gentle approach of T'ai Chi works for you.

Schools of Thought

T'ai Chi has many different schools, but most of them teach similar techniques. However, as in all styles of martial arts, everyone thinks his approach is best. The most important schools include the following:

- **Chen:** Chen-style is thought to be the original T'ai Chi. Its founder, Wang Tsung Yueh, according to legend, is supposed to have traveled to Chen village and challenged its fighters. He won but was so impressed with their fighting skills that he incorporated their fighting techniques into his style of T'ai Chi, which for reasons that remain unclear, was named after the village instead of the founder.

- **Yang:** Yang-style, a direct descendant of Chen-style, is the most popular form of T'ai Chi. Its founder, Yang Lu Chan, learned the Chen-style in Chen village. He is credited with developing the push-hands exercise. He became an expert at T'ai Chi and traveled throughout China teaching his version of it. (This early PR may be why this is the most popular style of T'ai Chi.)

- **Sun:** This style derives from Yang-style. Its founder, Wu Yu Hsiang, combined the techniques of Yang-style T'ai Chi with other Chinese martial arts (internal-style Kung Fu) to create the Sun style of T'ai Chi.

- **Wu:** Famous for its uprooting and throwing techniques, this style also derives from Yang-style. Wu Jien Chuan, the founder of this style, taught it throughout Southern China.

- **Cheng:** This style of T'ai Chi is a more philosophical version than the others and is more concerned with one's spiritual, mental, and emotional development than one's physical skills.

- **Lesser-Known Styles:** Lesser-known styles include Fu, which is practiced mostly in China; Li, Hao, and Hsu are all uncommon.

THE SENSEI SAYS

T'ai Chi is one of the *Five Accomplishments* thought in traditional China to make a superior person. The other accomplishments are painting, poetry, calligraphy, and music.

T'ai Chi Concepts

T'ai Chi emphasizes an understanding of *yin-yang* (the idea that the world is made of conflicting yet harmonious elements) and similar concepts that underlie other martial arts. (See Chapter 11 for more information on the mind-body-spirit connection.) It is based on Taoist philosophy, which encourages a supple, flexible mind, and spirit.

The techniques of Chi Kung, breathing exercises for health and fitness, are often taught in conjunction with T'ai Chi, just as they're frequently taught along with Kung Fu. See Chapter 15 for further Kung Fu information.

The original principles of T'ai Chi practice still exist in its teaching today:

- ✔ Circular movement
- ✔ Continuity (The end of one technique is the beginning of another.)
- ✔ Movement of chi from inside to outside the body
- ✔ Movement (The T'ai Chi practitioner is never still.)
- ✔ Relaxation
- ✔ Slowness
- ✔ Suppleness
- ✔ Straight body
- ✔ Strong stances (characterized by *sinking* into the stances)

Dan tien

The concept of *dan tien* (also known as *tan tien*) roughly corresponds with the Japanese concept of *hara* (the location of your chi in your abdomen) and the Korean concept of *danjon* (your base or center from which all actions begin).

The dan tien is your center of gravity; the location of your chi. Finding your dan tien, and focusing on it, is important for performing T'ai Chi movements correctly. Finding your center helps you maintain a balance of mind, body, and spirit.

Extend chi

You can (and should) direct your chi outward. If you know where your dan tien is and you relax, your energy focus is naturally outward.

Chi comes into the body as well as leaving it, just as air enters your body and leaves.

Meditation

You may be encouraged to meditate as a practitioner of T'ai Chi, but you won't receive a prescription describing how to do it. In T'ai Chi, it is thought that the meditative mind is always meditative. If serenity of mind is achieved, it's always evident. A serene state of mind doesn't just happen for ten minutes after class when you close your eyes and visualize.

Use any meditation technique, not just sitting in the lotus position and emptying your mind. In fact, the practice of T'ai Chi may be the perfect way to meditate! See Chapter 11 for more on meditation.

The Typical T'ai Chi Class

Because each style of T'ai Chi is different, and each instructor is also different, classes are taught in different ways. In general, the approach is much less formal than in other traditional martial arts.

You may be expected to wear a T'ai Chi uniform, which is similar to what Kung Fu practitioners wear. Or you may just wear a T-shirt and loose fitting sweat pants. Soft shoes, not athletic shoes, are worn.

T'ai Chi has no ranking system. In general, at least five years of intense practice are needed before you're ready to lead a class or start teaching on your own.

The class time itself may be unstructured. Start and stop times may be flexible, and people may come and go during class. (In a traditional Karate school, this kind of behavior would net you 500 pushups! In T'ai Chi, the message is *relax.*)

What to expect

Warm up exercises may be done to help your chi flow before you begin the forms. After your chi is circulating nicely (a gentle sweat never hurts), you'll do a T'ai Chi form. The one form all T'ai Chi practitioners learn is called the *Long Form* and it goes on for 108 movements or just short of forever. Because not everyone has just short of forever to do a form, the *Short Form* was developed. It incorporates 24 movements from the Long Form and can be managed even by the chronically impatient. Different styles may do the forms slightly differently.

Beginning and intermediate students may repeat the form in order to begin perfecting the techniques. Advanced students may do a weapons form. Students who have learned the Long Form teach and perform push-hands exercises. (See the "Push hands" section, later in this chapter.)

Training tips

The art is practiced alone by doing forms and by doing partner exercises with another person at the more advanced level. The famous Long Form, which consists of 108 movements, can take half an hour to complete. The Short Form, a modified version of the Long Form, takes fewer than ten minutes to complete. Learning the Long Form can take six months or more just to memorize the techniques. Then it can take years to master it. (Well, wouldn't it be boring if you could learn the techniques and master them in three weeks?) The forms can be done faster to improve your timing and balance or slower to improve your agility and power.

Techniques of T'ai Chi

To warm up, and help your chi to circulate, you can do any of a number of basic stretching exercises. You can do static stretches, go for a brisk walk around the block, or perform warming up techniques that your instructor has devised.

Sinking a horse stance instead of a basket

One popular technique to help you warm up is to *sink* a horse stance. You move into a horse stance position, which is done by keeping your legs a little more than a shoulder's width apart. Your toes should point forward, and your knees should be slightly bent. Your body should be straight; your pelvis shouldn't be tipped forward (see Figure 23-1).

Feel your dan tien. Sink into the horse stance as you focus on finding and focusing on your dan tien. Instead of holding the position, like a static stretch, move into and out of it.

Free flows, not free throws

The techniques of T'ai Chi are smooth, even, free-flowing, continuous movements — not specific, direct techniques with a starting point and a stopping point, like a knife-hand strike in Karate.

Techniques such as Parting the Wild Horse's Mane are actually small forms in themselves, comprising a series of movements. These small forms aren't repeated over and over the way a side kick may be in a Tae Kwon Do class.

Instead, one movement flows into the next until the entire form is complete. The complete form may be repeated if you have an extra half hour or so to do it, but individual techniques aren't repeated, except perhaps at the beginning level when the practitioner is trying to learn what to do.

Figure 23-1:
Sinking into the horse stance.

The first movements

So you can get an idea of what the complete form looks like, Figure 23-2 features the first few movements of the Long Form. Remember, no two of the 108 movements are exactly alike:

- ✔ Strike Palm to Ask Blessings (see Figure 23-2a)
- ✔ Grasp the Bird's Tail (see Figure 23-2b)
- ✔ Single Whip (see Figure 23-2c)
- ✔ White Crane Cools its Wings (see Figure 23-2d)

Figure 23-2:
The first in
a series of
movements
from the
Long Form.

Push hands

Advanced practitioners of T'ai Chi — those who learned the Long Form — can do partner drills called *push hands*. These exercises teach you how to redirect an opponent's energy and to absorb the energy of a strike that's directed toward you.

Doing push hands increases your sensitivity to your partner, and by extrapolation, to your opponent, so you can understand how to defeat him. In essence, you try to push each other off-balance.

Single hand

As shown in Figure 23-3, two partners face each other. The partner on the left is usually the junior or less experienced partner.

1. You each extend your right leg so that both feet are parallel to each other and about ten inches apart.

2. Extend your right hands so that the backs of your hands touch each other.

3. The first partner (the partner on the left) pushes forward with his right hand.

4. You (the partner on the right) shift your weight back to absorb the force of the push, turning your upper body to the right to redirect the energy.

5. Then you shift forward and push toward your partner, who shifts back to absorb the force of your push, turning his upper body to the right to redirect the energy.

Each partner repeats and continues the process. The force of pushing remains constant.

Two hand

This technique is similar to the single-hand technique. You begin in the same way, with two partners facing each other, right legs extended, right feet parallel to each other about ten inches apart, and the backs of your right hands touching.

1. Place your left hand on your partner's right elbow. Your partner does the same to you.

2. Turn both palms forward and press toward your partner. The partner absorbs the force by shifting back.

3. Your partner rolls her palms forward and does the same, such as pressing forward, to you.

The process is repeated (see Figure 23-4).

Figure 23-3:
Push-hands
technique,
single-hand
variation.

Figure 23-4:
Push-hands
technique,
two-hand
variation.

T'ai Chi history

You've heard of the Shaolin Temple, the birthplace of martial arts in China? For T'ai Chi practitioners, however, the temple that counts is the Wu Dang Shan Monastery. Located in central China, the Wu Dang Shan Monastery was a meeting place for Taoists who taught internal-style martial arts.

Although history credits the Taoist Chang San Feng as the founder of T'ai Chi more than 800 years ago, T'ai Chi was brought to the Wu Dang Shan Monastery in the mid-fifteenth century. Apparently, though, the Wu Dang Shan monastics were jealous of the Shaolin Temple, because they were involved in burning it to the ground. This was not the only conflict between practitioners of Kung Fu and practitioners of T'ai Chi. (And you thought T'ai Chi was a gentle art!)

Part IV
The Part of Tens

The 5th Wave — By Rich Tennant

For gosh sakes, Jerry! I told you blues and country-western tapes just aren't appropriate for a Tae-Kwon Do class.

In this part . . .

In these short chapters, you can find out what to look for in an instructor, discover some rules for learning, take some advice from the master (that would be me), and see a list of some favorite martial arts movies — popular among martial artists around the world.

Chapter 24

Ten Rules for the Martial Arts Classroom

To become successful as a martial artist, you have to commit yourself to learning. But sometimes, bad habits can prevent you from getting the most you can from your instructors, your fellow students, and your school. By following these guidelines, you can learn martial arts to the best of your ability.

Listen More than You Talk

Too often the sound of your own voice can drown out what the teacher (or a fellow student) is saying. Listen to what the teacher says. Think about it. Only if you still don't understand should you ask. But remember to ask at the right time and place. In many traditional martial arts classes, interrupting class in order to ask questions isn't considered appropriate. Instead, save your questions for before or after class.

Watch and Learn

In addition to listening to what the teacher is saying, watch what the teacher is doing. Try to mimic the way that the teacher performs techniques. Many questions could be answered and problems solved if students would simply do what the teacher (and the senior students) are doing.

In some old-fashioned schools, the teacher doesn't even talk. He simply performs the techniques, and over time, after seeing the techniques done correctly often enough, the student discovers how to do it right. This teaching technique is rare these days. Few instructors expect you to learn without talking to you and correcting your performance.

Watch the other students as well. Often, especially in the case of behavior and etiquette, they can teach you without even knowing they're teaching you. Imitate what the senior students do (unless the instructor makes the senior student do 50 pushups for it). If everyone rises and bows when the head instructor walks in the room, you should probably do the same even if no one has told you to.

Finally, watch yourself. Look at what you're doing as you do it. (For this, a mirror or camcorder is essential.) As you perform techniques, make certain that you're completing them correctly, so that your feet are in the right place and your body is balanced correctly.

Visualize

Creative visualization can lead to martial arts success. Imagine performing your form perfectly. Imagine scoring clean points against your sparring partner. Before class, take a moment to clear your mind and then think about having a perfect practice. After class, relax and take a moment to go over what you did and think about how you can improve your performance next time.

Accept Criticism

If you're performing your techniques incorrectly, you need to know it. Your instructor isn't doing you any favors by overlooking poor technique just because you're a nice person. Not correcting your performance can be dangerous, giving you the confidence that you're doing techniques in an effective way, when really you aren't. Performing techniques incorrectly can also cause damage to your body by overstressing your joints or causing strains and sprains. So when you think your instructor wouldn't know praise if it came and hit her upside the head, just remember that when you're facing a couple of street punks, you'll be glad she was hard on you.

Most students have days when all they want to do is go home and cry because, according to the instructor, nothing they do is right. Just accept that these days happen and then kick the heavy bag after class to blow off steam. Try to return to the next class with a positive, open mind.

If you really feel like your instructor only criticizes and never praises, ask her to tell you what you're doing right. Martial arts instructors are only human, and sometimes, they forget that you need to know that you have some talent.

Often, instructors simply come by and "fix" what you're doing wrong by moving your hand into a different position or pushing your feet farther apart. Some instructors use a wooden stick (a *shinai*) to make corrections. If you still don't understand what you're doing wrong, ask the instructor (or a fellow student). But wait for the appropriate time to ask.

Practice, Practice, Practice

You can't master martial arts techniques without practicing. Sometimes, though, you don't realize just how much practice the techniques require. Most instructors agree that, although you can get the feel for a technique pretty quickly and may even perform it pretty well after a few dozen repetitions, you don't actually master a technique until you've done it correctly at least two or three thousand times, probably more. (Yes, I said a thousand.) That's many, many kicks. So don't get frustrated if you're still having trouble doing a side kick if you've only been attempting it for three months. You have several more months to go.

Respect Yourself (And Others)

The martial arts don't care what you do outside the training hall. So it doesn't matter if you're a well-respected neurosurgeon recently nominated for a Nobel Peace Prize. The little high school squirt who is your senior belt still knows more than you do; respect her for it. Also respect yourself and your abilities, no matter what they are. You can best show this respect by always being courteous to your instructor and your fellow students and by trying your hardest at every training session.

Remember That Persistence Beats Talent

No matter how inept you are, if you keep trying, you can do better than the most talented students who never try. Persistence is at the heart of learning the martial arts. No matter how many times you fail, you must pick yourself up and keep trying. Your fellow students will respect you for it, and you will respect yourself, too. Even better, you'll discover how to master the techniques and achieve your goals simply by persisting.

Persisting is made easier if you also do some goal-setting. You have to know what you want in order to keep trying to get it. Set some long-term martial arts goals, such as earning a black belt or competing for a national title and some short-term goals, such as improving your kicking speed.

Eat Humble Pie

Who among us hasn't enjoyed the spectacle of watching an arrogant jerk get his comeuppance? It's really fun to see the mighty fall. Just remember, though, that it may be you the next time. Even the best martial artists fall down, forget their forms, and lose sparring matches to lower belts. By remaining humble, these minor setbacks don't turn into major humiliations. Humility is also necessary to learning. If you think that you know it all, you may never discover anything new. A good martial artist knows that there's always plenty to discover.

Cultivate Patience

To become a truly accomplished martial artist, along with practicing your techniques thousands of times and persisting in the face of failure, you have to cultivate patience. Every martial artist can describe plateaus in his training. You may have plateaus, too. No matter how hard you try, you just can't master that kick, you just can't throw that one partner, and you just can't lose that five pounds. You need to be patient. You can't achieve a black belt overnight (and what would it really mean if you did?). Through patience, you can achieve your martial arts goals. Remind yourself of that every now and then.

Have Fun

Martial artists tend to talk about martial arts in solemn, serious tones. And learning the skills that can maim other people is indeed serious. Discovering how to defend yourself is a big responsibility. But don't forget that martial arts are also a ton of fun. Maybe not every class is full of belly laughs but enjoy it anyway. It's a pleasure discovering what your body can do. Kicking a target as hard as you can is fun. Throwing your best friend to the mat is a grin. Don't forget the fun.

Chapter 25

Ten Qualities a Good Instructor Must Have

In This Chapter

▶ Understanding that teaching requires commitment and enthusiasm

▶ Identifying the characteristics of a good instructor

▶ Avoiding the martial arts instructor from the Stone Age

Good martial arts instructors can be found in plenty of places. Some have their own schools. Some teach at another person's school. Some teach for the local parks and recreation program. Some hold classes in their living rooms or at a nearby park. But all good instructors have certain qualities that you want to look for.

You should look for these qualities when you're choosing an instructor. You should also try to cultivate these qualities yourself because someday you may become the instructor. Keep an eye open for the following ten qualities when you want to find an instructor.

Commitment

A good instructor is committed to his art and to teaching it. Although many good instructors don't or can't make their living by teaching martial arts and therefore hold down other jobs, make sure teaching is more than just a hobby. A good instructor doesn't miss many sessions, arrive late all the time, or turn the teaching over to students. The instructor makes teaching a priority in his or her life. Check also to see that the instructor places an important emphasis on teaching by attending seminars and workshops or at least staying informed about the best methods for teaching a wide, diverse variety of students.

Patience

Just as a good student has patience while trying to master the techniques of martial arts, a good instructor has patience while trying to teach the techniques. Nothing is more demoralizing to a student than an instructor who is visibly annoyed with how slowly she is picking up a technique. Nothing is more likely to make it harder for the student to learn the technique. Martial arts students are like small children — they need to be handled with a certain amount of care and consideration.

Enthusiasm

A good instructor loves the martial arts. Even though she may have been practicing Karate for 15 years, it's still a blast. Her enthusiasm must extend to teaching, as well. Just because a person enjoys martial arts and excels at them doesn't mean she necessarily teaches well. And some of the best instructors aren't necessarily the most spectacular martial artists. But they do love what they do.

Humor

Many old-school martial arts instructors cultivate serious, grave demeanors. Even though this behavior is fine sometimes, a martial arts instructor must be able to unbend a little. If something really funny happens in class, check to see if he can laugh about it. Although it's important to keep discipline (a martial arts class can be dangerous otherwise), being able to smile when things don't work perfectly is often a better response than making everyone do 50 pushups. (Although making everyone do 50 pushups can sometimes be the right answer, too.)

Although having a sense of humor is important for an instructor, beware of the class that's always a barrel of laughs. This class may not have much learning going on. And that's why you came, isn't it?

Acceptance

A good martial arts instructor accepts diversity among her students. Although an instructor may demand or expect a certain amount of loyalty and a certain standard of behavior, she also treats all students equally regardless of gender, race, or age. At the same time, a good instructor understands how to accommodate for people's different needs and is open to discovering how to better help her students.

Creativity

Being a good instructor requires a certain willingness to bend the rules and look at things creatively. A resourceful teacher helps students get the most from their training. For instance, a creative instructor can create a modified *form* (often called *kata* or *hyung,* this is a precise pattern of martial arts movements) for a disabled student to do. He can develop self-defense techniques that can be used by the elderly or the young. Being able to solve a problem creatively is a definite advantage in martial arts.

Selflessness

When a martial artist begins teaching, to some degree he gives up refining his own skills. This doesn't mean an instructor gives up practicing, but it does mean that he devotes more time to helping others achieve their martial arts goals rather than focusing on his martial arts goals. For instance, when it comes tournament time, an instructor coaches his students rather than competing, even if he truly loves to compete. A good instructor is instinctively selfless (although this quality can be learned.) ***Note:*** An instructor who feels in competition with his students can be damaging.

Respect

Just as students must have respect for themselves, their instructors, and their fellow students, a good instructor must also respect her students (all of them) regardless of their abilities. It's easy to work with the talented students; it's not so easy to work with the klutzes. But an instructor who respects all her students helps them all develop to the best of their abilities. The instructor respects those abilities even if they're limited.

Knowledge

A good instructor thoroughly knows the martial art she is teaching. Although you may practice an art for an entire lifetime and still not know everything about it, a teacher maintains an extensive knowledge of the techniques and how they're done. She also has knowledge of teaching techniques. Not every student learns the same way. Some students develop skills by being told, some by being shown, and some by trying the technique themselves, over and over. A good teacher recognizes these learning styles and teaches in such a way that all students can benefit. To certify that she has the required knowledge, make sure a martial arts instructor holds certain credentials. In general, a second- or third-degree (minimum) black belt from a respected ranking organization is necessary. Also check to see if the teacher has experience teaching under a supervising instructor. Trophies and awards aren't necessary but can show that the instructor is involved in all aspects of martial arts.

Focus

A good instructor has intense focus. When she is teaching, that's what she is doing. When she is judging a student's performance, that's what she is doing. She isn't distracted by a ringing telephone; she isn't so disorganized that she forgets what time class starts. She is focused and ready to successfully conduct a class. A focused teacher also serves as a role model for the students, who soon learn that to be successful in martial arts they must be equally focused. At the same time, a good teacher remains aware of what is happening around her, so that even if she is leading class, she notices that the kid in the last row just got punched in the nose and has a nosebleed.

Chapter 26

Ten Tips from the Master

In This Chapter

▶ Understanding the importance of setting goals

▶ Discovering and developing your chi

▶ Setting a positive example

A good martial artist possesses certain qualities that others respect and admire. In many martial arts, these qualities are clearly set out. For example, in Tae Kwon Do, an instructor expects all students to cultivate the Five Tenets (courtesy, integrity, perseverance, self-control, and indomitable spirit). Other martial arts have slightly different expectations. But if you cultivate the following ten qualities, no matter what style you study, you can be a good martial artist.

Setting Goals

Martial arts are conducive to goal setting. As you learn more, you earn higher ranks. But you can't achieve a higher rank if you don't have goals. When you set goals, establish specific goals not only about what you plan to do but also when you plan to do it. For instance, a goal may be to earn a black belt. This goal is specific, but it needs a time limit. So you may find out how long it generally takes for a student to earn a black belt with consistent practice and make that time frame your goal. Remain realistic: No matter how talented someone is, no one earns a black belt after six months of practice. At the same time, just because you don't achieve your goal in the time that you've allotted doesn't mean that you can give up.

Committing to Training

Martial arts training isn't like aerobics. It's a way of life. Therefore, commit to training frequently and consistently. If you're not ready to set aside a certain amount of time each week for your practice, then you're not ready for martial arts. Make your commitment extend even to those times when it's difficult to practice, such as when you're busy at work or your wife has just left you. Your commitment can help you overcome many obstacles, not only in your training, but also in everyday life as well.

Learning to Breathe

Every martial arts instructor has a story about the student who holds his breath during the entire class, turns blue, and practically passes out. Learning to breathe helps build your endurance, so you can get through class, perform the techniques, and de-stress after (or even during) a difficult day. Essentially, you must breathe out during the exertion phase of a technique (when you're actually doing the strike or throw). If you master this skill, the breathing in comes automatically. (If you focus on breathing in, you can cause yourself to hyperventilate, which is almost as bad as turning blue and passing out.)

Finding and Using Your Chi

Your *chi* is your life force or energy. Your chi is located in your abdomen. Think of it as resting just above your navel. Concentrate on this part of your body as your base, the place where your energy and focus comes from. Close your eyes and imagine summoning your chi from this place. Tighten your abdomen to push your chi up and out of your body. The *kiai* (shout) is an expression of your chi.

Developing a Good Kiai (Shout)

Martial artists use the *kiai* (or shout) to summon their chi and focus their energy on a goal or technique. For example, a person getting ready to break a board may kiai just before striking in order to summon the energy and focus to perform the breaking technique successfully. However, many martial artists use their lungs or diaphragm to scream instead of using their chi, located in their abdomen, to kiai. To develop a good kiai, think of expelling all your breath forcefully while tightening your abdominal muscles. To practice doing your kiai, touch your body a few inches above your navel. As you let out a breath, push in on this spot with your fingers. Your shout comes from that spot.

Being a Good Role Model

Remember that as you make your way through the ranks, the students who join the school after you look up to you as a senior student. Set a good example. Behave as your school policy dictates. Perform in class to the best of your abilities and with your most intense effort at all times. Attend rank tests even if you're not testing in order to support other students. Help others, especially new students, become familiar with what's expected of them. Take the time to help other students develop their skills, too. If you're a woman, you may make a special effort to encourage other women. If you're a young student, you may encourage the other young students.

Contributing to the Art

At the higher black belt ranks, to achieve the next degree, a martial artist doesn't simply have to demonstrate certain techniques and perform a certain *form* (a precise pattern of martial art movements) correctly. He also gives back to the art in concrete ways. You can give back even before you're a black belt.

Black belts give back to the art by opening new schools in areas where they don't exist, by serving in martial arts organizations, and by spreading the word through speaking, seminars, and writing. (Not all black belts do all these things, of course.)

Lower ranking students can offer to help teach classes, promote a martial arts tournament, or simply encourage friends and family members to discover the art.

Honoring Your School

Even when you're outside the training hall, you represent your school. Don't take this responsibility lightly. Always respect your school and represent your school honorably. This means only using your martial arts techniques in self-defense. Also don't use any teaching techniques until your instructor has given you permission to do so. When you participate in a tournament, conduct yourself with grace and dignity even if the judge is a total idiot and the referees are all blind. Make your instructor proud that you're a member of her school.

Discovering All Aspects of Martial Arts

You owe it to the art that you're trying to master to learn all of its aspects. Most martial artists prefer certain parts of training. For example, I love sparring. I'd just spar all day, but I also know that self-defense practice, forms, and techniques practice are also essential to my success as a martial artist. So I give them equal time. I can still like sparring best, but I don't neglect my forms.

Furthermore, take time to discover something about the history of martial arts, especially your particular style, and the culture that gave rise to it. This action shows that you respect your art and all the people who have gone before you.

Accepting Hard Training

If becoming a martial artist could be accomplished by touching your toes five times a day, everyone would do it. But the fact is, it requires hard training to be a martial artist. In addition to giving your best effort in your ordinary class sessions, you can participate in more difficult training, which can help you grow as a martial artist. For example, many schools have advanced training classes for advanced students. These classes are more difficult, with harder techniques and a higher level of intensity. You always have the option not to go, but how can you develop your potential if you skip them? If your art participates in organized competition, then you can participate in a tournament now and then, even if you never win. If your instructor sponsors a special training workshop, make every effort to attend. With your instructor's approval, you can go to training camps and seminars to hone your skills.

Hard or difficult training is simply training that's more advanced or more intense than usual. It's not training where the instructor smacks you with a stick as hard as she can.

Chapter 27

Ten Cool Martial Arts Movies

In This Chapter

▶ Finding out about martial arts movies

▶ Discovering which stars to watch

A ll martial artists have their favorite martial arts movies, and then they have their favorite non-martial arts movies. This is because what makes a good martial arts movie (many cool techniques that you can try out in class next time) doesn't necessarily constitute high art. Even if the plot is terrible, a martial arts movie can be good if it shows many great martial arts moves, has fight scenes every couple of minutes, or captures the spirit of martial arts in some way, even if it's a cheesy way.

Why Watch Them?

As one martial artist points out, most martial arts movies are distinguished by their mediocrity. So why watch them? Because what else are you going to do after you've wiped yourself out from hard training? They're good for a belly laugh. Besides, it's fun to see the fight scenes and pick out the techniques you can do. Also, some of the actors are pretty cute.

Although many martial arts movies have boring, overused, or silly plots, that's not the main attraction. The main attraction is seeing martial arts in action. And even if the acting is wooden and unbelievable, the martial arts moves are cool and exciting.

Martial arts movies have come a long way from the 1970s, when the best you could hope for was a badly dubbed movie from Hong Kong. Even people who aren't martial arts fans enjoy some of the newer martial arts movies, which have better acting, more believable plots, and better cinematography.

Who Can You Watch?

Jet Li is the new Bruce Lee. Bruce Lee, of course, is the old Bruce Lee. Michelle Yeoh, who is actually an actor who learned martial arts and not the other way around, is a ton of fun. Cynthia Rothrock wins many votes. Almost everyone agrees that Jackie Chan is the funniest to watch. Then the standbys — Jean Claude van Damme and Steven Seagal — are old fan favorites. If either of these guys is involved, you know the bad guys are in trouble.

What to Watch

I conducted an admittedly unscientific poll to find out the favorite martial arts movies of martial artists. The following movies are their overwhelming favorites:

- ✔ *Best of the Best* Something like 97 sequels to this Eric Roberts' movie have been made, but it's still the best of the *Best of the Best*.

- ✔ *Bloodsport* Jean Claude van Damme makes it clear how the movie got its name.

- ✔ *Crouching Tiger, Hidden Dragon* The women take center stage in this art house flick that's become a cult favorite even among non-martial artists.

- ✔ *Enter the Dragon* You can't call yourself a martial artist until you've seen this Bruce Lee classic.

- ✔ *Hard to Kill* Steven Seagal makes it clear how the movie got its name.

- ✔ *Karate Kid* No one can forget "wipe on, wipe off." This movie inspired countless kids to take up martial arts.

- ✔ *The Matrix* Even though *The Matrix* isn't a traditional martial arts movie, and Keanu Reeves is no martial artist, this movie gets a thumbs-up from most martial artists.

- ✔ *Rapid Fire* Brandon Lee showing how he may have been good enough to rival his father.

- ✔ *Romeo Must Die* One of the first films released in the United States with Jet Li as the lead character. You can't say Kung Fu is a soft martial art after seeing him in action.

- ✔ *Rush Hour* Jackie Chan shows why he packs them into Hong Kong movie houses. No one's as funny as this guy.

Part V
Appendixes

"Here's a tip — if you hear yourself snoring, you're meditating too deeply."

In this part . . .

Appendix A gives you a glossary of common martial arts terms. Appendix B lists books, martial arts equipment and supply houses, and organizations and associations specific to martial arts.

Appendix A

Glossary

Aikidoka: A person who practices Aikido.

angles of attack: A concept of self-defense that relies on understanding what part of the body is being attacked. That part of the body is then defended in a specific way, regardless of whether the attack is being carried out with a kick, punch, stick, or knife.

animal martial arts: Traditional Chinese martial arts that incorporate the qualities of animals and attempt to emulate their movements; animals include snake, dragon, leopard, crane, tiger, and monkey.

baro (Korean): Return to starting position.

belt: Refers to the belt that a martial artist wears. The color of the belt denotes whether the artist is a beginner, intermediate, or an advanced student. Black belt is usually the highest rank.

Bodhidharma: Indian monk who created Zen Buddhism and is traditionally given credit as the person who brought martial arts to China.

bu (Japanese): War or combat.

budo (Japanese): Ways of combat. The practice of learning fighting arts as a way of life.

bugei (Japanese): Art of combat. The practice of learning the most efficient method of killing or stopping an opponent in a real combat situation.

bujutsu (Japanese): Same as bugei. See "bugei."

bunkai (Japanese): The application of techniques.

bushido (Japanese): Ethical code followed by Japanese samurai.

chareyhet (Korean): Attention!

Chi (Chinese): Life force; internal energy. Martial artists summon their chi in order to focus their minds on a difficult goal or problem. The chi, which is located in the abdomen, flows through the body in meridians or channels. If these channels become blocked, the chi is blocked and a person can become ill or uncomfortable. Using chi helps any physical action become stronger and more effective.

chi-chi: Attacks to the vital points.

ching (Japanese): Controlled chi; the physical power that results from chi.

chuan bi (Korean): Ready! A command that means students should assume the *ready* stance.

chu gyo nim (Korean): Teacher.

circular motion: Using an indirect rather than direct line of approach or attack.

courtesy throw: A practice throw that the opponent doesn't try to prevent.

cuong nhu tuong thom: Vietnamese word for yin-yang. See "Yin-Yang."

dai-Sensei (Japanese): Teacher.

dan: Black belt rankings.

danjon (Korean): The location of the chi in the abdomen.

dan tien (Chinese): The location of chi in the abdomen.

dau (Chinese): Command meaning *begin*.

degree: Black belt rankings. Also called *dan*.

dero dohras (Korean): Turn around. In certain circumstances, the student turns around, facing away from the instructor (such as when he is being judged after a performance), and this phrase will be used to instruct the student to do so.

dim mak: Death touch; purported ability of some martial artists to kill or maim an opponent by merely touching an opponent's vital point — one of several spots on the human body that are particularly vulnerable to an attack.

Do (Korean, Japanese): Path or way.

dobok (Korean): Traditional uniform.

dogi (Japanese): Traditional uniform.

dojang (Korean): Martial arts training hall.

dojo (Japanese): Martial arts training hall.

Eighteen Weapons, the: Traditional weapons used in Chinese martial arts since the 1200s; includes sword, spear, halberd, staff, hook, and related weapons.

empty hand: Refers to martial arts styles that don't use weapons and rely on hands, elbows, knees, and feet for defense.

enryo (Japanese): Indifference to death; one who is indifferent to death is nearly invincible in battle.

Escrimador/a (Spanish): A person who practices Escrima. (Add the *a* at the end to refer to a girl or woman.)

etiquette: Showing proper respect or courtesy to the martial arts instructor, one's fellow students, and the art itself.

examinations: Tests of a martial artist's prowess required before he can advance in rank.

Five Ways of Kung Fu: According to Bruce Lee, the methods — strikes, kicks, locks, throws, and weapons — that could be used against an opponent.

form: A predetermined pattern of techniques that martial artists memorize and practice to demonstrate grace and agility.

fudoshin (Japanese): Ability to be calm and detached at all times, no matter what's happening.

gaku (Chinese): Certificate given on successful completion of rank examination.

gi (Japanese): Traditional uniform.

go (Japanese): Term meaning hardness and action.

grappling: Techniques for throwing, locking, holding, and wrestling an opponent rather than kicking and punching.

gup (Korean): Ranking below black belt.

Guru (Chinese): Wise person or teacher.

hajime (Japanese): Begin! Used to start a sparring match, or to instruct a student to perform a *kata* (form).

hakama: Wide trousers worn in certain martial arts styles.

Hanshi (Japanese): Term of respect reserved for high-ranking black belts.

hara (Japanese): The location of chi (abdomen).

haragei (Japanese): The ability to locate and use one's chi.

hard styles: Martial arts that use striking, linear techniques.

harmony: The balance of two opposites; a basic principle in martial arts.

hatsu geiko (Japanese): Special training period that starts on New Year's Day and helps participants begin the New Year appropriately.

heijo-shin (Japanese): A focused but calm mind.

hidden teachings: Those techniques not taught to all students but reserved only for the most advanced, most trusted individuals.

hogu (Korean): Safety equipment.

hontai (Japanese): A state of readiness.

huyet: Vital points.

hyung (Korean): Form. (See "form.")

in-yo: See "Yin-Yang."

ippon (Japanese): Full point. Term used in matches to score techniques.

ju (Japanese): Softness and yielding; flexibility of mind and body.

jutsu: Term indicating a style of martial arts that emphasizes combat effectiveness rather than a way of life.

ka: Suffix used to denote *practitioner of.* Thus, *Kareteka* is one who practices Karate.

kaiden (Japanese): Teaching certificate awarded to a student when she has mastered an art.

kamidana (Japanese): Altar to the *kami,* which are spirits and deities, placed at the front of the training hall.

Karateka: A person who practices Karate.

kata (Japanese): Form. (See "form.")

keiko (Japanese): Martial arts training in general but with the intention of continually attempting to improve.

kensei: Silent *kiai* or *shout,* used when mental or emotional demands are placed on the practitioner and a traditional shout can't be used.

Ki (Japanese): See "Chi."

kiai (Japanese): The shout that releases and directs chi.

kihop (Korean): The shout that releases and directs chi.

kime (Japanese): Ability to focus single-mindedly on one goal.

kokoro (Japanese): Heart or spirit.

kumite (Japanese): Free-style sparring.

kune (Chinese): Form.

kup so (Korean): Vital points.

kwan: School.

kwan jang (Chinese): Head instructor of a school.

kwoon: School.

kyu: Ranking below black belt.

kyu/dan: The entire system of classifying martial artists by rank. Nonblack belts are at the kyu rank, which may have many divisions such as white belt, green belt, blue belt. Black belts are at the dan level, often referred to as "degrees." These go by number. A "second dan" is a higher rank than a "first dan."

lei-tei (Chinese): Platform on which martial arts are performed for spectators.

linear motion: Direct techniques that move in a straight line to the target.

ma-ai (Japanese): Judgment of the distance between the practitioner and the opponent; this distance is crucial for knowing what techniques to perform when.

makiwara board: Piece of training equipment used to condition knuckles; usually made of a post covered by a piece of fabric.

martial arts: Name given to various fighting systems, usually of Asian origin, that teach combat techniques.

metsuke (Japanese): Eye contact.

Michi: Path or way.

muga: The ability to focus so completely on the act at hand that nothing can interfere with its completion.

mushin: No mind; an open mind; a mind that's not concerned with appearances.

poomse (Korean): Form.

rank: Level of mastery that a martial arts student has achieved, usually indicated by belt of various colors.

sa beum nim (Korean): Teacher.

safety equipment: Gear designed to be worn during sparring to protect martial artists from injury.

Samurai: Japanese warriors in the service of the great warrior class families.

sen: Taking control of a combat situation through the application of strategy.

sensei (Japanese): Teacher.

Seven Stars: The opponent's weapons, according to Bruce Lee; hands, feet, knees, elbows, shoulders, thighs, and head.

Shaolin Temple: Chinese monastery popularly believed to be the birthplace of Asian martial arts.

shiai-jo: Training hall.

shomen: The front of the room, housing the *kamidana,* which is traditionally bowed to.

Sifu (Chinese): Teacher.

Sijo (Chinese): The founder of a martial arts school or style.

soft styles: Martial arts that rely on passive, evasive movements rather than direct, linear attacks.

suki: Loss of focus.

sutemi: The warrior's awareness of the need for self-sacrifice.

Tao: Path or way.

te: Hand; usually refers to martial arts that originated in Okinawa.

Tengu: Mythical creatures who inhabited the Asian mountains and taught martial arts to humans.

to-shin: Striking skills.

um-yo: See "Yin-Yang."

vital points: Areas on the body that are particularly vulnerable to attack.

vo: (Vietnamese): Begin.

vo phuc (Vietnamese): Traditional uniform.

vo su (Vietnamese): Teacher.

Yin-Yang: The perception that the universe is driven by opposing forces; essentially, the universe is made of conflicting yet harmonious elements, such as night and day; yin is symbolic of the negative and the destructive, while yang is symbolic of the positive and the creative.

zazen meditation: Popular form of meditation in which one simply tries to empty one's mind of thoughts.

Appendix B

Sources and Resources

* *

*I*f you want to learn more about a martial art, you can pick up one of the books or magazines listed in this Appendix. If you're interested in meeting other people like you, then consider joining a martial arts organization after looking through the organizations that I've listed complete with contact information. Or if you need to get a cool new Japanese sword, you came to the right place, as you'll find martial arts suppliers in the "Martial Arts Supplies and Equipment" section in this Appendix.

Books

General

Corcoran, John. *The Martial Arts Sourcebook*. San Francisco: Harper Perennial, 1994.

Crompton, Paul. *Complete Martial Arts*. New York: Bantam, 1989.

Draeger, Donn. *Comprehensive Asian Fighting Arts*. Boston: Tuttle, 1981.

Farkas, Emil and John Corcoran. *The Overlook Martial Arts Dictionary*. New York: Overlook Press, 1986.

Lawler, Jennifer. *Martial Arts Encyclopedia*. McGraw-Hill, 1996.

Lawler, Jennifer. *Martial Arts for Women*. Wethersfield, CT: Turtle Press, 1998.

Lewis, Peter. *Myths and Legends of the Martial Arts*. Rpt. London: Prion Books, 2000.

Yates, Keith. *Warrior Secrets: A Handbook of the Martial Arts*. Los Angeles: Paladin Press, 1985.

Styles

Bennett, Gary. *Aikido: Techniques and Tactics.* Champaign, IL: Human Kinetics, 1997.

Cho, Henry. *Korean Karate: Free Fighting Techniques.* Boston: Tuttle, 1968.

Draeger, Donn. *Modern Budo and Bujutsu.* Boston: Tuttle, 1996.

Hallander, Jane. *The Complete Guide to Kung Fu Fighting Styles.* Burbank, CA: Unique Publications, 1985.

Hickey, Patrick M. *Karate: Techniques and Tactics.* Champaign, IL: Human Kinetics, 1997.

Ho'o, Marshall. *T'ai Chi Chuan.* Santa Clarita, CA: Ohara Publications, 1986.

Inosanto, Dan. *Jeet Kune Do: The Art and Philosophy of Bruce Lee.* Los Angeles: Know Now Publishing, 1980.

Kotsias, John. *The Essential Movements of T'ai Chi.* Brookline, MA: Paradigm, 1989.

Lawler, Jennifer. *Secrets of Tae Kwon Do.* McGraw-Hill, 1999.

Lee, Bruce. *Tao of Jeet Kune Do.* Santa Clarita, CA: Ohara Publications, 1975.

Moeller, Mark. *Foundations of Karate-Do.* Indianapolis, IN: Masters Press, 1995.

Park, Hwan and Tom Seabourne. *Jujitsu: Techniques and Tactics.* Champaign, IL: Human Kinetics, 1997.

Presas, Remy. *Modern Arnis.* Santa Clarita, CA: Unique Publications, 1983.

Reay, Tony. *Judo: Skills and Techniques.* Wiltshire, England: Crowwood Press, 1985.

Shaw, Scott. *Hapkido: Korean Art of Self-Defense.* Boston: Tuttle, 1996.

Smith, Joseph Wayne. *Wing Chun Kung Fu.* Boston: Tuttle, 1992.

Suenaka, Roy and Christopher Watson. *Complete Aikido.* Boston: Tuttle, 1997.

Wiley, Mark V. *Filipino Martial Arts.* Boston: Tuttle, 1994.

Wong, Douglas. *The Deceptive Hands of Wing Chun.* Burbank, CA: Unique Publications, 1982.

Fitness and Training

Canney, J.C. *Health and Fitness in the Martial Arts.* Boston: Tuttle, 1992.

Inosanto, Dan. *Guide to Martial Arts Training.* Los Angeles: Know Now Publications, 1989.

Urquidez, Benny et al. *Training and Fighting Skills.* Burbank, CA: Unique Publications, 1989.

Philosophy

Morgan, Forrest E. *Living the Martial Way.* Fort Lee, NJ: Barricade Books, 1992.

Musashi, Miyamoto. *The Book of Five Rings.* Edited by Hanshi Steve Kaufman. Boston: Tuttle, 1994.

Nelson, Randy, ed. *The Overlook Martial Arts Reader.* New York: Overlook Press, 1989.

Reid, Howard and Michael Croucher. *The Way of the Warrior: The Paradox of the Martial Arts.* New York: Overlook Press, 1995.

Sun T'zu. *The Art of War.* Edited and with a foreword by James Clavell. New York: Bantam, 1983

Weapons

Daniel, Charles. *Traditional Ninja Weapons and Ninjitsu Techniques.* Burbank, CA: Unique Publications, 1986.

Fernandez, Cacoy. *Iron Butterfly — Balisong Knife.* Burbank, CA: Unique Publications, 1985.

Huey, David. *Spearplay.* Burbank, CA: Unique Publications,1986.

Suh, In H. *Fighting Weapons of Korean Martial Arts.* Burbank, CA: Unique Publications, 1989.

Yamashita, Tadashi. *Advanced Tonfa.* Santa Clarita, CA: Ohara Publications, 1987.

Yamashita, Tadashi. *Bo: The Japanese Long Staff.* Santa Clarita, CA: Ohara Publications, 1986.

Yamashita, Tadashi. *Dynamic Nunchaku*. Santa Clarita, CA: Black Belt Communications, 1989.

Yamashita, Tadashi. *Martial Arts Weapons Demonstrations*. Santa Clarita, CA: Black Belt Communications, 1989.

Yang, Jing-Ming. *Introduction to Ancient Chinese Weapons*. Burbank, CA: Unique Publications, 1985.

Yumoto, John. *The Samurai Sword*. Boston: Tuttle, 1958.

Magazines

Black Belt. 24715 Avenue Rockefeller, Santa Clarita, CA 91355. (661) 257-4066 or (800) 266-4066.

Journal of Asian Martial Arts. 821 West 24th Street, Erie, PA 16502. (814) 455-9517.

Martial Arts and Combat Sports. 4201 Vanowen Place, Burbank, CA 91505. (818) 845-2656.

Martial Arts Illustrated. 19751 Figueroa Street, Carson, CA 90745. (310) 851-9409.

Martial Arts Supplies and Equipment

Asian World of Martial Arts (www.awma.com) 11601 Caroline Road, Philadelphia, PA 19154-2177. (800) 345-2962.

Bu Jin Design (www.bujindesign.com) Clothing and equipment designed especially for women. (866) 444-3644. Fax: (303) 444-1137.

Century Martial Art Supply (www.centuryma.com) 1705 National Blvd, Midwest City, OK 73110-7942. (405) 732-2226.

Everlast (www.everlast.com) Sporting goods. Can be found in retail stores. 1350 Broadway, #2300, New York, NY 10018.

Fairtex (www.fairtex.com) Muay Thai equipment. 2995 Junipero Serra Blvd., Daly City, CA 94014. (888) 512-7727. Fax: (650) 994-9021.

Health in Balance (www.home.earthlink.net/~healthbalanc/) Supplies especially for women. 647 Hillsborough Street, Oakland, CA 94606. (510) 452-2990.

Kwon, Inc. (www.kwon.com) 3755 Broadmoor, SE, Grand Rapids, MI 49512.

Macho Products, Inc. (www.macho.com) 10045 102nd Terrace, Sebastien, FL 32958. (800) 327-6812.

Pil Sung Martial Art Supply (www.pil-sung.com) 6300 Ridglea Place, Suite 1008, Fort Worth, TX 76116. (817) 738-5408.

Ringside, Inc. (www.ringside.com) 9650 Dice Lane, Lenexa, Kansas 66215. (877) 4-Boxing.

Title Sports (www.titlesports.com) Sporting goods. 14371 West 100th Street, Building C, Lenexa, KS 66215. (800) 999-1213. Fax: (913) 492-7546.

Turtle Shells (www.turtle-shells.com) Protective sports bras and chest protectors for women. P.O. Box 5266, Edmonton, OK 73083. (800) 999-0927.

Organizations and Associations

Association of Women Martial Arts Instructors. (http://members.aol.com/AWMAI/home.html) P.O. Box 7033, Houston, TX 77248.

International Combat Hapkido Federation (www.ichf.com) (828) 683-1744.

International Kickboxing Federation (www.ikfkickboxing.com) P.O. Box 1205, Newcastle, CA 95658. (916) 663-2467.

International Sport Karate Association (www.iska.com) P.O. Box 90147, Gainesville, FL 32607-0147. (352) 374-6876. Fax: (352) 378-4454.

Jiu-Jitsu America. 2055 Eagle Avenue, Alameda, CA 64501.

National Association of Professional Martial Artists (www.napma.com) 5601 116th Avenue North, Clearwater, FL 33760. (800) 973-6734.

National Guang Ping Yang T'ai Chi Association. (www.guangpingyang.org) P.O. Box 1721, Nevada City, CA 95959. (415) 989-5665.

Professional Karate Association. (www.professionalkarateassociation.com) 3290 Coachman's Way, Roswell, GA 30075.

Professional Karate Commission (www.pkcheadquarters.org) P.O. Box 796, Anderson, IN 46015.

United Martial Arts Referees Association (www.umara.com) P.O. Box 371, Bordentown, NJ 08505.

USA Karate Federation. (www.usakarate.org) 1300 Kenmore Boulevard, Akron, OH 44314

United States Amateur Kickboxing Association. (www.uskba.com) (972) 562-3590.

United States Ju Jitsu Federation. (www.usjujitsu.net). 3816 Bellingham Drive, Reno, NV 89511

United States Judo Association. (www.usja-judo.org) 19 North Union Boulevard, Colorado Springs, CO 80909.

United States Martial Arts (www.mararts.org) 8011 Mariposa Ave., Citrus Heights, CA 95610. (916) 727-1486.

United States Tae Kwon Do Union. (www.ustu.com) 1750 East Boulder Street, Colorado Springs, CO 80909.

World Judo Federation. Kodokan. 16-30, Kasuga, 1-Chome Bunkyo-ku, Tokyo, Japan.

World Kickboxing Association (www.kickboxing-wka.co.uk) 63 Gravelly Lane, Erdington, Birmingham, B23 6LR, England. 44-0-121-382-2995.

Index

• A •

active Chi Kung (exercise), 203
active-isolated stretching (AI), 214
aerobics, 11, 97–98, 275
agility, 23, 178, 199, 224, 251
Aikido (martial art)
  breakfall, 237
  breathing, 237
  chi, 237
  competition, 131, 236
  controlling technique, 17
  curriculum, 238
  flexibility, 239–240
  footwork, 244
  form, 243
  hard versus soft style, 236
  history, 248
  immobilization, 238, 245, 246
  joint lock, 235
  kick, 235
  meditation, 237
  overview, 17, 235
  physical considerations, 236
  punch, 235
  purpose, 235
  rank, 236–237
  roll, 241–242
  self-defense, 238–239
  stance, 243–244
  stretching, 239–240
  techniques, 243–248
  throw, 17, 235, 238, 246–248
  uniform, 237
  weapon, 238
Aikidoka (Aikido practitioner), 239, 331
alertness, 37, 84
alive hand, 254, 255
am-duong, 29
anemia, 96
anger, 35, 36, 177
angles of attack, 252–253, 331
animal martial arts, 27–28, 199–200, 201, 331
Ap chaki (kick), 218
arm lock, 233, 245, 246
armor, full-body, 76, 85, 250
Arnis (martial art), 20, 249
arrow, 160
assertiveness, 24
assistant instructor, 51, 56
association, martial arts. See professional organization
Atemi (Aikido technique), 238
attack by feinting, 297
attention stance, 187, 254–255
attitude, 57, 70, 81–82, 92–94
awareness, 117, 118, 167, 251
axe kick, 219

• B •

back fist punch, 202
back fist strike, 221
back kick, 193
back stance, 187, 215–216
back stretch, 100
backward roll, 241, 267
bag gloves, 77
balance, 173–174, 278, 295
banana bag, 79
baro, 331
basic scarf hold, 232
beauty, 24
beginning student
  analyzing, 43
  belt, 43, 67, 68
  common injuries, 87
  fear, 82
  goal, 61–63
  paranoia, 119
  physical contact, 82
  T'ai Chi Chuan, 306
belt, 43, 67–68, 69, 236–237, 331. See also specific belts
big people
  Escrima, 251
  Judo, 224
  Karate, 183
  Kung Fu, 198, 199
  power, 101
biting, 128, 130
black belt
  beginning student, 68
  cost of promotion, 59
  degrees, 68, 69, 332
  giving back to sport, 325
  length of time to achieve, 58
  misconceptions, 12
  overview, 68
  promotion test, 70
  registration with police department, 12
  women, 52
black hakama, 74
bladed weapon, 160
block, 189, 208, 216–217, 257–260

blocking pad, 79
blue belt, 67–68
bo, 77, 163, 164, 195
board breaking, 13–14, 79, 136, 139, 210
boasting, 171–172
Bodhidharma (founder, Zen Buddhism), 20, 207, 331
body drop, 229–230
body-shifting, 256
bokken, 77, 238
books, martial arts, 9, 34, 337–340
Booth, Donald (founder, New Horizons Black Belt Academy of Tae Kwon Do), 133
bowing, 174, 186
Boxer Rebellion of 1900 (Chinese nationalist rebellion), 16, 207
boxer sit-up, 107, 108
breakfall, 225, 227–228, 229, 237, 267–268
breathing
  Aikido, 237
  chi, 153, 204, 265
  controlled, 152
  energy level, 64
  Hapkido, 265
  overview, 324
  rooted-tree, 153
  spirituality, 152–153
brick breaking, 13–14
broadsword, 162, 163, 208
broken bone, 87, 190
broken scarf hold, 232
bruise, 87
bu, 331
Buddhism (Eastern religion), 15, 18, 151, 222
budo, 331
bugei, 331
bujutsu, 331

bunkai, 186, 331
bursitis, 87
bushido, 331

• C •

camaraderie, 25, 48, 179–180
Capoeira (martial art), 291, 294
carbohydrates, 94
cardio-kickboxing, 11, 275
cardiovascular training, 97–98, 277, 279
Carradine, David (martial artist), 39
central point, 265
chain martial arts school, 49
chainwhip, 160, 164
Chan, Jackie (martial artist), 328
Chan, Yang Lu (founder, Yang-style T'ai Chi), 304
Chang kwon chigi (strike), 221
character building
  chi, 28–29
  Chinese martial arts, 33–35
  Five Tenets, 11, 32–33, 149, 174–177, 210
  fudoshin, 35–36
  heijo-shin, 36–37
  importance, 30
  Japanese martial arts, 30–32
  Karate, 32
  kokoro, 37–38
  Korean martial arts, 32–33
  Resolute in Five Respects, 30–32
  Tae Kwon Do, 32–33, 149
  Taoism, 33–35, 147–149
  the Way, 147–149
  yin-yang, 29–30
chareyhet, 4, 331

chashi, 206
chat group, 42
chest protector, 76, 85
chi
  Aikido, 237
  blocked, 264
  breathing, 153, 204, 265
  central point, 265
  Chi Kung exercises, 203–204
  dan tien, 305
  definition, 331
  extending, 305
  Hapkido, 263, 264–266
  heijo-shin, 37
  Kung Fu, 198
  meridian, 301
  overview, 28–29, 324
  shout, 29, 114, 265–266
  T'ai Chi Chuan, 301, 305, 307
  tapping, 29, 114, 153
  vital points, 264
chi sao technique, 202, 205
chi shing chung, 206
chi-chi, 331
chikaraisha, 185–186
Chiki chaki (kick), 219
children
  behavior in school, 55
  choosing friends, 117
  competition division, 141
  gun, 166
  safety, 84
China, 19, 28, 162, 207
Chinese boxer, 197
Chinese martial arts, 14–16, 33–35, 147
ching, 331
Choi, Hong Hi (founder, Tae Kwon Do), 19, 209
Chojun, Miyagi (founder, Goju-Ryu), 184
chokehold defense, 125–128
Chongul ja sae (stance), 215

Choo muk dung chigi
(strike), 221
Choy-Li-Fut (martial art),
200–202
chu gyo nim, 331
chuan bi, 331
Chun, Yim Wing (founder,
Wing Chun), 202
chung do kwan, 212
Chung kwon chigi (punch),
220–221
circular attack, 272
clamp hand, 254
class. *See also* school
consulting doctor, 22
eating snack before lesson,
64, 95
energy level, 64
ethical behavior, 148
getting through first
lesson, 64
schedule, 53
uniform rules, 75, 170–171
visualization, 152
watching, 43–44, 53
class/degree system, 69
close-range weapon, 161
club, 161
club, martial arts, 48, 50
code of conduct, 23
combos, 280
community college, 47, 49
competition. *See also*
tournament
Aikido, 131, 236
benefits, 32
board breaking, 139
cost, 140
divisions, 140–142
elbow strike, 284
emotional muscle
memory, 158
equipment, 140
Escrima, 138

expectations of students,
139
form, 134
getting permission to
enter, 139
giving best performance, 32
grand championship, 140
importance of winning, 133
integrity, 175
Judo, 131, 135, 223, 224
Karate, 135–136, 193
knee strike, 284
Kung Fu, 136
mistakes, 134
Muay Thai, 137–138,
276, 281
nervousness, 133, 158
preparation, 144–145
process, 140
purpose, 131–133
rules, 145
school selection, 57
scoring, 135, 136, 138,
139, 211
self-control, 170
smash, 193
sparring, 134–138
spectators, 140
stress, 133
Tae Kwon Do, 138, 211,
212–213
training, 132, 144–145
uniform, 140
visualization, 152
weapon, 77
composite weapon, 160
concealed weapon, 167
concentration. *See* focus
confidence. *See* self-
confidence
Confucianism (philosophical
belief), 18, 222
contact. *See* physical contact
continual motion theory, 268

control level of self-defense
chokehold defense, 126, 127
double-wrist grab
defense, 122
lapel-grab defense, 124
overview, 119, 120
seated defense, 129
shirt-grab defense, 124
shoulder-grab defense, 123
sleeve-grab defense, 123
wrist-grab defense, 120–121
controlled breathing, 152
controlling technique, 17
corner throw, 228
counterattack level of
self-defense
chokehold defense, 126, 127
double-wrist grab
defense, 122
lapel-grab defense, 125
overview, 119, 120
prone defense, 129–130
seated defense, 129
shirt-grab defense, 125
shoulder-grab defense, 123
sleeve-grab defense, 123
wrist-grab defense, 120–121
courtesy, 32, 48, 51, 174–175
courtesy throw, 332
crescent block, 189, 217
crescent kick, 193, 219
criticism, 316–317
cross block, 257–260
cross punch, 282, 284
crunches, 105, 106, 227
cuong nhu tuong thom, 332
cut, 87

dagger hand, 254
dai-Sensei, 332
dan tien, 305, 332
danjon, 265, 305, 332

dau, 332
deadly force, 112
death touch, 142
defensive kick, 284
deflection, 208
degree, black belt, 68, 69, 332
demonstration, 52, 64, 77, 175
demotion, 69
dero dohras, 332
diet
    changing eating habits,
        94–95
    consulting dietician, 95–96
    drinking water, 64, 71–72,
        86, 95
    goal, 66
    promotion test, 71
    safety, 86
    snacking before class, 64, 95
    supplements, 96
    training guidelines, 94–96
    weight loss, 65–66
dietician, 95–96
dim mak, 142, 332
disability, 22, 43
disarming opponent, 260–261
discipline
    benefits of martial arts, 25
    controlling body, 33
    developing, 153–156
    good school, 48
    mental, 13–14
    obeying teacher, 27
discount, tuition, 58
disengaging technique, 269
dislocation injury, 87, 88
do, 10, 332
dobo, 45, 73, 332
doctor, 22, 24, 25, 96
dogi, 237, 332
dojang, 47, 210, 332
dojo, 47, 186, 332
Doll rye chaki (kick), 219
domestic violence, 114
double end bag, 79

double kick, 217
double knife-hand block, 217
double-wrist grab defense,
    121–122
downward block, 189
dragon, 27–28
Drunken Monkey (Kung Fu
    style), 200

• *E* •

eating habits, 94–95
eclectic martial arts,
    290–291, 292, 294–295.
    See also Jeet Kune Do
eight-direction exercise, 240
elbow
    control, 272, 273
    smash, 193
    strike, 202, 281, 284
emotion, 36, 157, 158, 176–177
empty-handed technique,
    166, 254, 259–261, 332
endorphin, 154
endurance
    benefit of martial arts,
        23, 178
    heavy bag, 213
    jump rope, 79
    Muay Thai, 277, 279
    preconditioning, 25
    Tae Kwon Do, 213
energy level, 64, 86, 95, 96
enlightenment, 34, 151
enryo, 332
enthusiasm, 320
entrainment, 158
environmental weapon, 159,
    166–168
equipment. *See also specific
    equipment*
    adjusting during drills,
        84–85
    competition, 140

cost, 59
Escrima, 250
evaluating, 54
good school, 48
home gym, 78–79
Jeet Kune Do, 293
organizing, 155–156
proper fit, 86
purchase from teacher,
    59, 74
resources, 340–341
safety, 59, 76–77, 85–86,
    281, 334
sparring, 76–77
escape level of self-defense
    chokehold defense, 126
    double-wrist grab
        defense, 122
    lapel-grab defense, 124
    overview, 119, 120
    seated defense, 129
    shirt-grab defense, 124
    shoulder-grab defense, 123
    sleeve-grab defense, 123
    wrist-grab defense, 120–121
Escrima (martial art)
    angles of attack, 252–253
    approaches, 250
    body-shifting, 256
    competition, 138
    development of mental
        attributes, 251
    empty-handed techniques,
        254, 259–260
    equipment, 250
    footwork, 256–257
    form, 252
    history, 262
    injury, 252
    overview, 20–21, 249–250
    physical considerations,
        251
    rank, 250–251
    self-control, 251

sparring, 252
stance, 254–256
techniques, 253–261
training, 252
twelve strikes, 253
uniform, 250
Escrima stick
blocks, 257–260
characteristics, 254
definition, 249
disarming opponent, 260–261
fighting styles, 250
holding technique, 254
left-handed people, 257
origin, 21, 161
strikes, 257
Escrimador (Escrima practitioner), 250, 332
espada y daga, 249, 262
ethical behavior, 32, 34, 148, 175
etiquette, 174, 332
evasion, 295–296
explosive power drill, 101–102

• F •

fall, 227, 268
fanning strike, 257
fast strike, 257
fats, 94
fear
beginning students, 82
confronting, 156, 157, 158
emotional muscle memory, 158
fudoshin, 35, 36
physical contact, 82, 84
feinting, 297
Feng, Chang San (founder, T'ai Chi Chuan), 312
fighting stance, 215–216, 282, 283

Filipino martial arts, 20–21, 262
fist, 254
fitness
assessment, 25
benefits of martial arts, 23, 178
books, 339
cardiovascular training, 97–98
commitment, 31
drinking fluids, 64
energy level, 64
Hapkido, 264
preconditioning, 25–26
safety, 86
speed training, 100–102
starting program, 92
strength-training techniques, 102–109
the Way, 148–149
weight lifting, 78, 102–103
Five Accomplishments (personal accomplishments), 304
Five Tenets (character-building techniques), 11, 32–33, 149, 174–177, 210
Five Ways of Kung Fu (methods), 332
flail, 77, 161, 164, 195
flexibility
Aikido, 236, 239–240
benefits of martial arts, 23, 178
building muscle mass, 102, 108
Escrima, 251
Hapkido, 264
Judo, 226
Karate, 183
Kung Fu, 199
Muay Thai, 276, 278
overview, 98–99
stretching exercises, 99–100, 213–214

Tae Kwon Do, 210
T'ai Chi Chuan, 303
flying side kick, 217, 218
focus. See also mindset
benefits of martial arts, 25
breathing exercise, 152
controlling body, 33
developing, 153–156
importance, 37
meditation, 151
promotion test, 71
shout, 114
teacher, 322
focus mitts, 79
foot protector, 77, 85
footwork, 244, 256–257, 295–296
force, deadly, 112
forearm protector, 77
form
Aikido, 243
Choy-Li-Fut, 200–201
competition, 134
definition, 15, 63, 64, 332
Escrima, 252
Jeet Kune Do, 290
Judo, 225
Karate, 184, 186
memorizing, 64–65
musical, 134
Tae Kwon Do, 211
T'ai Chi Chuan, 306–309, 307–309
team, 134
varying technique, 64
weapon, 134
forward roll, 242, 267
forward stance, 215
forward throw, 271
foul, 136, 138
fracture, 87
free sparring, 211, 252
free weight, 109
friendship, 25, 179

front kick, 99, 191, 192, 218, 285
front stance, 187, 215
front-split stretch, 214
fudoshin, 35, 36, 37, 332
full contact, 45, 83
full-body armor, 76, 85, 250
full-power sweeping strike, 257

• G •

gaku, 333
Gedan barai uke (block), 189
gi, 73, 186, 333
Gichin, Funakoshi (founder, modern Karate), 32, 183, 185
gloves, 76
go technique, 184, 200, 333
goal
  achievement steps, 63–66
  attainability, 63
  beginning student, 61–63
  changing, 50, 62
  daily life, 180
  determining, 50
  getting through first class, 64
  long-term versus short-term, 62–65
  marker, 65
  measuring, 62, 66, 67
  memorizing forms, 64–65
  motivation, 62
  overview, 26, 323
  perseverance, 318
  rank, 66, 67
  setback, 63
  sharing, 63
  Tae Kwon Do, 212
  weight loss, 65–66
Goju-Ryu (martial art), 184
Goshin jutsu (Judo technique), 225

grand championship competition, 140
grappling
  Choy-Li-Fut, 202
  definition, 18, 333
  heavy bag, 78
  Judo, 225, 228, 232–233
  Karate, 18
  Kung Fu, 208
  light contact, 82
  shoes, 75
  tatami mat, 79
Grasp the Bird's Tail (form), 308, 309
green belt, 24, 68
grip, 224, 268
groin protector, 76, 85
groundwork technique, 227, 232–233
guard position, 188, 208
gun, 165, 166
gup, 333
guro, 251
Guru (teacher), 333
Gyaku tsuki (punch), 190
gym, home, 78–79

• H •

Hadan maki (block), 217
hajime, 333
hakama, 237, 333
hand
  C-hand, 254, 260
  hand-to-hand combat, 291
  handwrap, 77
  strike, 220–221
  technique, 268
Hanshi (term of respect), 333
Hapkido (martial art)
  breakfall, 267–268
  breathing, 265
  chi, 263, 264–266
  conserving energy, 266

continual motion theory, 268
disengaging technique, 269
hand technique, 268
history, 263, 273
joint locking, 269–270
kick, 272–273
open mind, 264
overview, 19, 263
physical considerations, 264
punch, 272
roll, 267
self-confidence, 264
shout, 265–266
stance, 268
strike defense, 271–273
techniques, 266–273
throw, 270–271
thumb, 268
training, 267
vital points, 264
hara, 236, 237, 305, 333
haragei, 333
Harai-goshi (throw), 230, 231
hard-style martial arts, 134, 333
harmony, 147–148, 158, 333
hatsu geiko, 333
headgear, 76, 85
healing arts, 252
heart rate, 98
heavy bag, 54, 77, 78–79, 213
heavy contact, 83
heijo-shin, 333
Heitzman, Jeanne (martial artist), 82
Heung, Chan (founder, Choy-Li-Fut), 200
hidden teaching, 333
Hidenori, Otsuka (founder, Wado-Ryu), 185
high block, 217
high kick, 209
high punch, 190

high stance, 187
high-guard position, 188º
Hilot (Filipino healing art), 252
hip stretch, 100
Hoffman, Janalea (music therapist), 158
hogu, 333
hombu dojo, 186
home gym, 78–79
honesty, 32
Hon-kami-shiho-gatame (grappling technique), 233
Hon-kesa-gatame (grappling technique), 232
hontai, 333
Hon-yoko-shiho-gatame (grappling technique), 233
hook, 282
horse stance, 188, 216, 307, 308
hourglass stance, 188
how-to video, 41
Hsiang, Wu Yu (founder, Sun-style T'ai Chi), 304
Hugul ja sae (stance), 215–216
humility, 81, 93, 172, 318
humor, 320
huyet, 333
Hwarang (Korean nobles), 18, 222
hyperextension injury, 87
hyung, 15, 184, 333

•I•

immobilization, 238, 245, 246
inclusive school, 49
India, 20
indomitable spirit, 33, 38, 71, 72, 177
Indonesian martial arts, 20–21

injury. *See also* safety
  beginning student, 87
  breakfall, 225, 227
  common, 86–87
  contact styles, 45
  Escrima, 252
  following doctor's orders, 24
  instructor's attitude, 57
  joint lock, 270
  Judo, 225, 227
  pain during stretching, 99, 214
  practice, 94
  preconditioning, 26
  prevention, 84–88
  roll, 227
  submission signal, 226
  weight lifting, 88
inner thigh sweep, 230
integrity, 32, 148, 175
international tournament, 143
Internet, 41, 42, 295
interviewing students and instructors, 44–45, 56–58
introductory lesson, 55
intuition, 117–118
invitational tournament, 143
in-yo, 29, 333
ippon, 135, 333
irimi, 238
isometric training, 103–108

•J•

Ja yu dae ruyn sae (stance), 215–216
jab, 282
Japan, 16, 19, 162, 222
Japanese martial arts, 16–17, 30–32, 147, 184, 185
Jeet Kune Do (martial art), 289–290, 292–299. *See also* eclectic martial arts
ji do kwan, 212

jo, 163, 238
Jodan uke (block), 189
joint locking, 19, 214, 235, 269–270
ju technique, 184, 200, 333
judge
  breaking competition, 139
  Escrima competition, 138
  forms competition, 134
  Judo competition, 135
  Karate competition, 136
  Kung Fu competition, 136
  Muay Thai competition, 137
  promotion test, 70–71
  Tae Kwon Do competition, 138
Judo (martial art)
  agility, 224
  big people, 224
  breakfall, 225, 227–228, 229
  categories of techniques, 225
  combining techniques, 233
  competition, 131, 135, 223, 224
  flexibility, 226
  forms, 225
  grappling, 225, 228, 232–233
  grip, 224
  history, 223–224, 234
  injury, 225, 227
  Olympics, 224
  overview, 17, 223–224
  physical contact, 224
  pinning opponent, 232
  popularity, 17
  sparring, 225
  strength, 224, 226
  teacher, 223
  throw, 225, 228–232
  training, 225–226
judogi, 228
juice, 86, 95
Jujutsu (combat art), 234

jump rope, 79
jumping kick, 209
Jungdan maki (block), 217
jutsu, 234, 333

 • K •

ka, 18, 333
kaiden, 333
kaiken, 17, 162
Kali (martial art), 20, 249
kama, 195
kame, 185
kamidana, 174, 333
Kano, Jigoro (founder, Judo),
    17, 223–224, 234
Kansetu (Aikido technique),
    238
kan-shu, 185
Karate (martial art)
  block, 189
  board and brick breaking, 13
  character-building
    guidelines, 32
  competition, 135–136, 193
  definition, 183
  form, 184, 186
  grappling, 18
  guard position, 188
  history, 195
  kick, 190, 191–193
  knife-hand strike, 190
  mastery, 18
  Okinawan versus Japanese
    style, 184–185
  overview, 18
  physical considerations,
    183
  physical contact, 135–136
  punch, 189–190
  smash, 193
  sparring equipment, 76
  spirituality, 186
  spread to United States, 184
  stance, 187–188

sweep, 193
takedowns, 193, 194
techniques, 18, 187–195
throw, 193
training, 185–187
weapon, 16, 18, 194–195
Karateka (Karate
    practitioner), 18, 333
kata, 15, 184, 186, 333
Kata-gatame (grappling
    technique), 233
katame waza, 238
katana, 162
keiko, 334
Kempo (martial art), 185
Kendo (sword art), 77, 163
Kenpo (full contact), 184
kensei, 334
ki, 29, 235, 334
kiai, 29, 113, 114, 324, 334
Kiba dachi (stance), 188
kick. See also specific kicks
  Aikido, 235
  control, 272–273
  Hapkido, 272–273
  Jeet Kune Do, 297, 298
  Karate, 190, 191–193
  Muay Thai, 284–287
  self-defense, 165
  stretching, 99, 214
  striking post, 206
  Tae Kwon Do, 209, 210,
    217–220
  White Crane, 203
kickboxing, 11, 21, 276,
    280–281. See also
    Muay Thai
kicking target, 79
kihon, 186
kihop, 29, 113, 114, 334
Kim jae sae (stance), 216
kime, 334
Kime no kata (Judo
    technique), 225
knee bend stretch, 214

knee smash, 193
knee strike, 202, 284, 285
kneeling stretch, 239
knees, 102
knife
  block, 217
  hand, 129
  strike, 190, 221
  weapon, 161, 165
knuckle pushup, 104
koan, 151
koka, 135
kokoro, 37–38, 334
Kokutsu dachi (stance), 187
kokyu nage, 247, 248
Korea, 18, 19, 222
Korean Karate. See
    Tae Kwon Do
Korean martial arts
  character-building
    guidelines, 32–33
  Five Tenets, 11, 32–33
  jumping kick, 209
  overview, 19
  the Way, 147
  weapons, 222
Krav Maga (martial art), 291
kumite, 186, 334
kune, 208, 334
kung, 203
Kung Fu (martial art)
  block, 208
  categories, 198
  chi, 198
  Chi Kung exercises, 203–204
  competition, 136
  definition, 14, 15, 197
  Five Ways, 332
  grappling, 208
  guard position, 208
  history, 197, 207
  inner-style versus outer-
    style, 15, 198, 200
  Northern style versus
    Southern style, 15, 198

overview, 15
passing on of knowledge, 15
physical considerations, 199
physical contact, 199
popular styles, 199–203
stance, 208
techniques, 208
throw, 208
training, 204–206
weapon, 162, 206–208
kup so, 264, 334
Kuzure-kesa-gatame (grappling technique), 232
Kuzushi (Judo technique), 225
kwan, 212, 334
kwan jang, 334
kwoon, 334
kyu, 69, 334
kyu/dan system, 69, 334

• L •

lance, 161
language requirements, 2–3
lapel-grab defense, 124–125
law, 12, 112, 167
Lee, Brandon (martial artist), 328
Lee, Bruce (martial artist)
books, 338
development of Jeet Kune Do, 14, 289, 299
instructional setting, 47
movies, 328
popularity of Kung Fu, 197
teaching Chinese martial arts to non-Chinese people, 16
Wing Chun, 202
leg sweep, 230
lei-tei, 334
Li, Jet (martial artist), 328

library research, 40
light contact, 45, 82
linear attack, 272
lion, 28
listening, 92, 315
Llama (martial art), 203
local tournament, 143
Long Form (T'ai Chi form), 306, 307, 308–309
Long, Wong (founder, Northern Praying Mantis), 199
long-arm technique, 201
long-range weapon, 160, 161
long-term goal, 62–63, 65–66
Lost Monkey (Kung Fu style), 200
low block, 217
low punch, 190
low stance, 187
low-guard position, 188

• M •

ma-ai, 334
machine weight, 109
Mae geri (kick), 191, 192
magazines, martial arts, 40, 79, 142, 340
makiwara board, 79, 185, 334
Man, Yip (martial artist), 202
mantis claw, 200
mantra, 151
martial arts. *See also specific martial arts*
benefits, 1, 22–25, 156–158, 178–180
commitment, 31
definition, 334
diversity of people, 21–22, 180
giving back to sport, 173, 325
history, 9, 10, 20
increased popularity, 1

learning all aspects of sport, 326
misconceptions, 11–14, 170
mythology, 11
overview, 2, 10
preconditioning, 25–26
purpose, 10, 12–13, 23
representing to outside world, 169–170
requirements for success, 21
types, 14–21
way of life, 10, 11
martial arts club, 48, 50
mat, 54, 78, 79
Matsubayashi-Ryu (martial art), 184
Matsumara Orthodox (martial art), 184
Mawashi geri (kick), 191
medical problem, 22, 42, 43, 96, 303
medicine bag, 79
meditation, 150–152, 237, 305–306
medium-range weapon, 161
mei-hwa-chuang, 206
memorizing form, 64–65
memory, muscle, 36, 93–94, 157
mental discipline, 13–14
mental mindset. *See* mindset
meridian, 301
metsuke, 334
Michi (path or way), 334
middle guard position, 188
middle punch, 190
Middle Way (T'ai Chi Chuan practice), 15–16, 30
Mikazuki geri (kick), 193
mindset, 35–37. *See also focus*
mirror, 54, 78
moderation, 15–16, 30, 34
monkey, 28

Monkey Style Kung Fu
(martial art), 28, 200, 201
moo duk kwan, 212
mook jong, 205, 206
Morihei, Ueshiba (founder,
Aikido), 17, 235, 248, 273
Morote-seoi-nage (throw),
230, 231
motivation, 52, 62, 251
mouthguard, 76, 85
movies, martial arts, 41, 328
Mu Tau (martial art), 291
Muay Thai (martial art). *See
also* kickboxing
balance, 278
body conditioning, 277
cardiovascular training,
277, 279
competition, 137–138,
276, 281
endurance, 277, 279
flexibility, 278
history, 287
kick, 284–287
versus kickboxing, 21
medical problem, 42
overview, 21, 275
physical considerations,
275–276
punch, 282, 283
sparring, 280–281
stance, 282, 283
stretching, 278
striking pad, 79
styles, 276
sweep, 287
target areas, 137
techniques, 281–287
throw, 287
training, 276–279
weight lifting, 277, 279
workout routine, 279–280
Mui, Ng (martial artist), 202
muscle
abdominal, 105–107
deltoid, 104

hamstring, 88, 102
leg, 107–108
mass, 78, 88, 102–103,
108–109, 183
memory, 36, 93–94, 157
oblique, 105, 107
quadricep, 88, 102
soreness, 154
tricep, 104
mushin, 334
musical form, 134
Musubi dachi (stance), 187
mythology, 11

• **N** •

Nage no kata (Judo
technique), 225
nage waza, 238
naginata, 17, 163
Nakbeop (breakfall), 267–268
nami-juji-jime, 233
national tournament, 143
natural stance, 243–244,
255, 268
necessary force, 112, 166
neck lock, 233
neck stretch, 100
Neporent, Liz (*Weight Training
For Dummies*), 109
nervousness, 72, 133, 158
neutral stance, 282, 283
ninja star, 160, 161, 164
no contact, 45, 82
normal-cross strangle, 233
Northern Praying Mantis
(martial art), 199–200
nunchuk, 16, 160, 161,
164, 194
nutrition. *See* diet

• **O** •

obi, 186
offensive kick, 284
Oi tsuki (punch), 190

Okinawa (island), 195
Okinawan martial arts, 18,
184–185
older people
abilities, 3
competition division, 141
rank, 3, 69
self-defense, 116
style selection, 42
T'ai Chi Chuan, 42, 303
Olympics (sporting event),
212, 224
one-knee squat, 227
open mind, 92, 264
open stretch, 214
open tournament, 143
optimism, 33, 177
organization, professional,
155–156, 212, 341–342
Organizing For Dummies
(Roth, Eileen), 156
overhand punch, 283

• **P** •

padded attacker course, 291
pain, stretching, 99, 214
palm strike, 122, 221
Pandalag (Escrima training
method), 252
Pang, Liu (martial artist), 207
Pankration (martial art), 291
paranoia, 119
parks and recreation
program, 47, 49
parrying, 257
partial roll, 227
passive Chi Kung
(exercise), 203
patience, 150, 318
pelvic-tilt crunch, 105,
106–107
penalty, 135, 136, 138
perseverance
applying to daily life, 176
definition, 174, 175

developing kokoro, 38
goal, 318
importance, 317–318
indomitable spirit, 33, 177
muscle memory, 93–94
overview, 33
plateauing at intermediate
    belt, 68
promotion test, 71
Philippines, 20–21, 262
physical contact
  beginning student, 82
  Choy-Li-Fut, 201
  fear, 82, 84
  full contact versus heavy
    contact, 83
  intermediate student, 82
  Judo, 224
  Karate competition, 135–136
  kickboxing, 281
  Kung Fu, 199
  no contact versus light
    contact, 82
  preventing injuries, 84–88
  requesting lighter contact,
    83–84
  safety, 82–83
  self-control, 83
  style selection, 45
  Tae Kwon Do, 209, 211
  types, 45
  White Crane, 203
physical self-control, 176–177
physician. *See* doctor
plyometric drill, 102
PNF. *See* proprioceptive
    neuromuscular
    facilitation
poomse, 211, 334
postures, 243
power, 101–102, 105–107, 112
practice
  attitude, 94
  home gym, 78
  importance, 317
  injury, 94

muscle memory, 93
nervousness, 133
self-defense, 114, 116
tournament, 144–145
Praying Mantis, Northern
    (martial art), 199–200
prioritizing tasks, 155
professional Karate, 136
professional organization,
    56–57, 211, 212, 226,
    341–342
projectile weapon, 160, 161
projection, 246
promotion test, 59, 68–69,
    70–72, 158. *See also* rank
prone defense, 129–130
proprioceptive
    neuromuscular
    facilitation (PNF), 214
protein, 94, 96
provoking attack, 171
punch. *See also specific
    punches*
  Aikido, 235
  Choy-Li-Fut, 202
  Hapkido, 272
  Jeet Kune Do, 299
  Karate, 189–190
  Muay Thai, 282, 283
  Tae Kwon Do, 220–221
push hands exercise, 301,
    310–311
pushup, 103–104

qi, 29
Qi Gong exercise (Kung Fu
    exercise), 203–204

randori, 225
rank. *See also* promotion test
  Aikido, 236–237
  beginning student, 43

belt color, 67–68, 69
class/degree system, 69
competition division, 141
definition, 334
Escrima, 250–251
goal, 66, 67
history, 67
Jeet Kune Do, 290, 293
older people, 3, 69
overview, 67, 68–69
showing courtesy, 32
T'ai Chi Chuan, 306
rape, 115
reaction time, 100–102
ready stance, 255
rebreakable board, 79
reference check, 56, 57
regional tournament, 143
registered dietician, 95–96
rei, 186
religion, 10, 15, 149. *See also
    specific religions*
ren-zoku-waza, 233
resistance training, 102–103
Resolute in Five Respects
    (character-building
    guidelines), 30–32
respect, 48, 51, 317, 321
reverse kick, 193, 220, 285
reverse punch, 221
reverse side kick, 193,
    220, 285
rice flail, 161
ring, 145
Rofuse (Aikido technique),
    238
role model, 325
roll, 227, 241–242, 267
rooted-tree breathing, 153
rope up exercise, 105,
    106–107
Roth, Eileen (*Organizing
    For Dummies*), 156
round kick, 191
roundhouse attack, 272

roundhouse kick, 219, 285, 286
roundhouse punch, 202
round-robin, 144
runner's high, 154
ryu, 185

• S •

sa beum nim, 334
safety. *See also* injury
   alertness, 84
   attitude, 81–82
   avoiding attacks, 116–119
   equipment, 59, 76–77, 85–86, 281, 334
   kickboxing, 280–281
   physical contact, 82–83
   weapon, 159–160, 165, 166
salutation stance, 255, 256
Samurai (Japanese warriors), 16, 335
Sanchin dachi (stance), 188
Sangdan maki (block), 217
satori, 151
Savate (French form of fighting), 287
scarf hold, 232
Schlosberg, Suzanne (*Weight Training For Dummies*), 109
school. *See also* class
   affiliations, 56–57
   characteristics of good school, 48–49
   children's behavior, 55
   cost, 58–59
   determining own goal, 50
   facilities, 54
   Five Tenets, 174–177
   formal versus laid-back, 55
   giving back to sport, 173, 325
   importance of competition, 57

inclusiveness, 49
introductory lesson, 55
large, 51, 54–55
options, 47–48
philosophy, 30
physical contact, 45
selecting style, 41–42
size of training area, 48, 54
small, 54–55
student-teacher ratio, 54
time to achieving black belt, 58
types, 49–50
variety of teachers, 51
women, 52–53
scoring, competition, 135, 136, 138, 139, 211
Seagall, Steven (martial artist), 328
seated defense, 128–129
seated toe touch, 239
seiza, 186, 239
self-confidence
   benefits of martial arts, 23, 24, 157
   boasting, 172
   Hapkido, 264
   self-defense, 115
   tournament, 146
   visualization, 151–152
self-control
   anger, 177
   applying to daily life, 170
   competition, 170
   Escrima, 251
   fudoshin, 35–36
   overview, 33
   physical contact, 83
   safety, 85
   training, 170
   types, 176
self-defense
   aerobic-class martial art, 11
   Aikido, 238–239
   anticipating danger, 118

avoiding attack, 116–119
awareness, 117, 118
basic techniques, 120–130
beginner paranoia, 119
benefits of martial arts, 24
chokehold defense, 125–128
choosing friends wisely, 117
de-escalating conflict, 113
double-wrist grab defense, 121–122
empty-handed techniques, 165, 166
finishing fight, 115
high kick, 165
intuition, 117–118
Judo grappling technique, 232
justifiable threat, 112
knowing attacker, 114, 117
lapel-grab defense, 124–125
levels, 119–120
necessary force, 112, 166
older people, 116
overview, 111
philosophy, 111–115
practice, 114, 116
preparation, 115–116
program, 291
prone defense, 129–130
punch, 190
purpose of martial arts, 12–13
rape, 115
responding quickly, 118–119
restricted lifestyle, 116–117
seated defense, 128–129
self-confidence, 115
shirt-grab defense, 124–125
shoulder-grab defense, 123
shout, 113, 114
sleeve-grab defense, 123
small people, 116
smash, 193
sweep, 193
takedown, 193

throw, 193
walking away, 112, 113
weapon, 116, 165–166, 168
wrist-grab defense, 120–121
self-discipline. *See* discipline
self-esteem, 23, 157
selflessness, 179, 321
semicontact Karate, 135
seminar, 294–295
sen, 335
sensei, 5, 186, 335
seppuku, 162
Seven Stars (opponent's
    weapons), 335
sexism, 52
Shaolin Temple, 20, 207,
    312, 335
shiai, 223
shiai-jo, 335
shin protector, 77
shinai, 317
shirt-grab defense, 124–125
Shobayshi-Ryu (martial
    art), 184
shoes, 75
shomen, 186, 335
shootboxing, 291
shootfighting, 291
Shorin-Ryu (martial art), 184
Short Form (T'ai Chi form),
    306, 307
short-hand technique, 201
short-range weapon, 161
short-term goal, 62–63, 63–65
Shotokan (martial art), 185
shoulder
    grab defense, 123
    hold, 233
    immobilization, 245–246
    lock, 233
    stretch, 100
shout, 29, 113, 114,
    265–266, 324
Shul, Choi Yong (organizer,
    Hapkido), 19, 273
shuriken, 160, 161, 164

Shuto uchi (knife-hand
    strike), 190, 191
sickle, 195
side bend, 240
side four quarters hold, 233
side kick, 191, 192, 219,
    220, 285
side leg stretch, 214
sifu, 202, 335
sijo, 335
Silla Kingdom Korea, 18
Single Whip (form), 308, 309
sleep, 86, 96
sleeve-grab defense, 123
small people
    competition division,
        141–142
    Kung Fu, 199
    Muay Thai, 276
    power, 101, 102
    self-defense, 116
smash, 193
soft-style martial arts,
    134, 335
Sokaku, Takeda (martial
    artist), 273
solar plexus, 125, 190
Sombra Tabak (Escrima
    training method), 252
sore muscle, 154
Soto ude uke (block), 189
Spain, 21, 262
sparring
    board and brick breaking, 13
    competition, 134–138
    equipment, 76–77
    Escrima, 252
    Judo, 225
    Muay Thai, 280–281
    partner selection, 53, 83
    practicing for tournament,
        144
    reaction drill, 101
    safety, 83–85
    shout, 114
    showing opening, 101

stance, 187
style selection, 45
Tae Kwon Do, 211, 212–213
timing, 100–102
unequal partners, 83
women, 53
spear, 160
speed bag, 79
speed training, 100–102
spinning back fist, 283
spirituality, 147–153,
    173–174, 186
sprain, 87, 88
staff, 77, 160, 161, 164, 195
Stambaugh, Carol (martial
    artist), 36, 157, 158
stance. *See also specific
    stances*
    Aikido, 243–244
    Escrima, 254–256
    Hapkido, 268
    Jeet Kune Do, 295
    Karate, 187–188
    Kung Fu, 208
    Muay Thai, 282, 283
    Tae Kwon Do, 215–216
    T'ai Chi Chuan, 307, 308
    training, 107
Standing Monkey (Kung Fu
    style), 200
step sparring, 211
stick. *See* Escrima stick
sticky-hands technique, 199,
    202, 205
stomach throw, 228
Stone Monkey (Kung Fu
    style), 200
straight punch, 190, 202, 220
strain, 87
strength. *See also* weight
    lifting
    Aikido, 236
    benefit of martial arts,
        23, 178
    Escrima, 251
    Hapkido, 264

strength *(continued)*
  isometric training, 103–108
  Judo, 224, 226
  Karate, 185–186
  medicine bag, 79
  preventing injury, 88
  resistance training, 102–103
  Tae Kwon Do, 213
  training techniques,
    102–109
stress, 25, 33, 133, 149, 203
stress fracture, 87
stretching
  active-isolated, 214
  Aikido, 239–240
  exercises, 99–100, 214, 227,
    239–240
  improving flexibility, 99,
    213–214
  injury prevention, 87–88
  kick, 99, 214
  machine, 79
  Muay Thai, 278
  pain, 99, 214
  proprioceptive
    neuromuscular
    facilitation, 214
  Tae Kwon Do, 213–214
  T'ai Chi Chuan, 307
strike. *See* hand strike
Strike Palm to Ask Blessings
  (form), 308, 309
striking arts, 82
striking equipment, 79, 205,
  206
student. *See also* beginning
    student
  advanced, 43, 68, 81, 306
  courtesy, 174
  evaluating similarities to
    self, 56
  expectations at
    competition, 139
  female, 52–53
  intermediate, 82, 306

interviewing, 44–45
motivation, 52
ratio to teacher, 54
sharing goal, 63
teaching friend, 172
watching, 316
style selection, 39–46, 338
Subak (martial art), 19, 222
submission signal, 226
Sudo chigi (strike), 221
Sudo maki (block), 217
suki, 335
sumi-gaeshi, 228
Sumo wrestling, 10
supplement, vitamin, 96
supply resources, 340–341
sutemi, 335
sweep, 193, 194, 202, 287
sweets, 94
sword, 77, 161, 162–163
synchronization of rhythm,
  158

• T •

tabak, 262
Tae Bo (aerobic-class martial
  art), 11, 275
Tae Kwon Do (martial art)
  block, 216–217
  board and brick breaking,
    13, 210
  competition, 138, 211,
    212–213
  definition, 10
  endurance, 213
  Five Tenets, 11, 32–33, 149,
    174–177, 210
  forms, 211
  goal, 212
  green belt, 24
  hand strike, 220–221
  history, 19, 222
  kick, 209, 210, 217–220
  Olympics, 212–212

origin, 19
overview, 19
physical considerations,
  210
physical contact, 209, 211
punch, 220–221
sparring, 76, 211, 212–213
stance, 215–216
strength, 213
stretching, 213–214
styles, 210–213
techniques, 19, 214–221
training, 213–214
weapon, 210
Tae Kyun (martial art),
  19, 222
T'ai Chi Chuan (martial art)
  advanced student, 306
  beginning student, 306
  benefits, 302–303
  chi, 301, 305, 307
  components, 15
  dan tien, 305
  Five Accomplishments, 304
  form, 306–309, 307–309
  history, 312
  intermediate student, 306
  martial art versus
    exercise, 302
  medical problem, 303
  meditation, 305–306
  Middle Way, 15–16, 30
  older people, 42, 303
  overview, 15–16, 301–302
  physical considerations, 303
  popularity, 301
  principles, 304, 305
  push hands exercise, 301,
    310–311
  rank, 306
  stance, 307, 308
  stretching, 307
  styles, 303–304
  techniques, 307–311
  training, 306–307

uniform, 306
warming up, 307
weapon, 302
yin-yang, 304
Tai sabaki (Aikido technique), 238
Tai Sing (Monkey style), 200, 201
Tai-otoshi (throw), 229–230
takedown, 193, 194, 214
tall people, 198, 199, 210
tan tien, 305
tanto, 238
Taoism (Eastern philosophy), 33–35, 147–149, 173
tap out, 226
target heart rate, 98
tatami mat, 79
Te (martial art), 18, 195, 335
teacher
  accepting diverse students, 320–321
  assistant, 51, 56
  attitude, 57
  characteristics of good teacher, 51–52, 319–322
  commitment, 319
  cost, 58–59
  courtesy, 174
  creativity, 321
  criticism, 316–317
  demonstration, 52
  enthusiasm, 320
  expectations of women, 53
  female, 53
  finding, 51–52
  focus, 322
  getting permission to enter competition, 139
  giving back to sport, 173, 325
  head, 51
  independent, 49
  interviewing, 44, 56–58

Judo, 223
knowledge, 321–322
large school, 51
listening, 92, 315
motivation, 52
obeying, 27
philosophy, 30
promotion test process, 70
purchasing equipment, 59, 74
qualifications, 56–57
ratio to students, 54
respect, 51, 321
selflessness, 321
sense of humor, 320
seriousness, 51
sharing goals, 63
student teaching friends, 172
Tengu, 11
watching, 315–316
team form, 134
tear drop bag, 79
tendonitis, 87
Tengu (supernatural creatures), 11, 335
Thai martial arts, 20, 21
therapy, 156–158
throw
  Aikido, 17, 235, 238, 246–248
  Choy-Li-Fut, 202
  courtesy, 332
  Hapkido, 270–271
  Judo, 225, 228–232
  Karate, 193, 194
  Kung Fu, 208
  Muay Thai, 287
  Tae Kwon Do, 214
thumb, 268
Tibetan White Crane (martial art), 203
tiger, 27–28
timing, 93, 100–102
toe touch, 227
tomoe-nage, 228

tonfa
  block, 194, 195
  definition, 77
  illustration, 162
  origin, 17
  overview, 164
tori, 225
to-shin, 335
tournament, 57, 142–146. *See also* competition
traditional school, 49
traditional weapon, 161–165
training
  applying to daily life, 169
  attitude, 92–94
  books, 339
  cardiovascular, 97–98
  commitment, 31, 38, 92, 323–324, 326
  competition, 132, 144–145
  consistency, 91–92
  controlled breathing, 152
  developing kokoro, 38
  diet, 94–96
  endorphins, 154
  Escrima, 252
  Hapkido, 267
  hard, 31, 326
  intensity, 91, 98, 145, 152
  isometric, 103–108
  Jeet Kune Do, 293–294
  Judo, 225–226
  Karate, 185–187
  Kung Fu, 204–206
  Muay Thai, 276–279
  muscle soreness, 154
  options, 47–48
  resistance, 102–103
  scheduling sessions, 109
  self-control, 170
  size of training area, 48, 54
  speed, 100–102
  stance, 107
  starting fitness program, 92
  Tae Kwon Do, 213–214

training *(continued)*
  T'ai Chi Chuan, 306–307
  the Way, 148–149
  weapon, 159, 162
trapfighting, 291
trapping, 296, 297
Tse, Kou (founder, Monkey Style Kung Fu), 28
Tsukuri to kake (Judo technique), 225
tuition, 58
turn-back kick, 193, 220, 285
twirling strike, 257
two-handed shoulder drop, 230, 231
tying belt, 61
Tze, Kao (founder, Monkey style), 200
Tzu, Lao (founder, Taoism), 148

• U •

Uchi Ude Uke (block), 189
Uchi-mata (throw), 230
uke, 225
Ukemi (breakfall), 225, 227–228, 229
um-yang, 29
uniform
  Aikido, 237
  care, 75
  competition, 140
  cost, 59, 75
  Escrima, 250
  finding, 74–75
  home use, 74
  Jeet Kune Do, 74, 293
  Judo techniques, 228, 233
  overview, 73–74
  purchasing, 74
  shoes, 75
  T'ai Chi Chuan, 306
  wearing outside class, 75, 170–171
  women, 73

university, 48, 49
upper block, 189
upper four quarters hold, 233
upper-body twist, 240
uppercut, 202, 283
ura-omate, 29
Ushiro geri (kick), 193

• V •

Vale Tudo (martial art), 291
van Damme, Jean Claude (martial artist), 328
violence
  abuse, 156
  avoiding attack, 116–119
  de-escalating conflict, 113
  domestic, 114
  justifiable threat, 112
  knowing attacker, 114, 117
  misconceptions about martial arts, 12–13
  necessary force, 112, 166
  provoking attack, 171
  rape, 115
  walking away, 112, 113
visualization, 151–152, 251, 316
vital point-striking, 19, 214, 264, 335
vitamin, 96
vo, 335
vo phuc, 335
volunteering, 173

• W •

Wado-Ryu (martial art), 185
Wallace, Bill (martial artist), 183
water, 64, 71–72, 86, 95
the Way, 147–149, 173
weapon. *See also specific weapons*
  Aikido, 238
  books, 339–340

categories, 160
Choy-Li-Fut, 202
competition, 77
concealed, 167
cost, 59
demonstration, 77
development, 161
environmental, 159, 166–168
forms, 134
Japanese, 16–17
Karate, 16, 18, 194–195
Kendo, 77, 163
Korean martial arts, 222
Kung Fu, 162, 206–208
modern, 165–166
overview, 77, 160
range, 160–161
safety, 159–160, 165, 166
self-defense, 116, 165–166, 168
Seven Stars, 335
Tae Kwon Do, 210
T'ai Chi Chuan, 302
traditional, 161–165
training, 159, 162
weight class, 141–142
weight lifting. *See also strength*
  building muscle mass, 102–109, 179
  chashi, 206
  home gym, 78
  how-to book, 109
  injury, 88
  Muay Thai, 277, 279
weight loss, 23, 26, 65–66
Weight Training For Dummies (Neporent, Liz and Schlosberg, Suzanne), 109
whipping strike, 257
white belt, 43, 67, 68
White Crane Cools its Wings (form), 308, 309
White Crane (martial art), 203, 204

Wing Chun (martial art), 79,
    202–203, 205
winning spirit, 33, 71, 72
women
  black belt, 52
  chest protector, 76
  competition division,
    141–142
  expectations, 53
  kickboxing, 276
  power, 102, 112
  school, 52–53
  self-defense, 112, 115
  sparring partners, 53
  teacher, 53
  uniform, 73
  the Way, 148–149
  weapon, 17
wooden dummy, 202, 205
Wooden Monkey (Kung Fu
    style), 200
workshop, 294–295
wrist-grab defense,
    120–121, 269

wristlock, 233
Wu Dan Shan Monastery, 312
Wushu (martial art), 14, 197

yang, 29
yin, 29
yin-yang
  daily life, 173–174
  definition, 335
  moderation, 30
  overview, 29
  T'ai Chi Chuan, 304
  the Way, 148
YMCA/YWCA program, 49
Yoko geri (kick), 191, 192
younger people, 42, 141
Yueh, Wang Tsung (founder,
    Chen-style T'ai Chi), 304
yuko, 135
Yup chaki (kick), 219, 220

● **Z** ●

zazen meditation,
    150–151, 335
Zen Buddhism (Eastern
    religion), 15, 151
Zenkutsu dachi (stance), 187
Zhangfeng, Chang (founder,
    T'ai Chi Chuan), 15

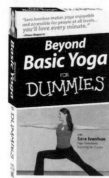

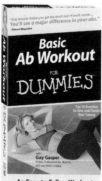

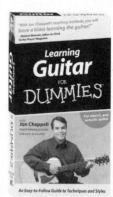

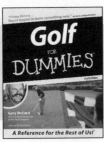
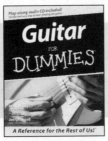

FOR DUMMIES®

A world of resources to help you grow

TRAVEL

0-7645-5453-0

0-7645-5438-7

0-7645-5444-1

Also available:

America's National Parks For Dummies
(0-7645-6204-5)

Caribbean For Dummies
(0-7645-5445-X)

Cruise Vacations For Dummies 2003
(0-7645-5459-X)

Europe For Dummies
(0-7645-5456-5)

Ireland For Dummies
(0-7645-6199-5)

France For Dummies
(0-7645-6292-4)

Las Vegas For Dummies
(0-7645-5448-4)

London For Dummies
(0-7645-5416-6)

Mexico's Beach Resorts For Dummies
(0-7645-6262-2)

Paris For Dummies
(0-7645-5494-8)

RV Vacations For Dummies
(0-7645-5443-3)

EDUCATION & TEST PREPARATION

0-7645-5194-9

0-7645-5325-9

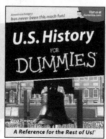

0-7645-5249-X

Also available:

The ACT For Dummies
(0-7645-5210-4)

Chemistry For Dummies
(0-7645-5430-1)

English Grammar For Dummies
(0-7645-5322-4)

French For Dummies
(0-7645-5193-0)

GMAT For Dummies
(0-7645-5251-1)

Inglés Para Dummies
(0-7645-5427-1)

Italian For Dummies
(0-7645-5196-5)

Research Papers For Dummies
(0-7645-5426-3)

SAT I For Dummies
(0-7645-5472-7)

U.S. History For Dummies
(0-7645-5249-X)

World History For Dummies
(0-7645-5242-2)

HEALTH, SELF-HELP & SPIRITUALITY

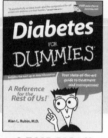

0-7645-5154-X

0-7645-5302-X

0-7645-5418-2

Also available:

The Bible For Dummies
(0-7645-5296-1)

Controlling Cholesterol For Dummies
(0-7645-5440-9)

Dating For Dummies
(0-7645-5072-1)

Dieting For Dummies
(0-7645-5126-4)

High Blood Pressure For Dummies
(0-7645-5424-7)

Judaism For Dummies
(0-7645-5299-6)

Menopause For Dummies
(0-7645-5458-1)

Nutrition For Dummies
(0-7645-5180-9)

Potty Training For Dummies
(0-7645-5417-4)

Pregnancy For Dummies
(0-7645-5074-8)

Rekindling Romance For Dummies
(0-7645-5303-8)

Religion For Dummies
(0-7645-5264-3)

Available wherever books are sold. Go to www.dummies.com or call 1-877-762-2974 to order direct